Human Rights and Diverse Societies

Human Rights and Diverse Societies: Challenges and Possibilities

Edited by

François Crépeau and Colleen Sheppard

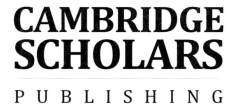

CAMBRIDGE SCHOLARS

PUBLISHING

Human Rights and Diverse Societies: Challenges and Possibilities,
Edited by François Crépeau and Colleen Sheppard

This book first published 2013

Cambridge Scholars Publishing

12 Back Chapman Street, Newcastle upon Tyne, NE6 2XX, UK

British Library Cataloguing in Publication Data
A catalogue record for this book is available from the British Library

ISBN (10): 1-4438-5137-X, ISBN (13): 978-1-4438-5137-4

TABLE OF CONTENTS

ACKNOWLEDGEMENTS

Advancing human rights while celebrating the diversity of cultures, communities and traditions is a complex and dynamic task. This book owes its origins to the Echenberg Global Conference on Human Rights and Diverse Societies, organized by the McGill Centre for Human Rights and Legal Pluralism in October 2010. As an international conference, it brought together diverse scholars, judges, politicians, policy makers, journalists, students and members of civil society. The conference examined a wide range of issues, including policies and practices of multiculturalism, human rights concepts and discourse, religious and cultural diversity, individual and collective rights and new approaches to governance. This book project includes contributions from a number of the conference speakers who work in diverse institutional, practical and scholarly contexts on these critical issues.

Accordingly, we wish to extend our sincere thanks to the Echenberg Family Foundation and its founders, Penny and Gordon Echenberg, whose commitment and generosity made possible the convening of the global conference. We also wish to express our appreciation to Dean Daniel Jutras of the Faculty of Law, McGill University for his continued support for human rights education and community outreach. We are also deeply indebted to Dr. Nandini Ramanujam, Executive Director of the Centre for Human Rights and Legal Pluralism, who played a central role in organizing the Echenberg Global Conference on Human Rights and Diverse Societies and worked closely with us in advancing this book project.

The book could not have been completed without the dedicated and professional assistance of Bethany Hastie, a doctoral candidate and O'Brien Fellow at the Centre for Human Rights and Legal Pluralism and Faculty of Law of McGill University. We also wish to extend our gratitude to Dia Dabby, a doctoral candidate at the Faculty of Law, McGill University; Stephanie Hachez, Aisenstadt Fellow (2012)(B.C.L. Student, Université de Montréal); and, Cécile Capela-Laborde, Aisenstadt Fellow (2013) (B.C.L.-LL.B. student, Faculty of Law, McGill University), for their excellent and dedicated research and editorial assistance in the completion of this project. We also wish to acknowledge permission to reprint chapters 6 and 12 provided by the *Human Rights Quarterly* and *Inroads* respectively.

The cover artwork was done by Wendy Sheppard of Cobourg, Ontario (Canada) specifically for the book and celebrates the theme of diversity and the human condition. We wish to thank her for generously sharing her artwork with us.

We view this book as part of an ongoing societal engagement to explore new ways of respecting the diversity of humankind, safeguarding the protection of collective identities and honouring our normative commitments to human rights.

Colleen Sheppard & François Crépeau
Montreal, Quebec
October 2013

Introduction

Human Rights and Diverse Societies: Challenges and Possibilities

François Crépeau and Colleen Sheppard

This book addresses the timely and important question of how to understand human rights in a world of increasing diversity. It has always been a challenge to reconcile the differences that exist between and within societies and to work towards peaceful coexistence. The effects of globalization and the increasing mobility of persons and peoples have further deepened and multiplied the sites of interaction between different cultures, religions and ethnicities. These changes have been a source of enrichment, as multiculturalism, interculturalism and diversity permeate our daily lives. Yet, they have also revealed important societal cleavages, different conceptualizations of human rights and divergent values and beliefs about moral, ethical, cultural and religious issues. In societies characterized by diverse social, ethnic, religious and cultural communities, it becomes critical to examine how to reconcile the tensions between respect for group-based identities and differences, the robust protections of individual rights and freedoms and the maintenance of community solidarity and social cohesion. It is these tensions, mediated through debates about the interaction between human rights and diversity that this book addresses.

Over sixty years after the *Universal Declaration of Human Rights*, it has been widely observed that 'human rights' resonate differently in various settings. The mainstream narrative of the universality of human rights has been challenged in the face of increasingly diverse societies. Thus, questions recur regarding the global and localized application of human rights standards in diverse societies. In thinking about diversity, moreover, it is important to recognize that it refers not only to ethno-national or religious considerations and contradictions, but also to post-colonial environments where linguistic, cultural and group-based differences endure sometimes in the face of changed structural and institutional settings. In eschewing any simple reconciliation of human rights and universalism, this book aspires to identify alternative frameworks that can facilitate the conceptualization of, and help find solutions to, the complex global human rights issues in diverse societies. In engaging with both the theoretical perspectives that question the 'universality' of human rights as well as assessing the practicality of diverse applications of human rights, this collection of essays explores how human rights can be employed to empower historically excluded/marginalized groups. It also examines how human rights can be invoked to further social inclusion. The essays reveal that the claim for universality of human rights is aspirational, but complicated by the need to apply human rights in diverse (and diversifying) societies. Taking diversity into account in thinking about the universal aspirations of human rights protection requires us to reframe the question. Rather than asking whether human rights are universal, we need to ask how the universal principles underlying human rights are practically and tangibly realized in diverse contexts and communities.

This book emerged out of an international conference on human rights and diverse societies, which attracted scholars and activists from around the world to discuss complex issues linked to human rights and social diversity. Despite the vast array of panel topics on issues from education to national security, a number of common themes emerged, creating a collective conversation about human rights in an increasingly diverse world. Recurrent themes included: the adequacy of our current conceptual human rights frameworks; the role of context in defining, implementing, problematizing and enforcing human rights; the power of narratives to untangle the complexities of the nuanced issues at the core of human rights realities; and the struggle to ascribe meaning to commonly-used amorphous concepts, such as human dignity, inequality, hatred, intolerance and exclusion. The panels also queried whether the entrenched dichotomies between universality and particularity, global and local, modern and traditional, developed and developing, religious and secular, and reality and rhetoric have been, can be or should be challenged and reframed in the human rights context.

Among the many themes explored at the conference, the need for dialogue amongst and within societies was prevalent. A culture of dialogue aimed at facilitating understanding and building new, harmonious frameworks for promoting human rights within and across societies is a necessary and important step in advancing human rights in today's pluralistic world. This book, therefore, seeks to contribute to this new culture of dialogue and to continue the conversations started during the conference. It endeavours to bring together various perspectives and ideas on the new world of human rights, to challenge assumptions and propose new ways to understand human rights in an increasingly pluralistic world.

Part I of the book begins with some preliminary reflections on human rights discourse in diverse societies. The chapters address questions such as: to what extent are human rights universal? How do diverse societies around the world conceptualize human rights and deal with the implementation of human rights policies and norms? What alternative frameworks exist that could facilitate the conceptualization of and help find solutions to global human rights issues? In Chapter 1, Peter Leuprecht probes the meaning of 'universality' vis-à-vis human rights. While discussing the challenges of conceptualizing human rights as universal and indivisible, Leuprecht posits the idea of a dialogic "alliance of civilizations." Rejecting the idea that human rights are a Western-crafted concept, Leuprecht explores the ways in which there is a common understanding of human rights across societies. In Chapter 2, Boaventura de Sousa Santos examines the "fragile hegemony" of human rights discourse, and critiques dominant conceptions of human rights as decontextualized, monolithic and imbued with a linear triumphalism. Thus, he argues for the development of a counter-hegemonic conception of human rights that could subvert the hegemonic vision and resonate with the needs of those who have been dispossessed of power and marginalized in our global world. In Chapter 3, Colleen Sheppard also examines the importance of engaging with human rights discourse, while critiquing it. She acknowledges the positive and normative significance of human rights globally, yet emphasizes the need to be vigilant in ensuring that human rights discourse goes beyond rhetoric to improve the lives of individuals and communities. She further argues for a critical analysis of the terminology of human rights law, and an unpacking of the ideological underpinnings of the language used to describe human rights issues and struggles. Both the substantive and procedural dimensions of human rights enforcement also require critical reflection, to ensure that current categories and processes for redressing rights violations do not limit our abilities to forge new categories and innovative approaches. This first part of the book, therefore, provides insights into the importance of human rights discourse, while emphasizing that its power to advance social justice depends on our continued ability to re-imagine and recreate its meanings to address the global challenges of a changing world.

Part II explores the intersection of human rights and post-colonial theory. The experience of colonization has created additional tensions for post-colonial societies striving to preserve culture while also advancing human rights. In Chapter 4, drawing on case studies from India and South

Asia, Ranabir Samaddar examines the challenge of democratisation in post-colonial countries where societies remain divided. He highlights the critical need to build effective and functioning democracies in pluralistic societies rather than focusing on individual human rights. In this regard, Samaddar emphasizes the need to go beyond a mechanical adoption of representative democracy, and instead calls for a creative federalization of politics through a dialogic culture and emphasis on justice as much as rights.

Despite the advancement of human rights, significant tensions remain in terms of understanding how women's human rights are advanced or inhibited by particular cultural, religious and community practices around the world. In Chapter 5, Isabel Altamirano-Jimenez engages critically with these themes, using settler-colonialism as a framework to interrogate Indigenous women's rights. She maintains that inherent in the idea of universal human rights is a rejection of otherness and a tendency to rely on human rights as a tool to entrench racial and gender marginalization. Through this critical lens, Altamirano-Jimenez examines the violation of Indigenous women's rights. Chapter 6 also explores the intersection of women's rights and human rights; however, Vrinda Narain suggests that human rights frameworks have the potential to alleviate gender discrimination for women in marginalized communities. In particular, she uses a human rights framework as an analytical tool to challenge Muslim women's exclusion from equal citizenship in India, examining the disparity of protection provided under the *Indian Constitution* and the religious-based family law system as case examples.

Part III highlights the role of state-based institutions in advancing human rights, including governmental human rights institutions and educational institutions. One theme that emerges in this part is the complexities of asserting national identity in the face of internal diversity and societal transitions. In Chapter 7, Canadian human rights lawyer, Pearl Eliadis examines the idea of "super-culturalism," which she argues has been relied upon to assert the pre-eminence of a majority group and its cultural preferences. Focusing on Quebec, this chapter critically evaluates the politicization of "super values" and their implications for access to public services and human rights for minority groups, arguing for an increased focus on equality rights in the on-going debate surrounding pluralism and diversity. Struggling with similar issues, but in a very different geo-political and legal context, in Chapter 8, Anna Sevortian examines post-Soviet Russia and its struggles to recognize and respect diversity. This chapter touches on many aspects of the changing nature of diversity in today's Russia – ethnic, economic, and lifestyle – and their connection to significant human rights challenges. In Chapter 9, Yossi Yonah examines the role of education both as a contributing factor to social exclusion of minority populations, and also as a key site to effect change. He analyses the challenges associated with Israel's political development towards national patriotism, and the resulting polarization of politics, identity and social inclusion, particularly in relation to Arab minorities. In Chapter 10, New Zealand Race Relations Commissioner Joris de Bres explores the use of National Human Rights institutions as a local partner for United Nations bodies to promote and monitor compliance with international human rights standards. Drawing on the New Zealand Human Rights Commission as a case study, this chapter examines the ability of such institutions to engage effectively with issues such as race relations, cultural diversity and indigenous rights, and the potential of human rights commissions to contribute to harmonious relations in diverse societies.

The concluding section of the book, Part IV challenges us to think about emerging problems of "othering," social exclusion and human rights violations in a global, interconnected and mobile world. In Chapter 11, Didier Bigo critiques national security policies for having engendered human rights violations, particularly in the wake of 9/11. Chapter 12 tackles the issue of mistreatment and social exclusion linked to irregular migration –a critical human rights issue for States. Irregular migrants are increasingly subject to inhumane treatment. François Crépeau, UN Special Rapporteur on the Rights of Migrants, argues for a more humane approach to irregular migration in which the rights of migrants are secured and promoted. He further maintains that we need to re-conceptualize conceptions of citizenship and residency if we are to afford and recognize every person's right to human dignity. The promotion and protection of migrants' rights and how they compare to the rights of citizens is an important new frontier in the development of human rights policies globally.

Through critical reflection and a reexamination of the concepts, categories, institutions and frontiers of human rights, this book contributes to an ongoing dialogue about human rights discourse and theory. Yet beyond its contribution to scholarly debates, it is our hope that this book will contribute to the development of concrete, tangible and institutional strategies for advancing the protection of human rights in diverse societies.

PART I

REFLECTIONS ON HUMAN RIGHTS
DISCOURSE IN DIVERSE SOCIETIES

CHAPTER ONE

UNIVERSALITY AND DIVERSITY

PETER LEUPRECHT

The issue of universality, one of the three "pillars" of the human rights edifice, remains a contentious and contested ideal. In this chapter, I examine the concept of universality of human rights and then indicate three possible ways of advancing towards universal application of those rights.

Universality

The 1948 Declaration of Human Rights is called "universal." It addresses itself to every state and to every person. It strongly affirms the equal dignity of all human beings – the foundation of the whole human rights edifice. Since they are based on this fundamental principle, human rights are, of necessity, universal, valid for all human beings, the same rights for all; otherwise, they would not merit their name.

However, the truth is that human rights, proclaimed as universal, are far from being universally practiced and applied. According to the Preamble of the Universal Declaration, they are "a common standard of achievement for all peoples and all nations." Even, as such, they are not accepted by all governments and political leaders of the world. Some of them dispute the universality of human rights; according to them, different political, social, cultural and religious contexts give rise to different, but equally valid conceptions of human rights. Kofi Annan has, in my view rightly, stated that:

> [I]t was never the people who complained of the universality of human rights, nor did the people consider human rights as a Western or Northern imposition. It was often their leaders who did so.

Nevertheless, it must be admitted, on the one hand, that universality remains a difficult philosophical issue and, on the other hand, that the universal realization of human rights is an ambitious and rather elusive goal. In the *annus mirabilis* of 1989, the Council of Europe organized an important international colloquy on "Universality of human rights in a pluralistic world" (1990). Several of the speakers, especially the great African lawyer Kéba Mbaye, aptly referred to "the difficult advance of human rights towards universality" (Council of Europe 1990, 68). At the same colloquy, Kéba Mbaye stated that "universality implies diversity" (1990, 67) and in his final report Robert Badinter emphasized that "human rights can only flourish if they make allowance for cultural diversity" (Council of Europe 1990, 170).

I have found general discussions on the universality of human rights sometimes interesting, but often extremely theoretical and far removed from reality. The picture looks quite different if one takes specific rights, e.g. the right to life, freedom of expression or the right to food, and considers whether these are universal. I would add that during my years as Special Representative of the UN Secretary General for human rights in Cambodia, I had numerous occasions to discuss those rights with oppressed and poor people. I was struck by the way in which they, in particular women, powerfully put their problems in terms of human rights. Not once was I told these rights were "Western" and irrelevant to them; not on a single occasion did my interlocutors refer to "Asian values" as opposed to human rights.

Universality – One of the Three Pillars of the Human Rights Edifice

Three pillars support the structure gradually erected since World War II by the international community for the protection and promotion of human rights: universality, indivisibility and solidarity (Leuprecht 1997, 135).

Universality of human rights is the logical and inescapable consequence of the fundamental principle of the equal dignity of all human beings. It means: human rights for all, the same rights for all. It is essential to see and apply this principle in connection with that of the **indivisibility** of human rights, as was rightly stressed by the Vienna World Conference on Human Rights in 1993. Human rights form an indivisible whole, whether they be civil, political, economic, social or cultural rights. Only if the human being is guaranteed all these rights can he or she live in dignity. Indivisibility means: all human rights. Taken together, the two principles mean: all human rights for all. Admittedly, this is an extremely exacting goal.

The third pillar, frequently forgotten or neglected, is that of **solidarity.** The realization of universal and indivisible human rights will be extremely difficult or even impossible in a society that does not practice solidarity, in which every member defends his or her rights and forgets those of the others. Human rights are not only the rights of each and every one of us; they are also and above all the rights of others. The way in which we perceive, approach and meet the other will have a strong, positive or negative, impact on his or her enjoyment of human rights. Particularly in Western societies, it seems essential to transcend an essentially egoistic, individualistic and acquisitive approach to human rights. Solidarity in the defence and promotion of human rights must be practiced at the domestic and at the international level. The international community is responsible for the joint and collective protection of those rights.

Three Possible Ways of Advancing Towards Universal Application of Human Rights

1. Challenging the Predominant Western View of the History of Human Rights

The concept and term of "human rights" is historically young. It is true that it arose in the West, in the late 18th century. However, many of the fundamental underlying ideas have been present long before in different cultures and civilizations, particularly the ideas of reason, justice, dignity and recognition of, and caring for, the human being. Certain Western countries like to describe themselves as the birthplace ("la patrie") of human rights. There is also a lot of talk about the Christian or Judeo-Christian roots of human rights. At the same time, according to stereotypes and clichés prevailing in the West, non-Western cultures and civilizations are perceived as strange, so "other," and according to some, the very idea of human rights is alien to them. It is essential to overcome Western parochialism, often paired with a high degree of arrogance and superiority complex.

It is worthwhile to look thoroughly into non-Western cultures and civilizations, e.g. ancient China and Islam (Leuprecht 2012). Humaneness, harmony and the idea of caring for fellow human beings and their suffering occupy a central place in the thinking of Confucius and Mencius. I agree with Louis Henkin, according to whom "there is no intrinsic tension between Confucianism and human rights" (1998, 313). Heiner Roetz regards the ethics of Confucius as a promising basis for the development of a human rights concept (2004, 109). He perceives the

Confucian ethical and political tradition as a precursor of human rights (2004, 115). According to him, the Chinese cultural tradition does not provide a convincing argument against the recognition of human rights, but can on the contrary foster it (1998, 192).

As far as Islam is concerned, simplistic minds are inclined to consider it as the natural and eternal enemy of human rights. The reality is, of course, much more complex. In fact, Islam has never been monolithic. On the contrary, it has a long history of doctrinal and cultural pluralism (Arkoun 2006, 23) and of tolerance of diversity (Bulliet 1996, 180). The "golden age" of Islam, in what we call the Middle Ages, is a particularly rich and fascinating period of Muslim history. It was a period of tremendous intellectual blossoming; at the time, the Muslim world was the first and not the third world, remarkably advanced in science, medicine and philosophy – far ahead of "Christian" Europe. Three outstanding thinkers seem particularly relevant: Avicenna (Ibn Sina), Averroes (Ibn Rushd) and Ibn Khaldun. They are representative of a world of humanism, rationality, moderation and tolerance, of a humanist, enlightened, rational and open Islam, quite different from certain caricatures of Islam presented in the West and from contemporary fundamentalist versions of Islam, which Mohammed Arkoun rightly qualifies as "explicitly anti-humanist" (2006, 22). The above-mentioned thinkers share a strong faith in the human being and human reason; they prove that the exercise of autonomous reason is perfectly possible in an Islamic environment, especially by means of *ijtihad*, personal judgment or personal effort of interpretation. They show an attachment to both religion and responsible human freedom. Unfortunately, Mohammed Arkoun seems to be right in asserting that from the $13^{th}/14^{th}$ to the 19th century, there has been a regression and a "dogmatic closure" in Islamic thought (2006, 144). However, it should be noted that since the beginning of the 20th century, advocates of Muslim reformism have been trying to resume, and to build upon, the great philosophical tradition of the golden age of Islam. At the above-mentioned Council of Europe Colloquy, Abdelwahab Boudhiba rightly stated:

> [C]ontrary to what is occasionally claimed without any evidence,...Islam is
> no stranger to the development of the doctrine of human rights – even less
> is it its enemy" (Council of Europe 1990, 31).

In 16th century Spain, well before the great human rights proclamations of the Enlightenment, the "discovery" not only of America, but also of the "other", the "Indian", provoked a great debate that raised fundamental questions about colonialism and the human nature, the dignity and the rights of that "other," the "Indian." Bartolomé de Las Casas in particular documented and denounced the crimes of the colonizers, courageously challenged prevailing doctrines and practices, rejected the argument of the superiority of European culture and vigorously asserted the equal dignity of the "other," the "Indian." It could be said that Las Casas "discovered" human rights through meeting the "other," the "indio."

2. Being Aware of Western Incoherence and Selectivity

One of the most shocking examples of past Western incoherence is the fact that countries that issued great human rights proclamations at the same time continued the practice of slavery. A more recent example is that of the "colonial clause" of the European Convention of Human Rights. In accordance with Article 1 of the Convention, "the High Contracting Parties shall secure to everyone within their jurisdiction the rights and freedoms" enshrined in the Convention. This is the fundamental principle of the universal application of the Convention *ratione personae*; the Convention does not limit itself to guaranteeing the rights of Europeans, but sets up a European regional system for the protection of universal human rights. However, Article 56 on the territorial application of the Convention stipulates:

> 1. Any State may at the time of its ratification or at any time thereafter declare by notification addressed to the Secretary General of the Council of Europe that the present Convention shall...extend to all or any of the territories for whose international relations it is responsible...
> 3. The provisions of this Convention shall be applied in such territories with due regard, however, to local requirements.

The incoherence is flagrant: the rights are secured to everyone under the jurisdiction of the Contracting States, but not, or at least not automatically, to those in the colonial territories. The drafters of the Convention were not unaware of this contradiction. On a proposal by Léopold Senghor, the Parliamentary Assembly of the Council of Europe voted in favour of the deletion of this provision,[1] but the Committee of Ministers decided to maintain it.

Nowadays, the "colonial clause" of the European Convention of Human Rights is practically irrelevant; however, its very existence is a striking example of European incoherence. Others could be added; I'll limit myself to one: Article 16 of the European Convention which allows the Contracting States to impose restrictions of the political activity of aliens. The notion of "alien" really does not have its place in the

Convention; nobody should be an alien in the land of human rights. Like Article 56, Article 16 runs counter to the basic principle enshrined in Article 1 of the Convention. It is a stain on the European Convention. However, all attempts to remove or amend it have been unsuccessful.

In spite of their declarations in favour of the indivisibility of human rights, Western countries in fact frequently practice their divisibility. Economic, social and cultural rights are far from enjoying the same degree of protection as civil and political rights. Canada is a telling example for the "failed promise" of economic, social and cultural rights; the Committee for Economic, Social and Cultural Rights which supervises the implementation of the Covenant concerning those rights has repeatedly criticized the fact that they have in fact been downgraded to simple policy objectives.

3. Opening up to the Other and Otherness

The statements by Kéba Mbaye and Robert Badinter, quoted above rightly, emphasized the need for reconciling universality and diversity. Accepting diversity, accepting the other and otherness, and "meeting the other's face" (to borrow from Emmanuel Lévinas (1991, 220)) is not a matter of course. For long periods of history, diversity has been perceived as a threat, a challenge or nuisance, and an obstacle in the way of racially, ethnically, culturally, linguistically or religiously homogeneous states and societies. Homogeneity was perceived and pursued as a prevailing objective. In Europe, from the late 18th to the first half of the 20th century, ethnocentric nationalism had a profound negative impact on the perception of diversity as well as on the situation of minorities and colonized and indigenous peoples. Although in the last fifty years there has been considerable progress with regard to the recognition of the value of diversity in domestic and international law, the forces hostile to diversity have not vanished. In spite of decolonization, imperialism, including cultural imperialism, has by no means disappeared. Edward Said has persuasively shown the centrality of imperialist thought in modern Western culture (1993). The UNESCO Convention on the Protection and Promotion of the Diversity of Cultural Expressions is an important step forward. However, it has been strongly rejected by the United States of America.

For an Intercultural Dialogue that includes Human Rights

Accepting diversity is an urgent necessity in the world in which we live. This need is recognized by international institutions and by men and women all over the world who are working for an "alliance of civilizations" and for dialogue among cultures and religions, thus countering the sinister prophecies of an inevitable "clash of civilizations" (Huntington 1996). Kofi Annan stressed the need of the dialogue of civilizations in these terms:

> The need for dialogue among civilizations is as old as civilization itself. But today, the need is more acute than ever. Individuals who live in fear and lack of comprehension of other cultures are more likely to resort to acts of hatred, violence and destruction against a perceived "enemy." Those who are exposed to the cultures of others and learn about them through communication across cultural divides are more likely to see diversity as a strength and celebrate it as a gift (Aboulmagd et al. 2001, 11).

A meaningful intercultural dialogue should include the essential issues of human rights. Whilst defending the universality of human rights, I believe that one can get to human rights by different ways and that the different cultures and civilizations of the world can and should contribute to the "common understanding" of human rights to which the Preamble of the Universal Declaration refers. The Western concept of human rights is certainly not the only valid one, Western practice even less.

References

Arkoun, Mohammed. 2006. *Humanisme et islam. Combats et propositions*. Paris : Vrin.

Bulliet, Richard W. 1996. "The Individual in Islamic Society." In *Religious Diversity and Human Rights*, edited by Irene Bloom, J. Paul Martin, and Wayne L. Proudfoot, 175-192. New York: Columbia University Press.

Aboulmagd, A. Kamal, Lourdes Arizpe, Hanan Ashrawi, Ruth Cardoso, Jacques Delors, Leslie Gelb, Nadine Gordimer, El Hassan bin Talal, Sergey Kapitza, Hayao Kawai, Tommy Koh, Hans Küng, Graça Machel, Giandomenico Picco, Amartya Sen, Song Jian, Dick Spring, Tu Weiming, Richard von Weizsäcker and Javad Zarif. 2001. *Crossing the Divide: Dialogue among Civilizations*. South Orange: School of Diplomacy and International Relations.

Henkin, Louis. 1998. "Epilogue: Confucianism, Human Rights and 'Cultural Relativism.' " In *Confucianism and Human Rights*, edited by William Theodore de Bary and Tu Weiming, 308-314. New York: Columbia University Press.

Huntington, Samuel P. 1996. *The Clash of Civilizations and the Remaking of World Order*. New York: Simon & Schuster.

Leuprecht, Peter. 1997. "General Course. Human Rights in the New Europe." In *Collected Courses of the Academy of European Law*, Vol. V, Book 2, edited by the Academy of European Law, 135-191. Dordrecht: Kluwer Academic Publishing.

—. 2012. Reason, Justice and Dignity. A Journey to Some Unexplored Sources of Human Rights. Martinus Nijhoff Publishers, Leiden-Boston.

Lévinas, Emmanuel. 1991. *Entre Nous. Dialogue sur le penser-à-l'autre*. Paris : Grasset.

Recommendation No. 24 of the Assembly (25 August 1950).

Roetz, Heiner. 1998. "Chancen und Probleme einer Reformulierung und Neubegründung der Menschenrechte auf Basis der konfuzianischen Ethik." In *Menschenrechte und Gemeinsinn – westlicher und östlicher Weg? Ergebnisse und Beiträge der Internationalen Expertentagung der Hermann und Marianne Straniak-Stiftung*, edited by Walter Schweidler, 189-208. Weingarten: Academia Verlag Sankt Augustin.

—. 2004. "Menschenrechte in China. Ein Problem der Kultur?" In *Das Recht, Rechte zu haben. Menschenrechte und Weltreligionen,* edited by Monika Rappenecker, 105-125. Freiburg: Tagungsberichte der Katholischen Akademie der Erzdiözese Freiburg.

Said, Edward. 1993. *Culture and Imperialism*. New York: Vintage Books.

Universality of Human Rights in a Pluralistic World. 1990. *Proceedings of the Colloquy organized by the Council of Europe in cooperation with the International Institute of Human Rights*. Strasbourg 17-19 April 1989. Council of Europe: N. P. Engel, Publisher.

Notes

[1] Cf. Recommendation No. 24 of the Assembly (25 August 1950). Adopted by 46 votes to 37. Cf. Recueil des Travaux Préparatoires de la Convention européenne des Droits de l'Homme, vol. V, p. 192.

CHAPTER TWO

HUMAN RIGHTS:
A FRAGILE HEGEMONY

BOAVENTURA DE SOUSA SANTOS

There is no question today about the hegemony of human rights as the discourse of human dignity. Nonetheless, such hegemony faces a disturbing reality. The large majority of the world population is not the subject of human rights. They are rather the object of human rights discourses. The question is, then, whether human rights are efficacious in helping the struggles of the excluded, the exploited, and the discriminated against, or whether, on the contrary, they make them more difficult. In other words, is the hegemony claimed by human rights today the outcome of a historical victory, or rather of a historical defeat? Regardless of the reply given to the previous questions, the truth is that, since they are the hegemonic discourse of human dignity, human rights are insurmountable. This explains why oppressed social groups cannot help but ask the following question: even if human rights are part of the selfsame hegemony that consolidates and legitimates their oppression, could they be used to subvert it? In other words, could human rights be used in a counter-hegemonic way? If so, how? These two questions lead on to two others. Why is there so much unjust human suffering that is not considered a violation of human rights? What other discourses of human dignity are there in the world and to what extent are they compatible with human rights discourses?

The search for a counter-hegemonic conception of human rights must start from a hermeneutics of suspicion regarding human rights as they are conventionally understood and sustained, that is to say, concerning such conceptions of human rights as more closely related to their Western, liberal matrix.[1] The hermeneutics of suspicion I propose is very much indebted to Ernest Bloch (1995 [1947]), as when he wonders about the reasons why, from the eighteenth century onwards, the concept of utopia as an emancipatory political measure was gradually superseded and replaced by the concept of rights. Why was the concept of utopia less successful than the concept of law and rights as a discourse of social emancipation?[2]

We must begin by acknowledging that law and rights have a double genealogy in western modernity. On the one hand, they have an abyssal genealogy. I understand the dominant versions of western modernity as constructed on the basis of an abyssal thinking that divided the world sharply between metropolitan and colonial societies (Santos, 2007b). The division was such that the realities and practices existing on the other side of the line, i.e. in the colonies, could not possibly challenge the universality of the theories and practices in force on this side of the line. As such, they were made invisible. As a discourse of emancipation, human rights were historically meant to prevail only on this side of the abyssal line, i.e. in the metropolitan societies. It has been my contention that this abyssal line, which produces radical exclusions, far from being eliminated with the end of historical colonialism, still continues to be there by other means (neo-colonialism, racism, xenophobia, permanent state of exception in dealing with terrorists, undocumented migrant workers or asylum seekers). International law and mainstream human rights doctrines have been used to guarantee such continuity. But, on the other hand, law and rights have a revolutionary genealogy on this side of the line. Both the American Revolution and the French Revolution were fought in the name of law and rights. Ernest Bloch maintains that the superiority of the concept of law and rights has a lot to do with bourgeois individualism. The bourgeois society then emerging had already conquered economic hegemony and was fighting for political hegemony, soon to be consolidated by the American and French Revolutions. The concept of law and rights fitted perfectly the emergent bourgeois individualism inherent both to liberal theory and to capitalism. It is, therefore, easy to conclude that the hegemony enjoyed by human rights has very deep roots, and that its trajectory has been a linear path towards the consecration of human rights as the ruling principles of a just society. This idea of a long established consensus manifests itself in various ways, each one of them residing in an illusion. Because they are widely shared, such illusions constitute the common sense of conventional human rights. I distinguish four illusions: teleology, triumphalism, de-contextualization, and monolithism.

The teleological illusion consists in reading history backwards. Starting from the consensus existing today about human rights and the unconditional good it entails, and reading the past history as a linear path towards such a result. The choice of precursors is crucial in this respect.

As Moyn comments: "these are usable pasts: the construction of precursors after the fact" (2010: 12). Such an illusion prevents us from seeing that at any given historical moment different ideas of human dignity and social emancipation were in competition, and that the victory of human rights is a contingent result that can be explained *à posteriori*, but could not have been deterministically foreseen. The historical victory of human rights made possible that the same actions which, according to other conceptions of human dignity, would be considered actions of oppression and domination, were reconfigured as actions of emancipation and liberation if carried out in the name of human rights.

Related to the teleological illusion is the illusion of triumphalism, the notion that the victory of human rights is an unconditional human good. It takes for granted that all the other grammars of human dignity that have competed with the human rights were inherently inferior in ethical and political terms. This Darwinian notion does not take into account a decisive feature of hegemonic Western modernity; indeed, its true historical genius, namely the way it has managed to supplement the force of the ideas that serve its purposes with the military force which, supposedly at the service of the ideas, is actually served by them. We need, therefore, to evaluate critically the grounds for the alleged ethical and political superiority of human rights. The ideals of national liberation – socialism, communism, revolution, nationalism – constituted alternative grammars of human dignity; at certain moments, they were even the dominant ones. Suffice it to think that the twentieth century national liberation movements against colonialism, like the socialist and communist movements, did not invoke the human rights grammar to justify their causes and struggles.[3] That the other grammars and discourses of emancipation have been defeated by human rights discourses should only be considered inherently positive if it could be demonstrated that human rights, while a discourse of human emancipation, have a superior merit for reasons other than the fact that they have emerged as the winners. Until then, the triumph of human rights may be considered by some as progress and a historical victory, and by others as retrogression, a historical defeat.

This precaution helps us to face the third illusion: de-contextualization. It is generally acknowledged that human rights as an emancipatory discourse have their origin in eighteenth century Enlightenment, the French Revolution, and the American Revolution. What is seldom mentioned, however, is that since then and until today, human rights have been used in very distinct contexts and with contradictory objectives. In the eighteenth century, for instance, human rights were the main language of the ongoing revolutionary processes. But they were also used to legitimate practices that we would consider oppressive if not altogether counter-revolutionary. When Napoleon arrived in Egypt in 1798, this is how he explained his actions to the Egyptians: "People of Egypt: you will be told by our enemies, that I am come to destroy your religion. Believe them not. Tell them that I am come to restore your rights, punish your usurpers, and raise the true worship of Mahomet."[4] And thus was the invasion of Egypt legitimated by the invaders. The same could be said of Robespierre who fostered Terror during the French Revolution in the name of piety and human rights.[5] After the 1848 revolutions, human rights were no longer part of the revolution imaginary and became rather hostile to any idea of a revolutionary change of the society. But the same hypocrisy (I would call it constitutive) of invoking human rights to legitimate practices that may be considered violations of human rights continued throughout the past century and a half and is perhaps more evident today than ever. From the mid-nineteenth century onwards, human rights talk was separated from the revolutionary tradition, and began to be conceived of as a grammar of depoliticized social change, a kind of anti-politics. At best, human rights were subsumed in State law as the State assumed the monopoly of the production of law and administration of justice. This is why the Russian Revolution, unlike the French and American Revolutions, was carried out, not in the name of law, but against law (Santos, 1995: 104-107). Gradually, the predominant discourse of human rights became the discourse of the human dignity consonant with liberal politics, capitalist development and its different metamorphoses (liberal, social-democratic, neoliberal, dependent, Fordist, post-Fordist, peripheral Fordist, corporative, state capitalism) and colonialism (neocolonialism, internal colonialism, racism, slave-like labor, xenophobia, etc.). And so we must bear in mind that the selfsame human rights discourse had many very different meanings in different historical contexts, having legitimated both revolutionary and counter-revolutionary practices. Today, we cannot be even sure if present-day human rights are a legacy of the modern revolutions, or of their ruins, if they have behind them a revolutionary, emancipatory energy, or counter-revolutionary energy.

The fourth illusion is monolithism. I elaborate on it here in greater detail having in mind the main theme of this book. The illusion consists in denying or minimizing the tensions and even internal contradictions of the theories of human rights. Suffice it to remember that the French Revolution's Declaration of the Rights of Man is ambivalent as it speaks of the rights of *man* and of the *citizen*. These two words are not there by chance. From the very beginning, human rights foster ambiguity by creating belongingness to two different collective identities. One of them is supposedly a totally inclusive collectivity, humanity, hence human rights. The other is a much more restrictive collectivity, the collectivity of the citizens of a given State. This tension has troubled human rights ever since. The goal of the adoption of international declarations and of regimes and international institutions of human rights was to guarantee minimal dignity to individuals whenever their rights as members of a political collectivity did not exist or were violated. In the course of the past two hundred years, human rights were gradually incorporated into the Constitutions and were re-conceptualized as rights of citizenship, directly guaranteed by the State and adjudicated by the courts: civic, political, social, economic, and cultural rights. But the truth is that the effective, ample protection of citizenship rights has always been precarious in the large majority of countries. Human rights have been invoked mainly in situations of erosion or particularly serious violation of citizenship rights.[6] Human rights emerge as the lowest threshold of inclusion, a descending movement from the dense community of citizens to the diluted community of humanity.

The other tension illustrating the illusory nature of monolithism is the tension between individual and collective rights. The United Nations Universal Declaration of Human Rights, last century's first major universal declaration, to be followed by several others, recognizes only two lawful subjects: the individual and the State. Peoples are only recognized to the extent that they become States. When the Declaration was adopted, it should be noted, there were many peoples, nations, and communities that had no State. Thus, from the point of view of the epistemologies of the South, the Declaration cannot but be deemed colonialist (Burke, 2010; Terretta, 2012). When we speak of equality before the law, we must bear in mind that, when the Declaration was written, individuals from vast regions of the world were not equal before the law because they were subjected to collective domination, and under collective domination individual rights provide no protection. At a time of bourgeois individualism, the Declaration could not take this into account. This was a time when sexism was part of common sense, sexual orientation was taboo, class domination was each country's internal affair, and colonialism was still strong as an historical agent, in spite of the drawback of Indian independence. As time went by, sexism, colonialism, and the crassest forms of class domination came to be acknowledged as giving rise to violations of human rights. In the 1960s, anti-colonial struggles were adopted by the Declaration and became part of UN affairs. However, as it was understood at the time, self-determination concerned peoples subjected to European colonialism alone. Self-determination thus understood left many peoples subjected to internal colonization, indigenous peoples being the paramount example. More than thirty years had to go by before the right of indigenous peoples to self-determination was recognized in the United Nations Declaration on the Rights of Indigenous Peoples, adopted by the General Assembly in 2007.[7] Lengthy negotiations were needed before the International Labour Organization approved Convention 169 regarding indigenous and tribal peoples. Gradually, these documents became part of the legislation of different countries.

Since collective rights are not part of the original canon of human rights, the tension between individual and collective rights results from the historical struggle of the social groups which, being excluded or discriminated against as groups, could not be adequately protected under individual human rights. The struggles of women, indigenous peoples, afro-descendants, victims of racism, gays, lesbians, and religious minorities marked the past fifty years of the recognition of collective rights, a recognition that has been always highly contested and always on the verge of being reverted. There is necessarily no contradiction between individual and collective rights, if for nothing else because there are many kinds of collective rights. For instance, we can distinguish two kinds of collective rights, primary and derivative. We speak of derivative collective rights when the workers organize themselves in unions and confer upon them the right to represent them in negotiations with the employers. We speak of primary collective rights when a community of individuals has rights other than the rights of their organization, or renounce their individual rights on behalf of the rights of the community. These rights, in turn, may be exerted in two ways. The large majority of them are exerted individually, as when a Sikh policeman wears the turban, an Islamic female doctor wears the hijab, or when a member of an inferior caste in India, a Brazilian afro-descendant or indigene takes advantage of affirmative action provided in their communities. But there are rights that can only be exerted collectively, such as the right to self-determination. Collective rights are there to eliminate or abate the insecurity and injustice suffered by individuals that are discriminated against as the systematic victims of oppression just for being who and what they are, and not for doing what they do. Only very slowly have collective rights become part of the political agenda, whether national or international. At any rate, the contradiction or tension vis-à-vis more individualistic conceptions of human rights is always there.[8]

Bearing in mind these illusions is crucial to build a counter-hegemonic conception and practice of human rights, particularly when they must be based on a dialogue with other conceptions of human dignity and the practices sustaining them. In order to better clarify what I have in mind, I will go on to define what I consider to be the hegemonic or conventional conception of human rights. I consider the conventional understanding of human rights as having some of the following characteristics: they are universally valid irrespective of the social, political and cultural context in which they operate and of the different human rights regimes existing in different regions of the world; they are premised upon a conception of human nature as individual, self-sustaining and qualitatively different from the non-human nature; what counts as a violation of human rights is defined by universal declarations, multilateral institutions (courts and commissions) and established, global (mostly North-based) non-governmental organizations; the recurrent phenomenon of double standards in evaluating compliance with human rights in no way compromises the universal validity of human rights; the respect for human rights is much more problematic in the global South than in the global North.

The limits of this conception of human rights become obvious in the responses it gives to one of the most important questions of our time. The perplexity it provokes grounds the impulse to construct a counter-hegemonic conception of human rights as proposed in this book. The question can be formulated in this way: if humanity is one alone, why are there so many different principles concerning human dignity and a just society, all of them presumably unique, yet often contradictory among themselves? At the root of the perplexity underlying this question is a recognition that much has been left out of the modern and Western understanding of the world.

The conventional answer to this question is that such diversity is only to be recognized to the extent that it does not contradict universal human rights. By postulating the abstract universality of the conception of human dignity that underlies human rights, this answer dismisses the perplexity underlying the question. The fact that such a conception is Western based is considered irrelevant, as, so it is claimed, the historicity of human rights discourse does not interfere with its ontological status. Generally embraced by hegemonic political thinking, particularly in the global North, this answer reduces the understanding of the world to the Western understanding of the world, thus ignoring or trivializing decisive cultural and political experiences and initiatives in the countries of the global South. This is the case of movements of resistance that have been emerging against oppression, marginalization, and exclusion, whose ideological bases have often very little to do with the dominant Western cultural and political references prevalent throughout the twentieth century. These movements do not formulate their struggles in terms of human rights, and, on the contrary, rather formulate them, often enough, according to principles that contradict the dominant principles of human rights. These movements are often grounded in multi-secular cultural and historical identities, often including religious militancy. It will suffice to mention three such movements, of very distinct political meanings: the indigenous movements, particularly in Latin America; the peasant movements in Africa and Asia; and the Islamic insurgency. In spite of the huge differences among them, these movements all start out from cultural and political references that are non-Western, even if constituted by the resistance to Western domination.

Conventional or hegemonic human rights' thinking lacks the theoretical and analytical tools to position itself in relation to such movements, and even worse, it does not understand the importance of doing so. It applies the same abstract recipe across the board, hoping that thereby the nature of alternative ideologies or symbolic universes will be reduced to local specificities with no impact on the universal canon of human rights.

References

Arendt, Hannah (1968). *The Origins of Totalitarism.* New York: Harcourt Brace Jovanovich.
—. (1990). *On Revolution.* London: Penguin Books.
Bloch, Ernst (1995). *The Principle of Hope,* Cambridge: MIT Press.
Burke R. (2010). *Decolonization and the Evolution of International Human Rights.* Philadelphia: Univ. Pa. Press
Eberhard, Christoph (2002). *Droit de l'homme et dialogue interculturel.* Paris: Éditions des Écrivains.
Hurewitz, J. C. (ed.) (1975). *The Middle East and North Africa in World Politics.* New Haven: Yale University Press.
Moyn, Samuel (2010). *The Last Utopia, human rights in history.* Cambridge, Mass: Harvard University Press.
Santos, Boaventura de Sousa (1995). *Toward a New Common Sense: Law, Science and Politics in the Paradigmatic Transition.* London: Routledge.
—. (2007a). "Human Rights as an Emancipatory Script?" Cultural and Political Conditions" *in* Santos, B. S. (ed.), *Another Knowledge is Possible.* London: Verso, 3-40.

—. (2007b). "Beyond Abyssal Thinking: From Global Lines to Ecologies of Knowledges", *Review Fernand Braudel Center*, XXX (1), 45-89.

Terretta M. (2012). "We had been fooled into thinking that the UN watches over the entire world": human rights, UN trust territories, and Africa's decolonization. *Human Rights Quarterly*. 34(2): 329–60.

Notes

[1] The liberal matrix conceives of human rights as individual rights and privileges civic and political rights. Upon this matrix, other conceptions of human rights evolved, namely those inspired by Marxist

or, more generally, socialist ideas that recognize collective rights and privilege economic and social rights over civic and political rights. On the different conceptions of human rights, see Santos, 1995: 250- 378 and Santos, 2007a: 3-40.

[2] Moyn (2010) considers human rights to be the last utopia, the grand political mission that emerges after the collapse of all the others. His insightful historical analysis on human rights is very convergent with my own.

[3] This point is also mentioned by Moyn (2010:89-90) who adds that neither Gandhi nor Sukarno or Nasser viewed in human rights doctrine an empowering instrument.

[4] "Napoleon's Proclamation to the Egyptians, 2 July 1798", cited in Hurewitz (ed.) 1975: 116.

[5]. For a detailed analysis of this issue, see Arendt, 1968 and 1990.

[6] This is what is happening today in many countries of the European Union, countries struck by the economic and financial crisis of the euro zone.

[7] Available at: http://www.un.org/esa/socdev/unpfii/documents/DRIPS_pt.pdf. Accessed 18 March 2013.

[8] Another dimension of the illusion of monolithism, not addressed in this book is the issue of the Western cultural premises of human rights and the quest for an intercultural conception of human rights. I address this dimension elsewhere. See Santos, 2007a. See also Eberhard (2002).

CHAPTER THREE

CRITICAL ENGAGEMENT WITH HUMAN RIGHTS DISCOURSE

COLLEEN SHEPPARD

Human rights discourse is pervasive and powerful. It is widely acknowledged as an important normative source of affirmation of the needs and concerns of individuals and groups, particularly those who are excluded from power and privilege in society. Human rights are also legally recognized at multiple levels, including the international, regional, national, local and institutional levels. The panoply of human rights instruments and the range of issues they address are impressive. In a global context where human rights are so widely endorsed, it is important to critically reflect upon the promise and the perils of an increasingly ubiquitous human rights discourse.

In this chapter, I highlight four critical reflections about human rights discourse, highlighting examples that address issues of diversity in the Canadian context. First, I maintain that it is important to ensure that the rhetoric of human rights does not mask the realities of systemic and ongoing violations of human rights. Second, a critical lens requires us to assess the terminology, words and language relied upon in our human rights debates. How does the vocabulary of human rights shape our understanding of the issues, or risk misrepresenting the dynamics of power, privilege and entitlement? A third critical reflection on human rights goes beyond the terminology to question the extent to which traditional human rights categories and concepts limit the kinds of *substantive* claims that are advanced. Indeed, post-colonial scholars have contributed to a rich and continuing debate about the limits of human rights law, recognizing both its transformational potential and the ways it is "fraught with conceptual and cultural problems" (Mutua 2008; de Sousa Santos, ch.2; Narain, ch. 6). Furthermore, even beyond the *substantive* limits of human rights discourse, it is important to re-evaluate the *processes* of human rights enforcement and to consider how we might

extend the relevance of the underlying norms of human rights beyond
formal legal channels and procedures to the everyday institutional and
social contexts of decision-making about exclusion, inclusion and respect
for fundamental human dignity.

Rhetoric versus Reality

One of the most apparent contradictions in the world of human rights is
the vast gulf between extensive legal endorsement of human rights by state
actors in international conventions, national constitutions and domestic
legislation and the persistent realities of widespread human rights
violations. Some have suggested that in a world of pervasive and
systematic violations of human rights, the "triumph of human rights" is
"something of a paradox" (Douzinas 2009, 2). Indeed, some of the most
comprehensive and generous enumerations of human rights are included in
documents where the likelihood of enforcement is quite low. It is striking,
for example, that international human rights conventions, which are often
difficult to enforce in national courts and tribunals, contain more
comprehensive protections than domestic laws. The *Convention on the
Rights of the Child*, for example, is the most widely recognized
international human rights treaty in history, with over 190 countries
having ratified, accepted or acceded to it, albeit with some state
reservations or interpretations (United Nations 2012a). The first legally
binding international instrument to incorporate the full range of human
rights, the UN Convention's protection extends to civil and political rights,
as well as economic, social and cultural rights. Such an extensively
endorsed statement of rights, however, stands in stark contradiction to the
widespread reality of rights violations for children in countries around the
world (Children's Rights International Network 2012). Similarly, although
women's rights are widely endorsed in the *Convention on the Elimination
of Discrimination against Women* (United Nations 2012b), they are
routinely violated, with violence against women, poverty and income
disparities on the increase. Furthermore, some national constitutions
contain extensive and comprehensive human rights protection without any
guarantees of effective enforcement. It is important, therefore, to resist the
assumption that the inclusion of human rights in legal documents means
that those rights are respected and protected in reality. One of the major
challenges of human rights in our times is the persistent and significant
gap between human rights on paper and human rights in reality.

In the Canadian context, two examples illustrate the risk of a gap
between rhetoric and reality. The first example concerns the continued

disproportionately high number of murders of Indigenous women in Canada. Despite a longstanding constitutional commitment to the rule of law and equality in the administration of justice in Canada, the 2004 Amnesty International report,entitled *Stolen Sisters: A Human Rights Response to Discrimination and Violence against Indigenous Women in Canada* (2004) documents systemic and pervasive violence in the lives of indigenous women – and tells the story of nine missing and murdered indigenous women and girls. Poverty, racism and social exclusion are identified as factors that contribute to heightened risks of violence in Aboriginal women's lives. The report also documents inadequate police protection and inequalities in access to government services – two critical components of equality in the administration of justice – and one of the most basic civil rights. Though the Canadian government has acknowledged the problem, a 2009 Amnesty update on human rights violations facing indigenous women concluded "[u]nfortunately, the federal government has shown little leadership in addressing the issue. Most of the positive measures initiated by individual police services or by provincial or territorial governments and have not been replicated nationally" (Amnesty International 2009, 4).[1]

A second example that highlights the gap between the rhetoric of human rights and the reality of continued violation of rights is workplace inequities. Despite anti-discrimination legislation prohibiting racial discrimination in employment since the 1960s and 70s, and employment equity legislation requiring affirmative action in federally-regulated workplaces and in many provincially-regulated workplaces through contract compliance programs, there are still vast disparities in workplace equality. A 2005 Québec government consultation document revealed an "unemployment rate in the black population twice that of the total population" (Ministère de l'Immigration 2005, 7), a higher percentage of seasonal work, and significantly lower average incomes. A 2009 study on the difficulties of workforce inclusion by North African Immigrants in Québec (Lenoir-Achdjian et al. 2009) exposed that according to 2001 Statistics Canada data, unemployment rates were 17.5 percent for Moroccans and 27.2 percent for Algerians, compared with the provincial average of 8.2 percent. Among Moroccans and Algerians who had lived in Quebec five years or less, the unemployment rates were even higher, at 33.6 percent and 35.4 percent, respectively. Compared to the national unemployment average of 7.4 percent (Statistics Canada 2011), this data raises serious questions about equitable access to employment in Canada.[2] Thus, it is clearly not enough to espouse human rights values or to affirm them in legal documents: we need to ensure that governments and citizens are held accountable and responsible for ensuring that the rights on paper are actualized. I have highlighted two Canadian examples to further underscore the need to remain vigilant in contesting the gap between rhetoric and reality, since Canada is often thought of as a beacon of hope in the domain of human rights. Yet, even in Canada, persistent gaps between rhetoric and reality persist.

Human Rights Terminology: How Words Shape Meaning

A second dimension of critical engagement with human rights insists on ensuring that human rights discourse is not used to misrepresent or skew the realities of power, privilege and entitlement. How does the language and terminology we use shape the ways in which we think about key issues and debates?

Scholars have critiqued the very idea of "rights" and rights discourse as indeterminate, as reducing complex societal issues to claims against the state, as rooted in the values of classical liberal individualism, as reflecting the biases of western colonial world views, to name just some of the many and compelling theoretical arguments (West 2011). Yet, rights discourse has also been embraced by those without power or privilege in society and praised for conveying a meaning more compelling than a language of needs, moral obligations, or interests (Williams 1987). The risk of rights being conceptualized exclusively in terms of individual claims has also been challenged through the reconceptualization of rights in relational terms (Minow, Nedelsky). And the alleged western philosophical bias of human rights has been questioned by those who find the roots of human rights concepts in non-western philosophy and law (El Obaid, Leuprecht). Legal anthropologists have also noted a "vernacularization" of rights discourse to local cultural and social struggles (Merry). The language of rights, therefore, has proven resilient and elastic – infused with multiple meanings linked to diverse and myriad contextual realities.

The statist focus of human rights claims has also been revisited. Human rights discourse emerged in the post-World War II era as a check on egregious violations of fundamental human dignity by state actors. Yet, it is striking that the International Declaration of Human Rights speaks about universal human rights as a:

> ... common standard of achievement for all peoples and all nations, to the end that **every individual and every organ of society,** keeping this Declaration constantly in mind, shall strive by teaching and education to promote respect for these rights and freedoms and by progressive measures, national and international, to secure their universal and effective

recognition and observance .... (UN Declaration 1948, *Preamble*; emphasis added.)

Human rights were conceived as a project whose responsibility extended from the macro to the micro level – from global and international to domestic and individual. Although the subsequent elaboration of international human rights obligations in the foundational human rights covenants (including, for example, the Covenant on Civil and Political Rights and the Covenant on Economic, Social and Cultural Rights) focused on state actors and formal law enforcement, there is a growing literature about the importance of extending human rights obligations to private actors (i.e. corporations). Through the lens of legal pluralism, the importance of understanding the interaction between formal and informal laws in the domain of human rights if effective enforcement of public law norms is to be achieved (Provost and Sheppard).

Turning to the Canadian context, an interesting example that helps us to reflect upon how terminology shapes our thinking and public debate on critical human rights issues is the idea of "reasonable accommodation" of religious diversity in public spaces. Indeed, this is an issue that resonates with public debates and controversies in many countries around the world (Elver 2012). In 2007, Québec Premier Jean Charest established the *Consultation Commission on Accommodation Practices Related to Cultural Differences.* The Commission (Bouchard and Taylor 2008) was a response to public debate and vocal opposition to legal decisions and a series of incidents involving the accommodation of religious minorities in Québec. Sparked in part by a legal decision invoking freedom of religion, that affirmed the right of a young Sikh boy to wear the ceremonial dagger known as the *kirpan* sewn under his clothing at school (*Multani* v. *Commission scolaire Marguerite-Bourgeoys* 2006), the fear over the slippery slope of accommodation materialized. Controversies had arisen about Muslim prayer space in public spaces, Muslim women wearing hijabs or niqabs, and the wearing of religious symbols at work. Similarly, in the wake of the Commission, the Québec government proposed a law delineating the limits of requests for accommodation in the provision of public services. Bill 94 (entitled *An Act to establish guidelines governing accommodation requests within the Administration and certain institutions*; 2011) outlined security, communication and identification justifications for requiring individuals to have their faces uncovered when seeking government services. The bill was a direct response to a small number of controversies involving Muslim women wearing the niqab or facial covering in public settings, such as schools and hospitals. The bill (which was not ultimately enacted) codified existing human rights jurisprudence, but emphasized the possibility of limiting accommodation.

In engaging critically with human rights discourse, it is important to question the terminology of human rights debates and public policy. It is significant that the government established a consultative Commission on *accommodation* rather than a Commission on *equality* or on *equitable inclusion*. The language of accommodation has the tendency to presume the legitimacy of dominant societal norms while casting those seeking accommodation as "others." With respect to "reasonable accommodation," who has the power to define what is "reasonable"? The appointment of two senior (albeit highly respected) white men to head the Commission sent a significant symbolic message in this regard. As Gwen Brodsky and Sheila Day, two scholars and legal activists have written in critiquing the notion of accommodation in anti-discrimination law:

> The difficulty with this paradigm is that it does not challenge the imbalances of power, or the discourses of dominance, such as racism, able-bodyism and sexism, which result in a society being designed well for some and not for others. It allows those who consider themselves "normal" to continue to construct institutions and relations in their image, as long as others, when they challenge this construction are "accommodated."
>
> … Accommodation does not go to the heart of the equality question, to the goal of transformation, to an examination of the way institutions and relations must be changed in order to make them available, accessible, meaningful and rewarding for the many diverse groups of which our society is composed. Accommodation seems to mean that we do not change procedures or services, we simply "accommodate" those who do not quite fit. We make some concessions to those who are "different," rather than abandoning the idea of "normal" and working for genuine inclusiveness (1996, 462).

In the context of the Québec debates on cultural and religious diversity, feminist scholars critiqued the language of "accommodation," suggesting that it "assumes and perpetuates a system of power whereby western "hosts" act as gatekeepers for non-western "guests." In this way, it "constructs certain ethno-cultural communities as perpetual outsiders and as threats to Québec identity rather than as integral to it" (Simone de Beauvoir Institute 2007). Many more examples could be raised to illustrate how language shapes meaning and understanding and to underscore the importance of identifying the biases and presumptions embedded in the language we use.

The Limits of Traditional Human Rights Categories and Concepts

A third way in which we can engage critically with human rights discourse – to ensure that traditional human rights *categories* and *concepts* do not limit the kinds of *substantive claims* that we make – often the complexities of social exclusion and structural inequality – does not fit neatly into *existing human rights categories.* Rather than ignoring the lessons of complex experiential knowledge that defies neat juridical categorization, we need to learn from it and challenge the coherence of legal categories and rights. To illustrate this concern, it is interesting to examine the categorical underpinnings of the legal concept of discrimination – a concept that is central to ensuring respect for minorities in diverse societies.

Legal protections against discrimination were first developed to redress historical concerns facing particular social groups, including racial, ethnic and religious minorities, and women. Human rights documents, therefore, were introduced to eliminate discrimination based on discrete grounds of discrimination, such as race, national or ethnic origin, religion, sex. Beyond the continued expansion of the list of recognized legal grounds of discrimination to include, for example, physical and mental disability, and sexual orientation, there has been a growing appreciation that individuals facing inequality often experience discrimination on more than one ground at the same time (Crenshaw 1989; Grabham et al. 2009; Sheppard 2011). The realities of exclusion and inequality are much more complex than the standard categories of anti-discrimination law. Gender-based discrimination, for example, affects different women differently and is deeply linked to other dimensions of their identity, including race, ethnicity, age, religion, sexual orientation, and disability. The same is true of all of the various grounds of discrimination and their interplay with other grounds. Economic vulnerability and social class also impact upon the multidimensional and complex character of discrimination.

Yet, legal remedies still too often force individuals to choose one dimension of their identity as the basis of their legal claim – sometimes different legal complaints procedures exist for different grounds of discrimination – forcing individuals to choose which dimension of their identity to focus on in raising issues of inequality and discrimination. Take the example of the women refused public services while wearing a face covering – or niqab in public is the discrimination she faces linked to her gender or her religion or a combination of both? Separating them into separate legal claims is impossible and risks misrepresenting her experiential reality of exclusion. To focus on religion is to negate the gendered realities of her situation – to focus on gender would ignore the critical role of religion. Concepts such as "multiple discrimination" and "intersectional discrimination" have emerged to describe the phenomenon of overlapping and intersecting inequality. They fundamentally challenge traditional legal approaches to grounds-based discrimination, but such challenges are essential to the continued evolution of equality rights.

While some scholars struggle to incorporate intersectional analysis into legal doctrines of discrimination, others suggest that the complexities of human identity render analyses based on the delineation of ever more complex categories or groups unworkable. They propose instead a fundamental rethinking of our conceptual frameworks and a shift away from claims rooted in discrete group-based categories. Though oppositional, both responses demonstrate a willingness to engage critically with human rights discourse and attest to a willingness to reexamine and revise legal categories when our understanding of the experiential realities of human rights so demand.

Rethinking Human Rights Implementation: Processes of Human Rights Engagement

Beyond the importance of challenging and transforming the *substantive* categories and concepts of human rights – critical engagement with human rights prompts a rethinking of *how, when, and where we engage with human rights*. In other words, it entails a critical reevaluation of the *processes* of human rights enforcement. The traditional paradigm of human rights focuses on formal law and the responsibility of the state to prevent human rights violations pursuant to retroactive legal processes and redress; it is a top down state-based model. There is growing recognition, however, that remedying systemic and structural inequalities and human rights abuses requires more participatory, preventive and proactive approaches. Indeed, some of the most effective strategies for implementing human rights do not rely on top-down, state-based retroactive strategies. Instead they are built from the bottom up and empower those at the bottom of institutional and social hierarchies. The effective enforcement of human rights, therefore, requires its integration into the institutional and community contexts of everyday life.

At a broader societal level, *process* issues are also critically important. In Canada, we live in a country of rich and diverse language, ethnic, racial, religious, regional, social, and cultural diversity. Recognition of multiple identities as integral to a conception of Canadian political nationality and citizenship must also go beyond the question of what substantive rights are recognized in our Charters to examine the further question of *how* diverse communities engage with each other. To this end, we need to nurture inclusive models of citizenship through democratic processes of governance and accountability that promote dialogue across the divides of difference that separate us. In James Tully's important work on Canadian constitutionalism in an age of diversity – he emphasized the importance of constitutionalism as a philosophy and practice that entails "the negotiation and mediation of claims to recognition" through dialogue within a context of "mutual recognition" (1995, 206, 209). We need a democratic constitutionalism that is attentive to adequate representation, mutual recognition, inclusive participation, consultation, and dialogue (Sheppard 2013). Critical engagement with human rights, therefore, requires attentiveness to institutional and social relations and the nurturing of relations of care, democracy and inclusive processes for governance in the public and private communities of everyday life.

References

Amnesty International. 2004. "Stolen Sisters: A Human Rights Response to Discrimination and Violence Against Indigenous Women in Canada." Accessed August 9, 2012.
http://www.amnesty.org/en/library/asset/AMR20/003/2004/en/c6d84a5 9-d57b-11dd-bb24-1fb85fe8fa05/amr200032004en.pdf.
—. 2009. "No More Stolen Sisters: The Need for a Comprehensive Response to Discrimination and Violence Against Indigenous Women in Canada." Accessed August 9, 2012.
http://www.amnesty.org/en/library/asset/AMR20/012/2009/en%20/194 3e1ef-1d45-4c42-a991-c6f0eea23a97/amr200122009en.pdf.
Assemblée Nationale du Québec. *Bill n°94: An Act to establish guidelines governing accommodation requests within the Administration and certain institutions.* 2nd Sess, 39th Leg, Quebec.
Bilge, Sirma and Olivier Roy. 2010. "La discrimination intersectionnelle: la naissance et le développement d'un concept et les paradoxes de sa mise en application en droit antidiscriminatoire." *Canadian Journal of Law and Society* 25(1) : 51-74.
Bouchard, Gérard and Charles Taylor. 2008. *Building the future: A time for reconciliation.* Montreal: Government of Québec.
Bowleg, Lisa. 2008. "When Black + Lesbian + Woman =/ Black Lesbian Woman: The methodological challenges of qualitative and quantitative intersectionality research." *Sex Roles* 59 (5): 312-325.

Children's Rights International Network. 2012. "Home." Accessed July 23. http://www.crin.org/.

Crenshaw, Kimberlé. 1989. "Demarginalizing the intersection between race and sex: A Black feminist critique of anti-discrimination doctrine, feminist theory and anti-racist politics" *University of Chicago Legal Forum*: 139-167.

Day, Shelagh and Gwen Brodsky. 1996. "The Duty to Accommodate: Who Will Benefit? " *Canadian Bar Review* 75: 433-462.

Douzinas, Costas. 2000. *The End of Human Rights.* Portland: Hart Publishing.

—. 2007. *Human Rights and Empire–The Political Philosophy of Cosmopolitanism.* Milton Park: Routledge-Cavendish.

Elver, Hilal. 2012. The Headscarf Controversy, Secularism and Freedom of Religion. Oxford: Oxford University Press.

Global Conference on Human Rights and Diverse Societies. 2011. Panel presentation at Echenberg Family Conferences, McGill Centre for Human Rights and Legal Pluralism in Montreal, October.

Grabham, Emily, Didi Herman, Davina Cooper and Jane Krishnadas, eds. 2009. *Intersectionality and beyond–Law, power and the politics of location.* New York: Routledge-Cavendish.

Haida Nation v. British Columbia (Minister of Forests), 2004 SCC 73.

Hannett, Sarah. 2003. "Equality at the intersections: The legislative and judicial failure to tackle multiple discrimination." *Oxford Journal of Legal Studies* 23(1): 65-86.

Ignatieff, Michael. 2001. *Human Rights As Politics and Idolatry.* Edited and with an introduction by Amy Gutmann. With Commentary by K. Anthony Appiah, David Hollinger, Thomas W. Laqueur and Diane F. Orentlicher, 101-116. Princeton: Princeton University Press.

Ignatieff, Michael. Tanner Lectures on human rights. http://www.tannerlectures.utah.edu/lectures/documents/Ignatieff_01.pdf

Kennedy-Dubourdieu, Elaine, ed. 2006. *Race and inequality–World perspectives on affirmative action.* Burlington: Ashgate.

Lenoir-Achdjian, Annick, Sébastien Arcand, Denise Helly, Isabelle Drainville and Michèle Vatz Laaroussi. 2009. "Les difficultés d'insertion en emploi des immigrants du Maghreb au Québec: une question de perspective." Choix IRPP 15(3). ISSN 0711-0685.

Ministère de l'Immigration et des Communautés culturelles. 2005. "Des valeurs partagées, des intérêts communs : la pleine participation à la société québécoise des communautés noires." Accessed August 9, 2012.

http://www.micc.gouv.qc.ca/publications/fr/dossiers/Consultation-communautes-noires-francais.pdf.

Monture-Angus, Patricia. 1995. *Thunder in my soul: A Mohawk woman speaks*. Halifax: Fernwood.

Multani v. *Commission scolaire Marguerite-Bourgeoys*, [2006] 1 SCR 256.

Mutua, Makai, 2008

Native Council of Nova Scotia v. *Canada (Attorney General)*, 2011 FC 72.

R. v. *Finley*, 2011 SKPC 16.

Razack, Sherene H. 2008. *Casting Out: The Eviction of Muslims from Western Law and Politics*. Toronto: University of Toronto Press.

Sheppard, Colleen. 2006. "Challenging systemic racism: Affirmative action and equity for racialized communities and Aboriginal Peoples in Canada." In *Race and Inequality: World Perspectives on Affirmative Action*, edited by Elaine Kennedy-Dubourdieu, 43-61. Burlington: Ashgate Press.

—. 2013. "Inclusion, Voice and Process-based Constitutionalism" *Osgoode Hall L.J.* 50, 557-574.

—. 2010. *Inclusive equality–The relational dimensions of systemic discrimination in Canada*. Montreal: McGill-Queen's University Press.

—. 2011. *Multiple Discrimination in the World of Work*. Working Paper No. 66. Geneva: ILO. http://www.ilo.org/wcmsp5/groups/public/---ed_norm/---declaration/documents/publication/wcms_170015.pdf.

Simone de Beauvoir Institute, Concordia University. 2007. "'Reasonable Accomodation': A feminist response." Accessed August 9, 2012. http://www.peoplescommission.org/files/poped/08.%20Simone%20de Beauvoir%20Statement%20EN.pdf.

Solanke, Iyiola. 2009. "Putting race and gender together: A new approach to intersectionality." *Modern Law Review* 72(5): 723-749.

Statistics Act, R.S.C. 1985, c. S-19.

Statistics Canada. 2011. "Latest release from the Labour Force Survey." Last modified July 8. http://www.statcan.gc.ca/subjects-sujets/labour-travail/lfs-epa/lfs-epa-eng.htm?WT.mc_id=twtB0063.

Tully, James. 1995. *Strange Multiplicity: Constitutionalism in an Age of Diversity*. Cambridge: Cambridge University Press.

UN Fundamental Principle 1. 2012. "Principle 1 - Relevance, impartiality and equal access." Accessed August 9. http://unstats.un.org/unsd/goodprac/bpaboutpr.asp?RecId=1.

United Nations. 2012a. "Convention of the Rights of the Child." Accessed August 9.

http://treaties.un.org/pages/ViewDetails.aspx?src=TREATY&mtdsg_n
o=IV-11&chapter=4&lang=en
—. 2012b. "Convention on the Elimination of All Forms of
Discrimination Against Women." Accessed 23 July.
http://treaties.un.org/Pages/ViewDetails.aspx?src=TREATY&mtdsg_n
o=IV-8&chapter=4&lang=en.
Universal Declaration of Human Rights, G.A. res. 217A (III), U.N. Doc
A/810 at 71 (1948).
West, Robin L. 2011. "Tragic rights: the rights critique in the age of
Obama." *William and Mary Law Review* 53: 713-746.
Williams, Patricia. 1987. "Alchemical Notes: Reconstructing Ideals from
Deconstructed Rights." *Harvard Civil Rights-Civil Liberties Law
Review* 22: 401-33.

Notes

[1] The 2009 Amnesty report also highlights the pervasive violations of economic and social rights in Indigenous communities (2009, 8). Of the 2500 reserves in Canada, one quarter of the water treatment systems on reserves pose a high risk to human health.

[2] Of significance as well is the fact that this type of data, so critical to understanding the realities of inequality, is at risk, given the Canadian government's decision to eliminate the long form Statistics Canada mandatory census. "Official statistics provide an indispensable element in the information system of a democratic society, serving the Government, the economy and the public with data about the economic, demographic, social and environmental situation" (UN Fundamental Principle 1 2012). On the importance of the census in Canadian society, see (*R.* v. *Finley* 2011), where the merits of the long form census were discussed in some detail; the Court ultimately found that the defendant had not her burden of proof with regard to the demonstration of the unreasonable breach of privacy. On the importance of the long form census for Aboriginal programs, see the recent case of (*Native Council of Nova Scotia* v. *Canada* 2011), where the applicants argued that changes to the 2011 survey are contrary to the Crown's constitutional and legal obligations to aboriginal peoples, infringe the constitutional and legal rights of aboriginal peoples to equality and non-discrimination, and will result in the Crown being unable to fulfill its duties under the *Statistics Act* (1985). The Federal Court dismissed the case.

PART II

POST-COLONIAL THEORY
AND HUMAN RIGHTS

CHAPTER FOUR

THE CHALLENGE OF DEMOCRACY IN DIVIDED SOCIETIES OF THE POST-COLONIAL WORLD

RANABIR SAMADDAR

I. The heterogeneous world of post-colonial democracy

Experiences of the third world suggest that in post-colonial countries, societies remain divided. Though China is exceptional, given its revolutionary independence and socialist history, my observations emerge from an overwhelming amount of evidence in the third world. This suggests that democracy, at least in its present institutional form/s, is unable to address the question of divisions in society or the complexities of rights. Now, we may begin by saying that divisions are not only divisions, but are reflections of social pluralities. However, these are not reflections in any ordinary mirror. They appear and function like fault lines and divisions in the mirror of power. Therefore, how to address the issue of plurality and how to make democracy appropriate and functioning in the context of pluralistic societies are significant challenges for human rights discourse.

The challenge is to re-transform divisions into pluralities, formal and informal partitions into accommodations, contest into dialogue, and power into desire (to co-exist). In societies ravaged by colonialism and post-colonial globalisation, where differences have been accentuated due to faulty resource planning and utilisation, global economic domination, agrarian disaster, and industrial breakdown, the challenge for democracy is to manage conflicts, protect the rights of the victims of conflicts, and make plural solutions possible.

The conventional wisdom is that the rule of law is essential for the realisation of rights. The critical question will initially be: Is the *rule of law* enough in these societies? At one level it seems to be the common wisdom of the international managers of peace and state building that most third world countries require a strong foundation of rule of law. By this, is meant regular elections, press freedom, an electoral system, independent judiciary, market freedom and limited economic regulation, certain constitutionally guaranteed individual freedoms, a strong police system and a criminal punishment code. Yet as we know, from the case of India and several other post-colonial countries, divides persist, different forms of domination such as linguistic, religious, cultural, economic, political, resource-centric, national, etc. persist, and these divides accentuate existing inequalities. In face of these divides, asymmetries, and inequalities, the formal institutional features just described become increasingly ineffective. Rights become increasingly governmentalized. They lose the fulcrum of justice. Consequently, large sections of the population lose faith in the rule of law.

The challenge here is to creatively democratise the society along with the political structure, not on the basis of market reforms (which indeed may be necessary but in a different way), but on the basis of justice, legal pluralism, and dialogic culture. These are elements to be found in the dialogic past of post-colonial societies, whose history lies in anti-colonial struggles and traditions of popular coalition building. The issue is: What will be the institutional forms of what can be called *experiments in new democracy*? As instances of the challenge, I wish to point out here three issues in institutionalising rights and democracy. These three issues will also substantiate the point about the challenge for democracy in our time. These issues are:

(a) Protection of minorities
(b) Politics of dialogue
(c) The issue of justice

While these issues reflect in a congealed manner the challenge for democracy in post-colonial situations, we have to ask: Can the discourse of rights lead to greater autonomy of social collectivities in a democracy? Can a dialogic framework replace the framework of centralisation of power? And finally, can democracy embody the norms of what can be called minimal justice? Based on Indian and general South Asian experiences of rule and resistance, this essay intends to deal with the challenge of rights and democracy in the post-colonial world.

II. Minorities in post-colonial democracy

We can take, *first*, the instance of minority protection. As we know, rights discourse in relation to minorities began in earnest with the United Nations Declaration of Human Rights, then the International Covenant on

Civil and Political Rights (ICCPR), then with other treaties and conventions, right up to the 1992 UN Declaration on the Rights of Persons Belonging to National or Ethnic Religious and Linguistic Minorities. The rights approach also got a boost from anti-colonial struggles, anti-fascist wars, and the emphasis on individual rights and constitutionalism. Later on came group rights. Europe also became an example. The treaty route had been important in Europe for the regional protection of minorities. Thus, with the treaties of Locarno and Rapallo began a long route that in the process created autonomous communities like in South Tyrol, followed by the Basle Charter, the European Court, the OSCE, and the arrangement of the Commissioner for protection of minorities. But why was this route not very successful in many countries in Asia or Africa? Of the several clues that may contribute to answering this question, we can mention a few: in the context of anti-colonial struggles, minority groups that contributed to the national alliance against domination now refuse to be silent spectators to majoritarian polities (either in Sri Lanka or India). Thus, accords for minority rights failed in Sri Lanka; bilateral treaties also failed or were only of limited success, such as the Pakistan-India joint accord in the form of the Nehru-Liaquat Ali pact. In short, minorities refuse to be satisfied with the legal status of being a minority and refuse to look for protection to a benevolent majority. Moreover, in many countries, they have not even been accorded this recognition (e.g. the Chittagong Hill Tracts population in Bangladesh). Riots have occurred. Government-backed pogroms have taken place.

Everywhere, the lesson is the same, namely that *minority population groups* demand the status of a *people*. The implication is that in a post-colonial context, democracy calls for shared sovereignty and a creative federalisation of politics. Sovereignty is shared by a new dialogic arrangement between different peoples, who become the constituents of what can be called a new federalism. The further implication of this is that the idea of justice becomes as important as the idea of rights. Though mainstream constitutional thinking has yet to welcome notions of pluralism, shared sovereignty, protection of common property resources, autonomy, decentralisation, and many other forms of direct democracy, a study of emerging critical juridical practices will show the trajectory of what we can call the possibilities of new democracy. Mechanical adoption of representative democracy may not work in such contexts. Again, India is a good illustration.[1]

The scenario of claims regarding minority protection is characterized by two developments. First, the ideology of nationalism brings into existence a nationalising state that thrives on fictive ethnicity, builds up a fictive ethnic core, makes majoritarianism the culture of the state, and encourages the belief in the minds of the members of the political class that strengthening republican nationhood is the way for the survival of communities through their integration with the nation. Because the search for a non-national state form, that is to say for a non-national form of political living, is seen as deviant political behaviour, minority rights are not seen as belonging to a category having rights to self-determination, which would form the core of group rights. They are not "rights;" instead they are treated as claims to "protection" by the State. Second, community rights are seen not as rights that redefine citizenship, but as factors that will enhance the republican spirit of the nation by reinforcing it with group participation. Since minority rights have emerged in this country only in the wake of the spread of the ideas of nationalism and republican democracy, minority rights have never appeared as an isolated item in a nationalist agenda. Identity politics are seen in terms of extra-territorial linkages, ethnicity (which by definition cannot be co-terminus with national territoriality), and the breakdown and formation of new states. In short, minority rights are considered to be challenging the state and the states-system. Against such a background, for critical theory the task of examining the juridical-political claims of the State regarding protection of minorities is important, but complex. This is more so in a context where the task of a democratic State to accord primary importance to individual rights is seen as not enough, simply because recognition of the individual is not enough today; and groups and communities have to be granted rights in order to make government work in a situation of diversity.

The strength of the discourse of minority rights has been that it is capable of drawing attention to the weaknesses of modern constitutionalism which acknowledges only individuals, legally guaranteed institutions and sometimes federal units (for example, states in India) as political actors. Communities are not accepted as legitimate actors. The defence of communities in India in the arena of juridical-political rights emanates from the imperative to defend communities and indigenous people from marginality in the wake of policies ushered in by the state in a climate of globalisation and economic restructuring. Protection becomes a key strategy particularly in non-dialogic contexts, where it appears that groups do not encourage tolerance; they produce hatred, and equality of rights becomes equality in hate acts. Multiculturalism, as a philosophy of diversity and as a policy response encourages accommodation of immigrant minority communities in the national community. The accommodation of differences generates a strategy of protection; the nationalising state adopts the strategy; yet as Sarah Joseph notes, it remains committed to a politics of assimilation, repression, denial, exclusion, and marginality (Joseph 1998). Protection, therefore, never addresses the issue of unequal power in society.

Protective mechanisms include of course the Indian National Human Rights Commission, and, wherever formed, the State Human Rights Commissions, as in West Bengal which passed the Protection of Human Rights Act in 1993. The Act constituting the Commissions does not show any awareness of the significance of group rights, with the result that whereas there is a National Commission for Minorities constituted under Section 3 of the National Commission for Minorities Act of 1982, a National Commission for the Scheduled Castes and Scheduled Tribes as referred to by/in Article 338 of the Constitution, and a National Commission for Women formed by Section 3 of the National Commission for Women Act of 1990, the National Human Rights Commission is based on the idea that human rights are fundamentally individual rights with special protective mechanisms for particular group rights. This disjunction results in a deficit in the mandate of the human rights mechanism. Similarly, the West Bengal Human Rights Commission (formed under the Human Rights Act of 1993) regulations do not require the Commission to develop any particular mechanism or procedure to safeguard group rights, and confines them to normal administrative and magisterial inquiry, implementation and follow-up procedure. Protection of group rights is "special," not "normal" – by implication an abnormal task. This explains the extraordinary co-incidence of institutional protection of human rights and daily violations of rights of minorities. Indeed, as the example of the Annual Report of the West Bengal Human Rights Commission (1999) suggests, the violations of human rights of individuals are very much violations of rights of individuals belonging to weaker and minority communities – Muslims, scheduled castes and women, particularly women belonging to these two groups. Unfortunately the table (in the said Report) on cases admitted by the Commission speaks of 51 custodial deaths that year, 95 incidents of rape and other indignities to women, 409 complaints against the police for abuses of rights, and 79 complaints against jail administration. The Report, however, does not provide a breakdown of the victims according to their community-identity (1999, 91-92). Nevertheless, the identities of the persons whose rights are being violated can be discerned from selective narratives in the Report, and the way in which these violations take place, extending from deaths due to rodent bites, sodomy, abuses in mental hospitals and jails, indiscretions by authorities including illegal arrests, demolitions by police, and firings, to non-implementation of recommendations and directives by appropriate authorities for redress.

It should not astonish us that the situation is so, considering that protection is a bureaucratic task and that therefore the members of the Commission are all nominated by the Government, which includes bureaucrats as well (Article 3.2 of the Act). The Commission, as expected, has stayed away from incidences of daily abuse, humiliation, and the sense of disempowerment that members belonging to minority communities face in their political-juridical-social existence. It is this disjunction (also because of the co-existence of the denial of political rights and the conceptualization of minority rights as fundamentally a cultural question as framed by Article 29 (1) of the Constitution) that the protective mechanisms of government cannot address.[2]

In order to understand the very limited nature of the institutional protection offered to the minorities in India – this disjuncture between the institutional language of protecting human rights, in particular minority rights, and the everyday domination of the minorities – it is necessary to look more deeply into the constitutional foundations of the current institutional order. In so doing, we can begin to explain the strange coincidences of everyday discrimination and suppression of minorities and the constitutionally guaranteed arrangements for the protection of rights, in particular minority rights. While the term "minority" was popular among all groups claiming special provisions and therefore invoked in the Constituent Assembly, the term "minorities" was removed altogether from the constitutional provisions dealing with group preference.[3] A benevolent majority community cast in the mould of easy-going, responsible, protective, self-sacrificing, and accommodative people, was going to be the best guarantee of minority protection, though theoretically in a constitutional democracy, minorities are to be the makers of their destiny, voicing their feelings, grievances, and opinions, and in the final judgment protector of their own interests. [4] The same model of protection was adopted to protect rights of weaker members or individuals within a group. The Shah Bano case of 1985 and the Muslim Women Act of 1986 exemplify this approach.[5] Similarly, this approach was repeated in the reorganisation of States. The report of the States Reorganization Commission, which was formed in 1954 and whose report came out in 1956, also based itself on the same strategy, namely quarantining the minority problem within a broad framework of equality and rights, and thus in this case, while it went some way in recognizing political identity of linguistic groups, it territorially contained linguistic minorities. Therefore, while it is true that in constitutional thinking there were two parallel ideas of nationalism and democracy (Mohapatra 2001), the disjunction we are speaking of here cannot be solely or mainly traced to this; rather, it has to be traced to the way in which nationalism and democracy, in their respectively republican and nationalist versions, combined to root out communitarian ideas, and along with this, to implement an effective programme of equality of groups.

It should not cause us surprise therefore that the National Minority Commission (and by the same token State Minority Commissions wherever set up) suffers from double jeopardy. First, it is enjoined to enforce and implement all the safeguards for the minorities provided in the Constitution, whereas we have seen that such safeguards are minor in the basic law itself (and the Commission does not have constitutional status).[6] Second, there has been a continuous campaign by some of the major political forces that the step of forming such a Commission has been divisive, that the term "minority" is imprecise and therefore that the government can use the Commission arbitrarily. Consequently, it has been suggested that it should be replaced with a National Integration and Human Rights Commission, merging the Human Rights Commission with it. It is in this way that the institutional process of protection of minorities has been conceptualised and defined.

The truth is that rights are not a pre-condition for political action; they can only be the end product. The protection of rights can strengthen the power of the weak only when it comes as the companion of mutual obligation, and when it is secured as the fruit of mutual recognition, politics of tolerance, decentralization, and autonomy. Otherwise, protection, as I have tried to explain, becomes a strategy of rule that makes government possible and only increases the power of those governing the unequal groups of population in a plural setting. To understand the strategic nature of such rule – the rule of the supreme community, *the nation,* over all other communities, the *majorities and minorities* – we must briefly recall what I have discussed relating to the dalits in the country. The advisory committee in the Indian Constituent Assembly had identified Muslims, Sikhs, Parsis, Anglo-Indians and Indian Christians as minorities. But dalits were never considered as minorities, for minority status to the dalits would touch the very power structure on which rule rested. A while back, Ambedkar had declared that the depressed classes were a minority – a status concealed by their inclusion in the Hindu society. This was during the time of depositions before the Simon Commission. On the political demand of a separate electorate for scheduled castes, the nationalist leadership had vehemently disagreed. The Poona Pact of 1932 between Ambedkar and Gandhi temporarily resolved the issue with the help of the principle of reservation. However, bitterness remained, as did other economic and political demands of autonomy. The constitution was a contract against the background of the rise of majorities and minorities.

Protection has turned out to be an effective governmental strategy with high stakes as it served to combine many aims in this milieu. It has meant administering a multicultural society of inequalities; it has served the fictive ethnic basis of the rule of law; it worked to deflect the dialogic notions of autonomy, self-determination and representation that form the core of the politics of justice; as a strategy, it allowed daily discrimination while stopping to some extent cataclysmic violence, and finally it allowed the replacement of the democratic question with the identity question. In this displacement, the ruled became the subject, the subject became the citizen, the citizen became the individual from a minority group, and the individual from the minority group became the representative of an ethnic stock. The histories of the minorities in India and in this region as a whole have become in this way part of the history of government, history of the procedures of a rule of law that bases itself on such transformation of identity. The functions of both care and protection have served that imperative. Government must identify the subjects with identifications, it must take care of them; in times of acute inequality, it must protect them. These two functions show the materiality of an unequal society and the materiality of rule over this unequal society.

III. Towards a dialogic democracy

Let us now briefly discuss the second issue – that of dialogue. Dialogue is of course not a new thing in post-colonial political history. As historians of popular constitutionalism tell us, dialogue was essential for anti-colonial struggles. Coalitions and fronts were built, yet the lessons were lost in the wake of decolonisation, specifically in the mad craze to build up the modern state, modern government, modern law, and a modern centralised sovereign apparatus (Samaddar 2010, 3-103). New fault lines appeared, while old ones were reinforced. We forgot our own past of dialogic justice. Institutional democracy has failed to a large extent in accommodating the notion of dialogue in these polities, or to put the matter differently, dialogues have remained beyond the institutional reach of representative democracy. It is important to think: why does dialogue tend to defy the institutional limits or forms of democracy and raise new issues beyond their pale? One reason is that though rights and justice are closely interrelated concepts, *rights belong more to the domain of law,*

while justice is more closely associated with dialogue. What begins as a
demand for justice can end in the codified form of a right. The democratic
discourse builds on the arguments of rights, and not on justice. Justice in
fact expands their frontier. Therefore, though democratic theory may
anticipate dialogue, and should anticipate it, the politics and practices of
dialogue contest the given institutional limits of democracy; to be truthful,
it challenges the democratic form because dialogic imagination is fuelled
less by the clamour for rights and more by the passion for justice. From
this, we can advance the second reason. The demand for justice leads
dialogic politics to inquire into democratic inadequacies, summed up in
the phrase "democratic deficit," to the extent that dialogic politics in the
form of peace politics begins questioning the hitherto accepted idea that
the given form of democracy heals conflicts. We have to ask: is the
traditional form of democracy inherently dialogic?

The UN Charter declares in article 55 that human rights are essential
for friendly relations among nations. But as we have seen, the post-
colonial narrative of democracy is complicated in this regard. We have to
think: what happens when democracies commit aggression in the post-
colonial region/s, or invade post-colonial countries, or conduct wars of
subversion for "humanitarian reasons" to overthrow autocracies or to roll
back communism, or to continuously arm themselves with nuclear
weapons? To keep peace, democracies wage war. If democracies do not
fight wars among themselves, they combine to fight war against others. In
fact, it is almost a law of democracy that an ideological Calvinism goads
democracies to launch wars against others. Thus, the existence of civil and
political rights, to a considerable extent, may not be a barrier to violence.
There are instances of countries where internally rights co-exist with
violent conflicts and civil wars.

In all these cases, democracy is more imagined than real because this
model of democracy does not encourage conversations and dialogue.
Democracy in the form of a national community can also be imagined. As
I try to show in my book *A Biography of the Indian Nation, 1947-97*
(2001), democracy facilitates the passage from the imagined features of a
collective community-hood to statehood by a double method. It resorts to
the concretisation of the features of a political community by laws and
institutions; it also makes this political community of democracy a matter
of imagination, almost beyond contest. Dialogic traces in the polity are in
this way effaced. An imagined democracy then becomes intolerant of
others, aggressively defines and protects its boundaries, and most
significantly, includes and excludes others emphatically from the
democratic nation, just as it had at one time excluded and later included

women and lower classes. In such a context, democratic resolution of conflicts may not fundamentally mean a broadening of dialogue, but a revision of the rules of the game whereby moderate elites of both sides try to marginalize old rules and old actors, and where the resultant process of negotiation is arrived at with hardly any public political debate. If the old agenda of contest was inspired by a mythological discourse of a democratic community, the new methodological politics are similarly a product of imagined consensus, which shuts out issues of justice, and which is indeed built on excluding these contentious issues. Thus, while the polity is sought to be made stable, the fundamentals of inclusion/exclusion remain – the contradictory goals of including the excluded but keeping them at the margin, transforming them into legitimate political actors, yet ensuring their externalisation. In this situation, conflicts do not die, they wait to reappear. Race, nation, class, language, religion, region … all conceivable forms of domination stare democracy in the face. Domination appears as order, while the desire for justice appears as anarchy.

Yet we have to note, if post-colonial experiences of democracy are any guide, order produces authority, authority produces violence, and violence provokes the desire for peace. But violence breaks down authority also, and the breakdown of the historically admissible form of authority leads to a collapse of the state. This is recognized socially as anarchy, and the desire for peace gets the phantasmagoria of a desire for lost authority, order, and thus the state. Thus Afghanistan, Rwanda, Cambodia, Somalia, Lebanon, erstwhile Yugoslavia – in all these countries restoring peace has been sought by restoring the state. The usual process has been the promulgation of a "peace constitution" (much like reconstructing post-war Japan), talks, interim power-sharing arrangement, a multilateral peacekeeping army, elections under international supervision, and the *restoration of the state*. The breakdown of the state is a universal phenomenon, so is its restoration. This had happened earlier in the forties, fifties, and sixties of the last century when in the wake of decolonisation the re-establishment of order became a priority. We can again think of the post-partition states or of the virtually partitioned states. Restoration of peace and the restoration of state in this way became the twin tasks of democracy. Probably the more significant conclusion that we can draw from this experience is that, since peace is restored in this condition through restoration of the state, and not primarily through plural dialogues, what we have is the return of the state on a weak and fragile basis, backed by a narrowly based consensus, and certainly not by a return of the dialogic politics/polity.

War and development have signalled in a democratic framework an all-enveloping and all-consuming notion of "gain," and consequently a majoritarian polity. International relations theory failed to understand the impact of war and development on patterns of dialogue, because it immersed itself too much in the neo-classical theory of utility and gain. Thus, it had no insights to offer on the dynamics of dialogue, an enduring feature of world relations in the second half of the last century. It had no answer to the following questions: what does the mediating agency of dialogue say about the war-peace continuum that it straddles? More important, is dialogue reducible to the status of being the language of negotiation? All that the international relations theory could do was to explicate various scenarios of bargaining in terms of rational choices. Thus, its own explanation of the dynamics of dialogue in terms of comparison of utilities, the "Pareto optimality," distributive bargaining, and integrative bargaining was of no relevance to the historical situation developing, particularly in the post-colonial world, amidst cold war, neo-colonialism, proxy wars, irreducible poverty, great power domination, and an increasingly global/fragmented scenario. The theory of rational bargaining tells us that each party has stable preferences, which are arranged along a single line of homogenous dimension utility. It of course acknowledges that though:

> (...) the bargainers (may) differ in their stockpiles of utility so that one is far wealthier than the other, this will have no impact on their evaluation of further units of utility, (and though) an additional unit will not be more valuable to the poor bargainer than to the wealthy one (Lockart 1979, 5).

Thus notions of justice, independence, equality, reparations, and human rights were not considered as calculable units of utility; yet, as we know, these have persistently influenced the fates of attrition, co-existence, and peace, and have provoked major demands for dialogue. We can follow the question further. Hence, for example, what again if parties do not have stable preferences either due to information deficiencies or changing perceptions because these parties, as new born states and nations, are in that seemingly endless twilight zone of "transition?"[7] While conflict theorists will put these to "limited perceptual capabilities of bargainers in actual conflicts" and "goals comprised of independent, and even conflicting constraints as opposed to homogenous utilities (that) cause some of the difficulties" (Lockart 1979, 43), the post-colonial experiences lead us to factors such as ideologies, values, and group ethos, which remain as powerful as the principles of calculation laid out by the theory of bargaining – a woefully inadequate supplement for a theory of dialogue.

It seems to me that if we have to step beyond the theory of bargaining in our effort at understanding the politics of dialogue, the key to such understanding is a rigorous probe into the war-peace and conflict-peace continuum.[8]

The question to be asked at this stage: will the restoration of a constitutional culture be enough to guarantee new dialogic practices and allow the latter a broader site? Going by the indications available now, the answer unfortunately seems to be negative. Not only are constitutions everywhere failing to be effective conflict-resolution mechanisms, they are on the contrary exacerbating these; constitution as a legal subject in post-colonial politics loses no time in demanding that the society acknowledge it as an autonomous political actor and it often, even before receiving an answer, sits at the top of political society.

In order to conduct a concrete analysis of that great failure, we have to abandon the centrality of sovereignty in the study of war and peace. The theory of sovereignty lends a centralized form to power, ignoring the myriad ways power forms to dominate and suppress people, and turn subjects into victims. To go back briefly to the issue of constitution, the Indian Constituent Assembly debates were clear as to how power was being formed. Groups, classes, estates, rebellious nationalities were not fighting each other to death. "War of all against all" was in fact suspended in favour of the "measuring of all against all" to found the commonwealth. It is a record of a will to compose various forms of power, of the postponement of that final fight, because society had to be run, citizens had to be ruled, and therefore the act of suspending bellicosity was scripted in the political document (the classic no war-no peace document).

In such context, constitution helps conversations for reconciliation and peace, but is never the principal dialogic site, simply because it does not encode what will be called "sovereign power." Dialogue undermines the fiction of a monolithic institutionalisation of power. Beneath the compact text of a constitution, one does not have to stretch ears far to hear the drum of wars of all kinds (caste, ethnic, religious, class), the violence, passions, enmities, revenges, also strains of illusive peace, desperate truce, reconciling acts, precarious friendships promising both war and peace, and finally the tensions that cut the social body, the decisive battles for which all are preparing. Sovereignty is not the explanatory principle here. Its role is to provide an image in which processes of war appear to be under control, processes of peace appear as harmless enough so as not to consume every organ with the fire of justice. Constitution and the fiction that it has given birth to and goes by the name of sovereignty aspires for the juridical-philosophical universality that lawmakers and philosophers have always dreamt and aspired for – the position between adversaries, the position of the centre and yet above the adversaries, the agency that imposes the armistice, the order that brings reconciliation. Dialogue poses before such politics questions about ways of power, about the visible brutality of law and of the possibilities of imagining new ways of conversation. In this relational context, new ideas of rights and justice are emerging; they form the terrain where new dialogic acts are shaping up, old divides are being interrogated and where quotidian conversation wrestles with the exceptional. At times, these conversations show dialogue as a strategy of rule, at others as the terrain of justice, rights, and peace.

IV. Justice and post-colonial democracy

Finally, we have the issue of justice. It is in this context that we can refer to the notion of dialogic justice that democracy must inhere: we can locate six broad principles of such dialogic justice. They can be also termed as principles of minimal justice:

(a) The victims of injustice must get the substantive recognition that injustice was done to them;
(b) The victims of injustice have to be assured of the conditions under which the undoing of injustice begins;
(c) There will be guarantee of these conditions;
(d) There will be custodianship of these guarantees;
(e) There will be conditions of innovations in and improvisations of existing pattern of rule;
(f) And finally, there will be federalisation of rules and practices of dialogue and authority, in other words plural forms of justice.

Minimal justice is arrived at dialogically. It is minimal, because it is historically obtained out of contests and conversations, and its rules are historically established. It may be propelled by higher aims, but as a social phenomenon or norm it rests on what has been historically possible and realised through practices of justice. It is important to mention here that while the judiciary and the constitution play their roles in the evolution of the norms of dialogic justice, these roles are not predominant. Rather, it is necessary to go back to the ways in which social dialogues have evolved over norms of justice. Minimal justice based on dialogic principles make justice not only dependent on the idea of the legality of rights, it also expands the idea of justice by enabling society to view justice in the broader light of entitlements, capabilities, and the collective social position in which the person seeking justice is situated. Collective social position indicates, among other things, the unequal social security position that a person may have, time spent in unpaid labour, recurring bad harvests, the position of women in such a milieu, where any unanticipated rupture in the patron-client relationship could bring disaster in the justice scenario, and the affected person's capability to access justice could be thereby severely affected.

It is important to take note of legal pluralism in this context as a condition of minimal justice, which as I have indicated, can be achieved through a dialogic route. Dialogue does not only indicate conversation between law and justice or law and politics, it also means dialogue between different legal imperatives, situations, requirements, traditions, and procedures. In natural resource management, management of the common property resources, indigenous people's economy and in several other related matters, the better approach may be to accept custom, which is the place of law, even though customary law has not always been rights and justice sensitive, particularly where issues of gender and caste are concerned. Custom always strengthens personalised authority, which may go against other values of the customary procedures of conflict settlement and management of common resources. In meting out justice, modern law bases its wisdom on statute, precedent, and doctrine, whereas custom identifies the source of its wisdom as social relations and the interrelations between duty, good custom, and ancient knowledge. Clearly therefore one cannot adopt legal pluralism uncritically – how much plurality it embraces is a question in point. Similarly, legal pluralism by itself cannot tackle the problem of natural resource management and cannot cope with diversity because it thinks that plurality by itself is the virtue and the all-weather answer to the search for effective legal routes to justice. Besides, it does not necessarily ensure dialogue and interchange of experiences. Yet, when we see howthrough the establishment of a single legislature for the whole of India in 1833 with authority to legislate for the entire country, the codification of laws in form of a single legal book between 1837-1860, a single succession act in 1865, and a contract act passed in 1872- just within one century the entire justice machinery was centralised and put in place ignoring many legal traditions and differential legal requirementswe can imagine the extent of centralisation of law and justice machinery, and the centralisation of the legal hold over the country.

In this connection, we also have to note that our notion of group justice is very unclear, law being oriented towards ensuring individual justice, thus ignoring not only the requirements of group justice against the backdrop of which the individual may be suffering injustice, but ignoring the aspect of capability that I also mentioned above. As one observer has pointed out, one of the features of the emerging scene of justice–in

November 1946 in Bengal, the masses of peasantry joined hands to demand a fair share of the crops produced, known as the *Tebhaga* movement, in 1973 villagers hug trees in order to save these trees by interposing their bodies between the trees and the contractors' axes in the hills of Uttar Pradesh–increasingly groups are demanding justice, to which our justice machinery has no response. Indeed, the Court, apart from framing a penal response, has no way even to respond to the emerging justice scene (Chaudhry 2003, 35). Not only do we need a perspective of group justice, we need to have reviews of laws such as the Land Acquisition Act of 1894, which enables the government to acquire group property and group territory for the "public good;" similarly, we need a review of the Indian Forest Act (1927), the revised National Forest Policy (1988), the Wildlife Protection Act (1972) (Chaudhry 2003, 35-61; Crawford 1994, 178-220), and a thorough review of what the constitution had meant by property rights.[9] Thus, we have had unequal legal-constitutional protection with regard to different property rights – private-individual, public-individual, public-group, and private-group.[10] The lack of clarity has resulted in one more failure. The constitution remains inadequate for ensuring justice for minorities who are increasingly victims of a majoritarian polity. The establishment of the National Human Rights Commission, the National Minorities Commission and similar commissions at the state level has proved inadequate, though these commissions were established in conformity with the Paris Principles, precisely on the ground that the normal procedure of individuated justice is inadequate to protect group rights and human rights in general. I have discussed elsewhere in some detail the reasons of the failure of these commissions to complement or supplement the Court in ensuring justice.

The governmental mode of justice in this way has blinded the justice machinery to layers of vulnerabilities, special situations, and the differential world of capabilities. In many areas, resource crisis has brought to public light the regulatory vacuum that has appeared along with the decline of the customary regulation system; special interest groups manipulate legal institutions and in matters of water control, legal complexities have defeated the need for justice. Thus, in the Ganga basin the upstream rich farmers have exploited at will the water available there, with the effect that the river now carries less water for the poor peasants downstream. We only have to see the water crisis in the Ganga delta that arises every dry season as an instance of what I have been arguing here. Similarly, the prospect of a rights-based healthy water management system is dim and the available legal frameworks are of little help. For inter-sector and inter-region water transfers, multiple uses, and water rights, we now clearly need a new dialogic approach beyond the usual commission and tribunal system. Likewise, we need a new dialogic framework to deal with the issues of justice emanating from the quarrels between native communities and the immigrants in many areas inhabited by the indigenous population. It is important that in all these cases we explore the possibilities of legal pluralism because it indicates the need for new approaches, the inadequacy of the usual formal laws, and an agenda for dialogue between different legal styles and approaches (Johnson 2003, 39-52; Boelens, Roth and Zwarteveen 2003, 125-158). We can even say that to negotiate different aspirations of different popular groups or ethnic communities, the way is not to espouse a monolithic constitutional approach, but a plural legal approach that allows for pluralism and pragmatism in negotiating issues of autonomy, self-determination, and separatism (Godoy 2003, 375-402).

In brief then, what I am advocating here is the requirement to take a close look at legal pluralism as one more possible way of ensuring dialogic justice, because unlike formal law, other forms of law may be more open-ended, at times bordering more on being norms than being laws. Other forms of law may be more local-specific, resource-specific, and time-specific (such as suited to the times of distress or grazing common, or one particular area). Thus, the need of the times is one of conversation between different legal systems, legal situations, and legal norms. Indeed, it is a big challenge if the State wants to ensure agrarian justice in the vast countryside, where the governmental wisdom of distinguishing the "occupied" and "unoccupied" areas and governmental actions against "encroachment" mark the revenue and property scene, and where the government is determined to stop the peasant rebels and agitators from directly ensuring agrarian justice by land redistribution.

I am not, of course, suggesting that legal pluralism is the quintessential dialogic form. Legal pluralism is only one major indication of how to conceptualise the dialogic form of justice. Legal pluralism must not be accepted as a dogma. The main point is to have practical dialogues between several legal situations and legal schools. More importantly, as a legal subject, an individual may be open to several legal remedies, several forms of legal justices, and as a legal subject s/he would have some space to decide what to opt for. This is already happening–the victims of a foreign multinational company's operations may have to decide where to seek justice: in the country of the multinational or in the country where the misdeed has been conducted. In any case, different situations of in/justice, different ways of conflict resolution and different ways of fixing standards are marks of any society. Centralised law, the Law, ignores the reality. The question is: can we imagine a situation of daily transactions of justice where different legal principles and ways are involved or, more importantly, where different legal authorities are involved and where pluralism is not mistaken for arbitrariness? Again, we already have such a situation in the interface between international law and national sovereign authorities, where universal principles do not always operate – in the case of extradition it may be treaty-bound, in some cases it may be UN-bound, and in some others the WTO may bind the parties in rules of trade. It is this relation that we must acknowledge as the cardinal principle of dialogic justice. In other words, we have two dialogic situations here–(a) a dialogue between different situations, methods, and authorities of law for different legal subjects, who may be groups or individuals, and (b) the same legal subject open to more than one legal remedy, situation, method, and authority. Dialogic justice points to the need for the sharing of sovereignty.

In short, justice is a historical category, and its criticality lies in this. The practice of justice makes it a historical category. It is therefore necessary to study closely the minute practices that make justice a reality and not simply a moral principle. The practices of justice show two possibilities of its form governmental form of justice and the dialogic form of justice.

The reason behind the overwhelming domination of the governmental form of justice is the legitimacy given to the governmental form by the constitution. Yet, even while examining the dynamics of the constitutional process, it is necessary to see how the constitutional power makes use of laws to set aside the dialogic possibilities of justice and introduce in their place a procedure that would rely endlessly on time-tested and time-driven institutions and methods.

The legal world produces the subject of justice, yet the justice-seeking subject, while caught up in the justice game, seeks more than a legal avenue. In as much as justice is sited in law yet exceeds law, the justice-seeking subject also combines in its subject-hood the reliance on law and the dialogic capacity to look for other avenues of justice. The political complementarities and oppositions are reproduced in the world of justice.

References

Bajpai, Rochana. 2002. "Minority Rights in the Indian Constituent Assembly Debates, 1946-1950." Working Paper. Queen Elizabeth House Working Papers Series. QEHWPS30.

Boelens, Rutgerd, Dik Roth and Margreet Zwarteveen. 2003. "Legal Complexity and Irrigation Water Control – Analysis, Recognition, and Beyond." In *Legal Pluralism and Unofficial Law in Social and Political Development*, edited by Rajendra Pradhan, 125-158. Volume II, papers of the XIIIth International Congress, Chiang Mai, Thailand, 7-10 April 2002. Kathmandu: The Commission on Folk Law and Legal Pluralism, Department of Anthropology, University of New Brunswick, Canada and The International Centre for the Study of Nature, Environment and Culture.

Chaudhry, Shivani. 2003. "Indigenous Community-Based Property Rights in India–Public or Private?" In *Legal Pluralism and Unofficial Law in Social and Political Development,* edited by Rajendra Pradhan, 35-61. Volume I, papers of the XIIIth International Congress, Chiang Mai, Thailand, 7-10 April 2002. Kathmandu: The Commission on Folk Law and Legal Pluralism, Department of Anthropology, University of New Brunswick, Canada and The International Centre for the Study of Nature, Environment and Culture.

Clinton, Robert L. 1991. "The Rights of the Indigenous People as Collective Group Rights." *Arizona Law Review* 32: 739-747.

Crawford, James. 1994. "Legal Pluralism and the Indigenous Peoples of Australia." In *The Rights of Subordinated Peoples*, edited by Olivier Mendelsohn and Upendra Baxi, 178-220. Delhi: Oxford University Press.

Crépeau, François. 2010. "Dealing with Migration–A Test for Democracies." *Refugee Watch* 35: 37-50.

Gautam, Ashwani Kant, comp. 2001. *Human Rights and Justice System.* Delhi: A.P.H. Publishing Corporation.

Godoy, Arnaldo Moraes. 2003. "Legal Pluralism and the Indigenous Issue in South America." In *Legal Pluralism and Unofficial Law in Social and Political Development*, edited by Rajendra Pradhan, 375-402. Volume II, papers of the XIIIth International Congress, Chiang Mai, Thailand, 7-10 April 2002. Kathmandu: The Commission on Folk Law and Legal Pluralism, Department of Anthropology, University of New Brunswick, Canada and The International Centre for the Study of Nature, Environment and Culture.

Horowitz, Irving Louis. 1973. *War and Peace in Contemporary Social and Philosophical Theory*. London: Souvenir Press.

Johnson, Derek Stephen. 2003. "Rapid Growth, Resource Crisis, and Regulatory Vacuum in the Gujarat Fishery–Can a Legal Pluralist Approach Help Save the Day?" In *Legal Pluralism and Unofficial Law in Social and Political Development*, edited by Rajendra Pradhan, 39-52. Volume II, papers of the XIIIth International Congress, Chiang Mai, Thailand, 7-10 April 2002. Kathmandu: The Commission on Folk Law and Legal Pluralism, Department of Anthropology, University of New Brunswick, Canada and The International Centre for the Study of Nature, Environment and Culture.

Joseph, Sarah. 1998. *Interrogating Culture - Critical perspectives on Contemporary Social Theory*. New Delhi: Sage.

Lockhart, Charles. 1979. *Bargaining in International Conflicts*. New York: Columbia University Press.

Lynch, Owen J. 2003. "Whose Nations? Whose Natural Resources? Towards Legal Recognition of Community-Based Property Rights." In *Legal Pluralism and Unofficial Law in Social and Political Development*, edited by Rajendra Pradhan, 199-209. Volume I, papers of the XIIIth International Congress, Chiang Mai, Thailand, 7-10 April 2002. Kathmandu: The Commission on Folk Law and Legal Pluralism, Department of Anthropology, University of New Brunswick, Canada and The International Centre for the Study of Nature, Environment and Culture.

Mahmood, Tahir. 2001. *Minorities Commission–Minor Role in Major Affairs*. Delhi: Pharos.

Macpherson, Crawford B., ed. 1978. *Property–Mainstream and Critical Positions*. Toronto: University of Toronto Press.

Mohapatra, Bishnu. 2001. "Understanding the Discourse on Minority Rights in Contemporary India." Paper presented at a seminar on Minority Rights in India organized by the International Centre for Ethnic Studies, Colombo, Sri Lanka and New Delhi, India, August 25-26.

Ostrom, Elinor. 1991. *Governing the Commons–The Evolution of Institutions for Collective Action*. Cambridge: Cambridge University Press.

Ram, Kalpana. 2000. "The State and the Women's Movement–Instabilities in the Discourse of 'Rights' in India." In *Human Rights and Gender Politics–Asia-Pacific Perspectives*, edited by Anne-Marie Hilsdon, Martha Macintyre, Vera Mackie and Maila Stivens, 59-79. London: Routledge.

Samaddar, Ranabir. 2001. *A Biography of the Indian Nation*. New Delhi: Sage.

—. 2010. *The Emergence of the Political Subject*. New Delhi: Sage.

Wadha, Shri R. K. 27 August 1947. Indian Constituent Assembly Debates. Volume V.

Walton, Prichard and Robert Mckersie. 1965. *A Behavioral Theory of Labor Negotiations– An Analysis of Social Interaction System*. New York: McGraw Hill.

West Bengal Human Rights Commission. 1999. *Annual Report, 1998-99*. Calcutta.

Notes

[1] To cite one more instance of the newness of the situation: democracy revolves around a *de jure* category, "citizens," and not people. In this condition, immigrants become a question mark. As the Canadian jurist François Crépeau tells us, migrants become a test for democracy (2010).

[2] Indeed, the entire justice system that includes constitution, laws, statutes, courts, commissions, and the implementation machinery under the executive carries the mark of the disjuncture. In this context, one has to only look at the various pronouncements of the justices on the state of the implementation of human rights of the victims. See in this connection the compilation of relevant acts, judgments, and statements (Gautam 2001).

[3] One member in the Constituent Assembly remarked, "I only wish, Sir, that the phrase 'minorities' should be wiped out from the history. The ten years that have been given to them is a sufficiently long period and I hope that when we meet in the short period within ten years, these minorities will come and say 'we are happy, we do not want anything'" (Wadha 1947, 209).

[4] Rochana Bajpai notes in detail the process in which the minority issue was marginalized in the resolutions of the Constituent Assembly as a result of the contradictory co-existence of two constitutional spirits – republicanism and the spirit of group interest (1999).

[5] (Ram 2000) in an essay discusses the case, and points out how state takes the role of the male custodian in defining the protection that the woman needs, and how this contributes to the identification of a religious community as a site of female identity.

[6] (Mahmood 2001) calls it "minor role in major affairs."

[7] In fact, Lockhart cites the work of (Walton and Mckersie 1965) to show how rational bargaining leading to expectations of "distributive bargaining" (division of spoils) or "integrative bargaining" (upgrading of common interest) are prevented by intra-party disagreements that make "commitments fuzzy and hinder integrative bargaining," thus making "attitudinal structuring" (influencing perceptions of the opponent) – one of the main goals of bargaining – almost impossible (1979, 13-15).

[8] In my (Samaddar 2001, 265-313), I discuss two instances of how bargaining becomes the form of contradictory and yet complimentary processes of relations between post-colonial nations marked by the war-peace continuum. Irving Louis Horowitz long back had shown how in philosophical and social thought the continuum had been an important object of inquiry (1973).

[9] On the ways in which the concept of property has been variously used: (Macpherson 1978).

[10] Owen J. Lynch discusses the typology by cross-referencing various property-rights systems (2002).

CHAPTER FIVE

HUMAN RIGHTS, SETTLER COLONIALISM AND THE PROBLEM OF UNIVERSALITY[*]

ISABEL ALTAMIRANO-JIMENEZ

In this chapter, I use settler colonialism as a framework to interrogate Indigenous women's rights, the production of the female victim and the threatening Other. I argue that because human rights are constituted on the rejection of Otherness (savage, Indigenous peoples), its emancipatory possibilities work both to simultaneously justify a subtle civilizatory mission, erase other subjectivities, and conceal the many marks of colonial, racial, and gender structural marginalization that Indigenous women have faced and continue to face. As gender and race are constitutive of concrete experiences, Indigenous women's conditions of life and circumstances are produced not only by the individual choices they make, but also by a structure of oppression involving race, colonization, regulations, patriarchy, and other forms of structural violence.

Although this structure of oppression is often constructed as inherent to the margins, the conditions for the violation of human rights are structurally embedded in existing modes of governance. Thus, the focus of this chapter is the simultaneous construction of Aboriginal women as both victim and threatening Other. The first narrative justifies state intervention to save the "powerless woman" victim of her harmful culture. The second one defines a threatening, unsettled body located outside state protection. Both victim subject and unsettled body are products of different modes of governance.

In the following sections, I provide a critical discussion of the limitations of the human rights framework in relation to settler colonialism. Next, I discuss how victim subject and unsettled body are

[*] A slightly different version of this paper has been published in *Prairie Forum* 36, Special Indigenous Human Rights Issue, pp. 105-125.

constituted by different modes of governance. Finally, I explore matrimonial property rights and violence against Indigenous women and show how in settler societies, the human rights discourse can work to transform the victim subject into a liberal subject and to conceal violence done to the threatening, deviant Other.

Settler colonialism, rights, and the threatening Other

Decolonial scholar Anibal Quijano (2000, 534) writes that one of the fundamental axes of colonialism was the social classification of people based on the idea of race, a notion that did not exist, as we know it today, before the colonization of the Americas. The author argues that the two historical processes that facilitated colonialism were the codification of difference, colonized and colonizers, and the constitution of a new structure for the appropriation of wealth, resources, and bodies.

Although colonial structures produced racial regimes, a growing literature insists on the need to distinguish different colonial processes. As a specific type of colonialism, settler colonialism relied on a logic of racial disappearance and spatial seclusion (Wolf 2006, 388). As a structure, settler colonialism heavily relied on the land, and Indigenous presence constituted a threat for the appropriation of land. The acquisition of land was founded on the violence that both emptied Indigenous territories of social relations and occupied the land with migrants' settlements (Veracini 2008, 365). Notions such as "vacant," "empty land," and "wilderness" functioned to erase prior Indigenous connections to the land. Settlements, on the other hand, provided colonizers with a sense of themselves as being local and a particular vision of the past, present and the future. Indigenous societies' or peoples "without history" were brought into existence to be governed.

Assumptions of settler's superiority flourished in the 19th century as well as narratives of progress, patriarchy and property. These narratives ordered the world and organized people along gender and racialized lines. Post-colonial feminists have pointed out that while categories have been understood as being homogeneous, this logic obscures what exists at the intersections, including violence perpetrated against Indigenous women.

Anne McClintock (1995), for example, argues that in the 19th century, sexual purity and morality became a controlling metaphor for racial, political, and economic power. Race, sexuality, and gender shaped the experience of colonialism and the boundaries of inclusion and exclusion. As a legacy of colonialism in Canada, bodies, particularly those of Indigenous women, served as a terrain in which sexuality, race and mobility were controlled. Indigenous women's bodies not only took the form of property, but were simultaneously considered "exotic," "savage," and a "working beast." In settler cities, Indigenous women's presence was criminalized and their bodies marked as "vagrant," "prostitute," and "wanderer" (Edmonds 2010; Sangster 1999). These categories define unsettled bodies that were a threat to settlers' space. These distinctive political categories remade Indigenous women's bodies and criminalized their presence in the city. The embodiment of these spatialized categories reveals the contradictory and violent operations of the settler state both to contain the reserve and maintain the racial and moral "hygiene" of the city (Edmonds 2010, 7).

By the time European empires were colonizing different regions of the world, the Enlightenment created the space for human rights as a theory and for who constituted the liberal subject: the White, propertied male. This definition excluded women and other rights seekers. Besides excluding potential rights seekers, the British system, for example, identified other social categories, which could probably never aspire to enjoy rights: the unproductive, the dispossessed, the residuum, and the unemployable (Rose 1999, 256).

The exclusion of non-European societies from international law in the 19th century was organized around the colonial binary civilized and uncivilized. Acceptance into the restrictive community of international law was based on outside communities' ability to resemble the European ideal. As Ratna Kapur argues (2006, 673), although past exclusions stand as examples of liberalism's inconsistencies, such exclusions continue to be at the heart of international law and have taken new forms. The establishment of human rights as a subject of international recognition dealing with the negative effects of industrialization was an important moment. For the first time, states' actions were subject to scrutiny and measured according to new ideas of human dignity and development. However, the belief in the transformative nature of human rights was based on a liberal project, which sought to advance individual rights as a means to move forward.

In *Politics Out of History* (2001, 10), Wendy Brown argues that since human rights emerged partly as a response to the "barbarism within Europe" during World War II, it is important to ask what are the implications of a universalized project for those who remain under colonial subjugation. Brown argues that this is particularly relevant because in the case of World War II, genocide committed against Europeans was witnessed with different lenses than genocide committed against the Other, the non-European. Thus, the idea that these rights are human centered raises the fundamental question of *who* is recognized as human (Grear 2010, 173). In Canada, while the advent of human rights created the space for legislations aimed at correcting discriminatory provisions, such legislations excluded Indigenous peoples. Even when Indigenous persons were invited to integrate into the settler society through voluntary or involuntary enfranchisement, substantive acceptance within the settler society was not guaranteed.

The acknowledgement that there are different types of obstacles facing different groups of people shaped the evolution of human rights. The second generation of rights recognized the right of individuals to preserve and develop their separate group identity within the process of integration. Although the decolonization movement after World War II challenged the very idea of a people subjugating another people and imposing an alien culture and politic-administrative system on others, decolonization did not extend to Indigenous peoples (Sanders 1995, 12-13).

In response to the exclusion of Indigenous peoples, a sustained Indigenous advocacy by organizations such as the Sami Council and the Inuit Circumpolar Conference made the space for Indigenous peoples. In asserting nationhood, Indigenous organizations introduced the question of Indigenous rights onto the political agenda. Since then, a substantive body of international jurisprudence aimed at recognizing Indigenous peoples' rights has emerged (Colchester 2002). Finally, after decades, in October 2007, the Universal Declaration on the Rights of Indigenous Peoples was ratified by numerous countries, but not by Canada, Australia, New Zealand, or the United States. More recently, in 2010, the Canadian government ratified this declaration.

Although human rights discourse has evolved over time, the process of recuperating the injured and the colonized into the settler state continues to be uneven, assimilationist, and exclusionary. According to David Kennedy (2004), human rights have come to occupy an emancipatory field only by marginalizing other projects. Moreover, the focus on the state and the emphasis on the public space leave the severe harms produced by non-state actors unaddressed. Many harmful practices are not recognized as violations until they are named and acknowledged by the legal human rights framework, which often lags behind what is being done by local courts and social movements. Moreover, the universalizing vocabulary promotes a one-framework-fit-all politics which does not necessarily end violence; rather, this vocabulary conceals, if not justifies, some forms of violence to the Other. From this perspective, the continuous marginalization of women from the sphere of human rights not only reveals a world of gender and racialized inequality, but also makes it difficult for women to address human rights violations in practice.

These inconsistencies are not unexpected outcomes. As Ratna Kapur (2006, 673) notes, this is the dark side of human rights. The process of transforming the colonial, racist state into one that is "caring" and "compassionate" has had important limits. In practice, the application of human rights to all "without distinction of any kind such as race, colour, sex, and language" (Art. 2) has served to conceal inequalities and to blame different groups of people for deviating from the "ideal, moral, liberal subject." In doing so, the human rights framework has not eliminated structural obstacles including racism, prejudice, patriarchy, social injustice, and economic inequalities. Combined, these structural obstacles continue to relegate Indigenous women to a secondary status. While human rights discourse has become a site for addressing ruptures and exclusions, it does so by bringing the past into the norms and values of present liberalism instead of questioning those very norms and values.

The victim subject and the unsettled Other: two sides of the same coin

As argued earlier, although the human rights law has come to occupy an emancipatory field, it does so by marginalizing other projects and other subjects. According to Ratna Kapur (2006, 675) there are at least three ways in which the Other has been addressed in human rights. The first is through the assimilation of the Other, the second is through the essentialization and naturalization of difference, and the third is through the justification of violence against the Other, who poses a threat to liberal societies. In the first instance, assimilation of the Other involves a diversity of mechanisms aimed at erasing cultural difference. In the Canadian colonial context, assimilation policies took the form of residential schools, forced enfranchisement, and control over membership on reserves. The extension of citizenship was determined by Indigenous people's ability to conform to civilized norms and to separate themselves from their Indigenous identity.

The second and third ways identified by Kapur are closely connected and can be seen as the two sides of the same coin. The naturalization of difference has a long history. In Canada, colonization was substantiated through the encounter with an uncivilized, immoral Other, who was incapable of sovereignty and government. Colonial rule naturalized a division of the world into the familiar places of inclusion and exclusion, colonizers and colonized, and men and women. Binary colonial discourses constructed Indigenous women's autonomy, work, and sexuality as indications of the backwardness of Indigenous cultures. These dichotomies defined the bodies that needed to be both regulated and contained.

In the contemporary period, narratives of progress, rights, and democracy have become a measure for the world. Exclusions and gender discrimination are blamed on non-Western cultures, and this situation allows the colonial state to simultaneously remain colonial and to portray itself as post-colonial. The Indigenous female victim is embedded in these narratives in which the settler state is not the source of violence. Rather, the female victim subject is constrained by "culture" and "tradition." The effectiveness of the Indigenous female victim is that it reduces the complexity of her subjugation. Saving her requires state intervention to modify her cultural identity (Newdick 2005, 74).

The other side of the victim subject is the threatening Other, the one who resists confinement, the one who was dispossessed, the unsettled body who resides at the margins of the settler cities, the female body is identified as "wandered", "sex worker", and "drug addict" who contaminates society. The racialized, gendered, and sexualized colonial construction of this subject combine to dehumanize her, to pre-empt her of subjectivity. This dehumanized body is excluded from state protection and her circumstances are not conceived of as a product of settler colonial governance. Rather, this unsettled body is blamed for her circumstances. While governing the victim subject focuses on intervention and individualization, the prison system is expanding to manage the risk posed by the dispossessed and ungovernable bodies. In settler cities, erasure, criminalization and confinement have operated to erase Indigenous presence and to give settlers roots.

These colonial constructions are part of a geopolitics of gendered and racialized inequalities that continue to problematize the universality of human rights. In order to provide some historical context to this discussion, let me turn to two issues facing Indigenous women in Canada. As Joyce Green (2001) points out, the case of Indigenous women shows the connection between law, gender, politics and the limits of the Canadian state and human rights.

Property, rights and unsettled bodies

Colonial constructions of race, the "Other", and the "savage", reflected European perceptions and worldviews and were the processes by which social groups were identified, assigned stereotypical characteristics, and coerced into social/spatial segregation. The colonial state regulated the "intimate spaces" of Indigenous women, men, and children through the interlinking of private and public spheres and body politics. As gender, race, sexuality and body are not only a reflection of colonialism, but also produced the colonial space.

Contrary to the construction of the victim subject, the negative circumstances facing Indigenous women are neither "cultural" nor limited to Indigenous communities. The settler state itself has long victimized Indigenous women. The best-known case of the exclusion of Aboriginal women is the *Indian Act.* This statute concerns registered "Indians," their bands, and the reserve system, was enacted in 1876 and provided Canada's federal government exclusive authority to legislate in relation to these peoples and their lands. This legislation was amended numerous times to further limit Indigenous peoples' autonomy and mobility and to expand the federal government's control over them. First Nations women have borne the burden of the *Indian Act.* In paternalistically defining who was and was not "Indian," the government took away the birthrights of First Nations women and their children. Colonial definition and governance also changed the construction of social provision and the boundaries of inclusion and exclusion within Indigenous communities. From this perspective, gender, race and sexuality are essential to understanding the differences between formal and *de facto* citizenship as well as the discourses and practices embedded in policy making and state structures.

The assumption that the fundamental dimensions of Canadian citizenship have been achieved ignores the fact that, in practice, Indigenous women have never had full citizenship rights either within their communities or within Canada. As a result, in contexts where discourses of equality and social rights have become more and more difficult to support, Indigenous women become a site of liberal intervention. I argue that in the Canadian context, assimilation is taking the form of property rights and individualization.

The election of the Conservative government in 2006 significantly shifted the terms of the Aboriginal policy debate in Canada. The Harper government represents not only a continuation of the market-based neo-liberal trajectory, but also a shift that will likely alter both the framework and nature of social policy discussions (Porter 2006). The Conservative agenda promotes a new type of social and economic order that ensures not only the continuation of privatization and individualization, but also the promotion of certain ways of intruding into the lives of families and women. In terms of the Aboriginal policy, the two pillars of the Conservative government are economic development and human rights. The issue of the division of on-reserve matrimonial real property is closely linked to that of land management.

This Aboriginal policy focuses on strategies and programs to alleviate aboriginal poverty that are grounded in "common sense" and the "acceptance of everyone's responsibility." Under the Conservative policy, *everyone* involved must accept responsibility and get equally involved. Unlike other governments, the Harper government has stated that a new relationship between Aboriginal peoples and the government is unnecessary, for all that is needed is to make the existing relationship work. The government's commitment to Aboriginal peoples focuses on *empowering* Indigenous citizens and *protecting* the *vulnerable* (Harper 2007). To the Harper government, the extension of the *Human Rights Act* to the *Indian Act* would protect Indigenous Canadians, particularly women.

The Conservative government's goal of privatizing property on reserves, so that valuable property can be sold, mortgaged, or used to fight poverty, is implicitly linked to the issue of matrimonial state property and housing. Aboriginal housing is a federal government responsibility and it has been noted that 43% of houses on reserve have substandard conditions including lack of fully operational bathrooms, drinking water, and heating. Indigenous women are overwhelmingly affected by the housing crisis on reserve, and their choices are either to stay in a violent relationship or to leave the reserve. Housing in the city is not necessarily secure or affordable, and with insufficient transition programs and shelters, many women are isolated from their families and networks of support.

The Canadian Government put forward an initiative aimed at dealing with matrimonial property in the event of marital breakdown and ensuring that First Nations women enjoy the same rights as other Canadian women. The Native Women's Association of Canada, a long time promoter of equality, decided to undertake a consultation. At the end, the organization did not support the bill. In its report on matrimonial property rights, this organization showed that Indigenous women do indeed experience greater disadvantages and are allocated less property title than men. The study also showed that a greater percentage of Indigenous women live off-reserve and that the differences between on/off reserve suggest that matrimonial real property has an uneven impact on where a child resides. Although the report acknowledged that matrimonial property rights would greatly benefit women, it also recommended the adoption of a more holistic approach for dealing with this issue. Moreover, the document stated that solutions must be found that are based on Indigenous peoples' traditions, accommodate human rights, and acknowledge the traditionally strong role of First Nations women in their communities (Native Women's Association of Canada 2008).

The bill dealing with matrimonial property was opposed by First Nations organizations because it promotes the liberal discourse on rights and private property. Moreover, it formally relies on the courts system, which does not consider conditions associated with lack of access to justice in northern communities. First Nations leaders were also concerned that, in practice, the legislation would be used mostly by non-Indigenous people to acquire long-term property interests on-reserve. Despite opposition, Bill S-4, *Family Homes on Reserves and Matrimonial Interests or Rights Act* was ultimately passed. It was claimed that this legislation would reduce violence against women. The law states that a "temporary" matrimonial property regime was imposed by the government on Aboriginal land to determine the period of time that a spouse can remain in the house. The law also called upon reserves to develop their own property structures, which would need government officials and communities' approval. However, no funding was provided to support Indigenous governments to design their own rules (INAD 2010).

Claiming to benefit Indigenous women and address gender inequalities, this legislation foregrounds individualization and private property. According to Janine Brodie (2010, 1589-90), individualization downloads responsibilities for systemic changes including economic crises and social challenges onto individuals and families. This approach treats all people the same and demands that they find the causes and solutions to their own circumstances whatever they are. At the same time, it works to normalize Indigenous peoples by disseminating individualist aspirations of private property, prompting self-improvement, and building community capacity. Property, as Paul Nadasdy (2003, 135) argues, reflects the norms and values embodied in a given society. Rescuing the female Indigenous victim invites distance from her own culture and assimilation into the settlers' norms and values.

The other face of the victim subject, the threatening, unsettled Other, invites other technologies of governance. While the victim subject is "invited" to take responsibility for herself on reserve, the threatening Other continues to be erased. Through legislations, regulations and symbolic practices, the settler city continues to unwelcome the "Indigenous, unsettled migrant." Stories of settlers' constructions of cities and pioneers, for example, have had the effect of reconfiguring spaces, bodies and expectations. As Penelope Edmonds (2010, 5) argues, this colonial reconfiguration not only constructed Indigenous peoples' presence in the city as an anomaly, but their bodies were also marked as being "inconvenient," "vagrant," and "prostitute," all categories that resulted from municipal codes, policing, segregation and violent operations. This pathologized and dangerous classification was constructed in opposition to the fixity of settler settlements and idealized bodies. In the same way, the violent acquisition of land was erased; in setter cities, repeated violence by police, structural racism, poverty experienced by and the acts of resistance of these Indigenous migrants go largely unnoticed. The fact that the victim subject coexists with this pathologized "Other" suggests a spatialized continuity between the reserve and the settler city. By moving between reserve and the city, the Indigenous Other transgresses this colonial construction and becomes vulnerable to overregulation, surveillance, policing and disappearance. Colonial legislations not only severely weakened the roles and position of Indigenous women in both Indigenous and Canadian society but also transformed them into landless, unsettled "Others."

According to the NWAC, this degradation of Aboriginal women's roles and responsibilities in society increased their vulnerability in a number of areas, including their vulnerability to being targeted for violence (Native Women's Association of Canada 2008, 2). Compared to other Canadian women, Aboriginal women are three times less likely to report that they have experienced some form of violence perpetrated by their spouse or partner. Aboriginal women are eight times more likely to be killed by their spouse after a separation. Violence, including sexual assault, whether inflicted by a spouse or a stranger, is one of the most fundamental transgressions of the human rights of Aboriginal women. Studies have shown that Indigenous women are not only more likely to face racialized violence and sexual exploitation, but that such violence goes unnoticed and unrecorded (Culhane 2003, 598).

Similarly, the Report of the Aboriginal Justice Inquiry of Manitoba (1999), for instance, noted that bias, prejudice, and hate have strong motivators for the violence perpetrated against Indigenous women. The document draws a correlation between violence and the negative images of Indigenous women in which their bodies exist for consumption, ownership and abuse. The levels of violence experienced by Indigenous women and girls represent a contemporary manifestation of these complex relations in which gender, race, class, and neocolonialism form a "dangerous intersection" (Smith 2005; Razack 2002). Over 500 Aboriginal women have disappeared, mainly in western cities. Racism, colonialism and erasure have shaped a settler society where Aboriginal women are not seen as victims of human rights violations. Rather, they have been seen as confronting the "natural consequence of the life style they have chosen to live" (Report of the Aboriginal Justice Inquiry of Manitoba 1999).

Settler society's neglect of these missing women signals how colonial racial, gender and sexualized constructions combine to dehumanize them. Indigenous women's inequality and racism in society contribute to a perception that they are easy targets; discriminatory and sexist policing has all too often rendered this perception reality. The mass media has played a key role in perpetuating this trend by often defining missing women as "prostitutes" or "drug addicts," instead of as women with personal biographies embedded in a set of relationships. Media reports of those located at the margins tell of sex, drugs, crime, violence, murder, and disease. Through the erasure of people's subjectivity, bodies can be criminalized for being licentious, violent, drug addicted. Managing social risk involves a way of thinking about and representing the world, quantifying an imagined future, and justifying particular forms of governance (Dean 1999).

As Dara Culhane (2003, 599) observes, overexposing the risk posed by these bodies is constitutive of a "regime of disappearance." According to the author, this concept describes a neo-liberal mode of governance that further marginalizes or erases different categories of peoples through strategies of erasure including silence, blind spot, displacements and abandonment, which have material, discursive, and symbolic effect on people. In exposing this selective process of erasure, it is important to note that racism and sexism continue to threaten Indigenous women's safety and security in Canadian cities.

Women began disappearing in western cities in the late 1970s, but these events were ignored both by the police and city officials. Although the Royal Canadian Mounted Police covers 75% of Canada's geography serving more than 630 Aboriginal communities , the lack of available data contributes to a major gap concerning the victimization of Aboriginal peoples (Royal Mounted Canadian Police). For example, it is known that police services only identified "White" persons. The lack of statistics that acknowledge the racialized victimization of Indigenous women has negative impacts on addressing this situation. Indeed, the lack of statistical inquiry in light of what needs to be addressed could be interpreted as another expression of erasure.

It was not until recently that advocates, journalists, and academics joined taken Indigenous women's families to raise awareness of these forced disappearances. In 2005, the Native Women's Association of Canada (NWAC) undertook the *Sisters In Spirit* initiative to increase Canadian society's attention to the taken Aboriginal women and to research the roots of violence they face. In doing so, Sisters in Spirit has articulated a critique and redefinition of dominant representations of Aboriginal women embedded in Canadian colonial history and society.

Similarly, Amnesty International's *Stolen Sisters Report* (2004), states that systemic patterns of racism and discrimination in Canadian society contribute to violence against women in a number of ways. According to this report, people constructed as having a "high risk lifestyle" are denied protection from violence because they are who they are.

In February 2009, the United Nations called upon the Canadian Government to investigate the alarming rise in incidents of missing and murdered Aboriginal women. In March 2010, NWAC released its research findings entitled "What Their Stories Tell Us," which provided evidence that 582 Aboriginal women and girls have gone missing or been murdered in Canada since the 1970s. The document states that many of the stories heard speak of the social, legal, and economic exclusion of Indigenous women. While some stories tell of poverty, abuse or addictions often associated with "high-risk" lifestyles, many of these women were vulnerable simply because they were Aboriginal women. As argued by Jacobs and Williams (2008, 134), they:

> (...) were simply in the wrong place at the wrong time in a society that poses a risk to their safety. They were targeted because it was assumed that either they would not fight back or they would not be missed.

This situation, in my view, reveals that there is no clear-cut distinction between the female victim and the threatening subject. Moreover, it challenges assumptions that Indigenous women's disappearance occurs *only* in spaces of violent eruptions. Instead, disappearance is a mode of settler governance and has taken different forms. From this perspective, we can argue that both the victim subject and the threatening Other are exposed to state violence. The difference is that the threatening Other's exposure to violence of the state is unmediated and unprotected by rights. The threatening Other is reduced to a life without humanity. While the victim subject is encouraged to distant herself from her culture, the threatening Other is a project of colonial dehumanization and the assertion of a settler, urban space. Both exist side by side.

Despite the importance of the work being done by Sisters in Spirit, the Canadian government cut off its funding to this initiative and instead poured $10 million to prompt change in the life of women experiencing violence or families that have not received justice. Both NWAC and Amnesty International observed that this amount is not enough to initiate real change. Both NWAC and Amnesty International have made recommendations to address violence against Indigenous women, and such recommendations associate inequalities, extreme marginalization, and racism with violence. Thus, change will not happen if all these different dimensions are not addressed. In my view, what is at stake is how the human rights discourse is framed and perpetuated, not how human rights can change people's lives. Some of the questions in this context are: who is held accountable when human rights interventions are used to assimilate the "Other?" How can people assert their subjectivity when the state itself dispossesses them of their human dignity? These are questions that we must consider. These are questions that require us to think about human rights' epistemic grounds.

Conclusion

In this paper, I problematized the human rights discourse and its universal assumptions. I argued that the emphasis on the state and suffering as a source of rights conceal the multi-layered experiences of class, race, religion, ethnicity, and/or sexual orientation. In rejecting Otherness, the human rights discourse works to codify people and places that are within and outside of the "modern notion of progress." Human rights emancipatory possibilities work both to simultaneously justify a civilizatory mission and to expel some racialized bodies from the world of rights. No right to have rights creates a vacuum that enables extreme, structural violence.

Although human rights have had the potential to mobilize a wide variety of people for change, rights depend on the social or political vision that informs them. The struggle for Indigenous women's rights reveals the inherent problem of universality and of how the discourse of rights is used by the state. The struggle to end state and non-state violence against these women is not merely a struggle for rights, but for human dignity.

Moving beyond the modernist understanding of human rights requires us to interrogate the colonial framework in which such rights are articulated and to include the "Other" in the conversation. At the same time, more than describing the positive content of humanity, community, and morality, human rights need to specify how these different dimensions can be constructed dialogically by recognizing difference instead of denying it. Confronting colonialism in history, knowledge and culture does not mean rejecting the principle of a humanist project. Rather it means that we construct knowledge based on the recognition of relationships and interrelations. If we continue to speak of human rights in hierarchical terms, their transformative power will always be limited. To be clear, this critique of human rights is a constructive one and aims at understanding their place in our contemporary, diverse world.

References

Amnesty International. 2004. "Canada: Stolen Sisters: Discrimination and Violence Against Indigenous Women in Canada." AMR 20/001/2004.

Brodie, Janine. 2010. "Globalization, Canadian Family and the Policy, and the Omission of Neo-liberalism." *North Carolina Law Review.* 88(5): 1559-1591.

Brown, Wendy. 2001. *Politics Out of History*. Princeton: Princeton University Press.

Colchester, Marcus. 2002. "Indigenous Rights and the Collective Conscious." *Anthropology Today* 18(1): 1-3. doi: 10.1111/1467-8322.00096.

Culhane, Dara. 2003. "Their Spirits Live with Us. Aboriginal Women in Downtown Eastside Vancouver Emerging into Visibility." *American Indian Quarterly* 27(3-4): 593-606. doi : 10.1353/aiq.2004.0073.

Dean, Mitchel. 1999. *Governmentality: Power and Rule in Modern Society*. London: Sage.

Edmonds, Penelope. 2010. "Unpacking Settler Colonialism's Urban Strategies: Indigenous Peoples in Victoria, British Columbia and the Transition to a Settler Colonial City." *Urban History Review* 38(2): 4-20.

Grear, Anna. 2010. *Redirecting Human Rights. Facing the Challenge of Corporate Legal Humanity*. Hampshire: Palgrave Macmillan.

Green, Joyce. 2001. "Canaries in the Mines of Citizenship: Indian women in Canada." *Canadian Journal of Political Science* 34(4): 715-738.

Harper, Stephen. 2007. "Speech on the Government Achievements for Aboriginal Peoples." Halifax: November 2. http:www.pm.gc.ca/.

Indian and Northern Affairs Canada. 2010. Family Homes on Reserves and Matrimonial Interests or Rights Act. http://www.aadnc-aandc.g.ca/eng/1317172955875/1317173115233.

Jacobs, Beverley and Andrea J. Williams. 2008. "Legacy of Residential Schools: Missing and Murdered Aboriginal women." In *From Truth to Reconciliation: Transforming the Legacy of Residential Schools*, edited by Marlene Brant Castellano, Linda Archibald and Mike DeGagné, 21-140. Ottawa: Aboriginal Healing Foundation.

Kapur, Ratna. 2006. "Human Rights in the 21st Century: Take a Walk on the Dark Side." *Sydney Law Review* 28(4): 666-687.

Kennedy, David. 2004. *The Dark Side of the Virtue: Reassessing International Humanitarianism*. Princeton: Princeton University Press.

McClintock, Anne. 1995. *Imperial Leather: Race, Gender and Sexuality in the Colonial Contest*. London: Routledge.

Nadasdy, Paul. 2003. *Hunters and Bureaucrats. Power, Knowledge and Aboriginal-State Relations in the Southwest Yukon.* Vancouver: UBC Press.

Native Women Association of Canada. 2008. *Reclaiming our Way of Being: Matrimonial Real Property Solutions.*
http://www.nwac.ca/sites/default/files/reports/NWACMRP.pdf.

—. 2010. *What Their Stories Tell Us. Research Findings from the Sisters in Spirit Initiatives.*
http://www.uregina.ca/resolve/PDFs/NWAC%20Report.pdf

Newdick, Vivian. 2005. "The Indigenous Woman as Victim of Her Own Culture in Neo-liberal Mexico." *Cultural Dynamics* 17(1): 73-92.

Porter, Ann. 2006. "The Harper Government: Towards A New Social Order?" *Socialist Projet e-bulletin* 21.
http://www.globalresearch.ca/index.php?context=va&aid=2494.

Quijano, Anibal. 2000. "Coloniality of Power, Eurocentrism and Latin America." *Nepantla: Views from South* 1(3): 533-580.

Razack, Sherene. 2002. *Race, Space and the Law. Unmapping a White Settler Society.* Toronto: Between the Lines.

"Report of the Aboriginal Justice Inquiry of Manitoba 1999," Aboriginal Justice Implementation Commission, accessed July 17, 2012, http://www.ajic.mb.ca/volume.html.

Rose, Nikolas. 1999. *Power of Freedom.* Cambridge: Cambridge University Press.

Sanders, Douglas. 1995. "State Practice and the United Nations Draft Declaration on the Rights of Indigenous Peoples." In *Becoming Visible- Indigenous Politics and Self-Government,* edited by Terje Brantenberg, Janne Hansen and Henry Minde. Proceedings of the Conference on Indigenous Politics and Self-Government in Tromsø, 8-10 November, 1993. Tromsø: University of Tromsø.

Sangster, Joan. 1999. "Criminalizing the Colonized: Ontario Native Women Confront the Justice System 1920-60." *Canadian Historical Review* 80(1): 32-60.

Smith, Andrea. 2005. *Conquest. Sexual Violence and American Indian Genocide.* Cambridge: South End Press.

Veracini, Lorenzo. 2008. "Settler Collective, Founding Violence and Disavowal: The Settler Colonial Situation." *Journal of Intercultural Studies* 29(4): 363-379.

Wolf, Patrick. 2006. "Settler Colonialism and the Elimination of the Native.'' *Journal of Genocide Research* 9(4): 387-409.

CHAPTER SIX

MUSLIM WOMEN'S EQUALITY IN INDIA: APPLYING A HUMAN RIGHTS FRAMEWORK[*]

VRINDA NARAIN

Introduction

This article evaluates the potential of a human rights framework as an analytical tool to challenge Muslim women's exclusion from equal citizenship in India (Universal Declaration of Human Rights 1948). Located at the intersection of community and nation, public law and private law, Muslim women are simultaneously included and excluded from the enjoyment of equal rights by the continuance of the personal law system. In sharp contrast to the formal guarantees of equality in the Constitution of India, this parallel system governing family law is explicitly discriminatory on the basis of religion and gender. Applying the framework of human rights offers the possibility of analyzing this disjuncture between formally guaranteed constitutional rights and state legitimized discrimination under the religious personal law.

Women across the globe, and particularly in the Asia Pacific region, are challenging laws, religious norms, and cultural traditions, drawing upon arguments of international human rights law, particularly the Convention on the Elimination of All Forms of Discrimination against Women (CEDAW) (Jivan & Forster 2005). In India, this engagement with international human rights law occurs at multiple levels. As claimants, women challenge the justice system to recognize their rights by appealing to norms of equality and anti-discrimination in both international and

[*] Narain, Vrinda. "Muslim Women's Equality in India: Applying a Human Rights Framework." *Human Rights Quarterly* 35:1 (2013), 91-115. © 2013 by The Johns Hopkins University Press. Reprinted with permission of Johns Hopkins University Press.

national law. Furthermore, at the level of the judiciary, the Supreme Court of India now explicitly incorporates the rules and principles of CEDAW where gaps exist in national legislation. Finally, the legislature has begun to initiate laws that are consistent with women's human rights. Despite such promising developments, the material reality of women's lives in India does not reflect much improvement, nor has the gap between formal rights and the actual status of women been narrowed as a result of this legalization of human rights (Kapur 2006).

This chapter considers the emancipatory potential of applying a human rights framework to the particular situation of Muslim women in India. It evaluates the possibility for Muslim women to move toward equality through the translation of ideas, such as human rights from a universal to a local context. It explores the possibility of universal norms of human rights to provide the normative framework to recognize their equality rights that, paradoxically, cultural relativist arguments might preclude in this particular context. Acknowledging the limitations of human rights, this article seeks to recover from the notion of human rights its ability to contextualize and situate violations of equality within larger structures of systemic discrimination and group disadvantage.

Contextualizing the particular situation of Muslim women is critical to the inquiry because of the fraught political context, and because the terms of the debate today are so highly dichotomized. We continue to see simplistic oppositions constructed between culture and universal human rights, gender equality and religious freedom in ways that tend to abstract the material realities of the everyday lives of Muslim women. It is necessary to challenge this tendency of geopolitical abstraction, as well as de-contextualization in analyzing social and cultural constructions.

Invariably, the framing of the debate around women, religion, and human rights focuses on misleading oppositional categories that must be challenged. Drawing from the insights of postcolonial theory, challenging the construction of binaries is critical to defend women's rights against those who deny their legitimacy on grounds of cultural inauthenticity. It is only by questioning these us/them, East/West binaries, and asserting the hybridity of Indian culture that we can begin to disrupt the assumption of cultural inauthenticity on which the denial of women's human rights is based (Cossman 1979).[1] Related to this challenge is the need to reinsert gender equality into the conversation. Rather than focusing on the religious freedom of the group to the exclusion of gender equality, framing the issue as one of contextualizing and balancing rights and interests is necessary. Structuring the debate in this way keeps a meaningful focus on women's equality rights, which is critical to uncovering previously hidden perspectives. Thus far, Muslim women arguably have been excluded from public debate and democratic dialogue and prevented from naming issues, defining their interests, or claiming their rights (Narain 2001; Daly 1978).

Challenging de-contextualization and abstraction of women's issues is the first step in crafting a legal response to their exclusion and inequality (McCalla Vickers 1989). When challenging the exclusion of Muslim women from the debate that defines their rights, it is necessary to be attentive to the contingency of categories and the need to extend the "woman question" to include other disempowered groups (McCalla Vickers 1989). Only then can there be an inclusive challenge to mainstream analysis and to the normative framework of human rights. Particularly in arguments of religious customs and rules that disadvantage women, the debate must be structured in a way that restores context and agency to women. Oppositional categories are called into question through such an inquiry. An analysis that relies on the category "Muslim women" must necessarily subject its own categories to constant critique and scrutiny, revision, interrogation, deconstruction, and reconstruction. Categories structure the questions asked and, inevitably, the conclusions reached (Wishik 1985). The importance of reinserting Muslim women's interests into the democratic dialogue becomes critical to reconstruct an understanding of law that can take into account their experiences.

The Constitution of India guarantees equality and freedom from discrimination.[2] It also guarantees religious freedom and protection of minority rights.[3] In sharp contrast to these equality guarantees, Muslim women are subject to explicit discrimination in the family, which is regulated by religious personal laws.[4] These laws discriminate on the basis of both religion and gender. The religious personal laws are justified under the right to religious freedom and the state's commitment to the protection of group rights.[5]

This explicitly discriminatory system and the contradictions between public formal equality and private discrimination are a compelling demonstration of the state's reluctance to uphold gender equality when it is presumed to conflict with group interests (Narain 2008).

In this way, the public-private dichotomy underpins the religious-secular binary. The state is committed to a policy of secularism in the so-called public sphere, but allegedly does not interfere with religious laws in the so-called private sphere, even when these laws conflict with constitutional guarantees (Narain 2008). Muslim women are simultaneously included and excluded from equal citizenship, as the state's guarantee of equality does not extend to the private sphere of the family. Thus, Muslim women are explicitly discriminated against within the family, and the state does little to enforce constitutional guarantees of equal citizenship in the family as part of its commitment to a policy of multiculturalism and accommodating Muslim groups' rights. Consequently, the state has created a differentiated citizenship, wherein it has differing obligations and duties to citizens based on gender and religious identity (Narain 2008).

The controversial *Shah Bano* case and the subsequent enactment of the Muslim Women's Protection of Rights on Divorce Act illustrate the ambivalent alliance between the state and male leaders of the Muslim community (Mohammed Ahmed Khan v Shah Bano Begum 1985; The Muslim Women's Protection of Rights of Divorce 1986). The *Shah Bano* case brought postcolonial India to the brink of a constitutional crisis over the issue of spousal support for divorced Muslim women (Pathak & Rajan 1989). Very briefly, the facts of the case are as follows: Shah Bano was a seventy-three year old Muslim woman who was divorced unilaterally by her husband when she sued him for spousal support under the general secular Indian law. He then appealed against the order for spousal support. He claimed that his religious law did not require him to comply with the court order for support, that as a Muslim he was not required to pay support for more than forty days and that the religious law absolved him of all support duties beyond this period. The Supreme Court, however, ruled in Shah Bano's favor, causing a strong reaction from religious leaders who eventually prevailed upon the government of that time. The religious leaders also convinced the government to abrogate the Supreme Court decision and to enact a new law regulating Muslim women's access to spousal support, absolving husbands of the duty to support and moving Muslim women further away from equal citizenship.[6]

Shah Bano raised questions of gender justice, minority rights, and the accommodation of difference. It tested the limits of constitutional rights and the commitment to fundamental organizing principles of India's multicultural democracy — secularism, religious freedom, and women's equality. The state absolved itself of the responsibility to enforce constitutional principles in the "private sphere" of the family, abandoning Muslim women to greater control by male religious leaders (Narain 2008).

The legal context

The Indian Constitution is a remarkable document with an explicit transformative agenda, drafted at a moment when the ideals and aspirations of human rights were compelling to the newly independent nation. Recognizing the role of law and the significance of rights in remedying the sharp inequities of colonial India — with its divisions of class, caste, gender, and religion — the Constitution incorporates notions of universal human rights (Narain 2008). Returning the imperial gaze meant that the status of women was central to the self-conscious project of modernizing nationalism. As in other postcolonial societies, law was understood to be the primary agent of social change, and accordingly, the Constitution incorporates notions of universal human rights, principles of equality, and non-discrimination (Narain 2008). In turn, the judiciary was understood to be responsible for bringing about change, regulating rights, and reforming religion to address inequities, particularly with regard to gender and caste. Secularism, equality, and religious freedom were the fundamental organizing principles of the newly independent multi-ethnic, multi-religious, pluralist democracy (Narain 2008). Taking its postcolonial constitutional mandate for social reform through judicial activism seriously, the Indian Supreme Court has been remarkably enthusiastic about interpreting the Constitution to reach decisions in favour of equality rights (Narain 2008).

Article 51(c) of the Indian Constitution directs the state to fulfill its obligations under international law.[7] In addition, Article 253 of the Constitution confers on Parliament the power to initiate legislation to implement international agreements, treaties, or conventions entered into with other countries, which include any decision made at an international conference or convention. These broad ranging provisions underscore the constitutional commitment to honour international rules and norms.8 In addition to these constitutional provisions, the Protection of Human Rights Act of (1993) was enacted by the Indian Parliament pursuant to the directive under Article 51 of the Constitution and in conformity with India's commitments under international human rights law.

The Supreme Court's increased use of international law and universal norms of human rights to interpret constitutional guarantees of women's substantive equality and freedom from discrimination is promising. Arguably, international law has a normative impact on states, as demonstrated by the adoption of international human rights norms by the Indian Supreme Court.

In *C. Masilamani Mudaliar*, the Supreme Court considered inequality in religious personal law, emphatically asserting the connection between constitutional rights to equality and India's obligations under international law to eliminate gender discrimination (*Masilamani Mudaliar v The Idol of Sri Swaminathaswami Thirukoil* 1996). In allowing the appeal, the court held that provisions of religious personal law that discriminate against women violate the equality guarantee and must be consistent with constitutional law. Turning to international law to support its decision, the Court underlined India's obligations under CEDAW to prohibit all gender-based discrimination and made specific mention of property issues (*Masilamani Mudaliar v The Idol of Sri Swaminathaswami Thirukoil* 1996). Significantly, women's human rights were seen as indivisible, as the Court insisted that the goal of development as outlined in the UN Declaration on the Right to Development (1986) signified the indivisibility of economic, social, and political rights. The Court stated:

> The human rights for woman, including girl child are, therefore, inalienable, integral and indivisible part of universal human rights. The full development of personality and fundamental freedoms and equal participation by women in political, social, economic and cultural life are concomitants for national development, social and family stability and growth culturally, socially and economically. All forms of discrimination on grounds of gender is violative of fundamental freedoms and human rights . . .
> Article 15(3) of the Constitution of India positively protects such Acts or actions. Article 21 of the Constitution of India reinforces "right to life." Equality dignity of person and right to development are inherent rights in every human being. Life in its expanded horizon includes all that give meaning to a person's life including culture, heritage and tradition with dignity of person. The fulfillment of that heritage in full measure would encompass the right to life. For its meaningfulness and purpose every woman is entitled to elimination of obstacles and discrimination based on gender for human development, women are entitled to enjoy economic, social, cultural and political rights without discrimination and on a footing of equality . . . but also all forms of gender-based discrimination should be eliminated (Masilamani Mudaliar 1996, 1709-10).

Specifically incorporating international law into constitutional law, the Court then strengthened its argument by turning to national legislation, the Protection of Human Rights Act, to reinforce the entrenchment of anti-discrimination principles of international human rights law into Indian constitutional law. In the Court's own words, "Thereby the principles embodied in CEDAW and the concomitant right to development became integral parts of the Indian Constitution and the Human Rights Act and became enforceable" (Masilamani Mudaliar 1996, 9).

Most important, the Court categorically asserted that India's reservations to CEDAW were not enforceable in light of Indian constitutional law and India's commitments to international human rights. The Court called on the state to make good its commitments to constitutional guarantees of anti-discrimination under Articles 14 and 15 of the Constitution, as well as its obligations to equality and anti-discrimination under human rights law (Masilamani Mudaliar 1996). Thus, the Court emphasized the link between national constitutional law and international human rights law to expand and enforce state accountability to all its citizens through the implementation of equality rights. Specifically, the court noted the duty of the state to remedy existing domestic legislation, laws, regulations, customs, and practices that discriminate against women (Masilamani Mudaliar 1996).

The Court stressed the purpose of law as an instrument of social change, noting the role of the Supreme Court in bringing about such change, and mandated the state to enforce constitutional rights. In using human rights law to interpret Indian constitutional law, the Court stated that

> Law is an instrument of social change as well as the defender for [sic] social change. Article 2(e) of CEDAW enjoins this Court to breath [sic] life into the dry bones of the Constitution, international conventions and the protection of Human Rights Act . . . to prevent gender based discrimination and to effectuate right to life including empowerment of economic, social and cultural rights to women (Masilamani Mudaliar 1996, 13).

In *Madhu Kishwar v. State of Bihar* (1996), which concerned the validity of customs and traditions that explicitly discriminate against women, the Court noted that customary laws of succession that deny women equality within the family raised the need for all national legislation to conform to both constitutional guarantees of gender equality and international norms of gender equality.9

Remarkably, citing India's obligations under international law, the Supreme Court explicitly stated that the rights to equality guaranteed under the Constitution must be read in conjunction with the provisions of CEDAW, as well as the Declaration on the Right to Development. Significantly, in this case, the Court used international law to expand and support its interpretation of constitutional guarantees of equality, non-discrimination, and social and economic justice.

Valsamma Paul v. Cochin University (1996) challenged the constitutional validity of affirmative action in government employment policies as a violation of equality and anti-discrimination guarantees. In dismissing the appeal, the Court ruled that remedial programs of affirmative action that respond to historic disadvantage were necessary to combat social and economic inequality. Together with asserting the constitutional legitimacy of affirmative action programs, the Court turned to CEDAW to establish the state's right to enact such remedial measures as were necessary to promote women's equality rights. Interestingly, the Court asserted that the government of India's reservations to CEDAW Articles 5(e), 16 (1), (2), and 29 "bear little consequence in view of the fundamental rights" to equality and the right to life, as well as the directive principles of the Constitution. The court in *Valsamma Paul* asserted that all forms of discrimination on the basis of gender violate fundamental freedoms and human rights.

Perhaps the most well-known case is *Vishaka v. State of Rajasthan* (1997), in which the Supreme Court considered the brutal gang rape of a female social worker in rural Rajasthan. The Supreme Court demonstrated its receptiveness to incorporating international law into domestic law, citing Article 51(c) of the Constitution and Article 253 as it turned to international norms to craft a legal response to sexual assault. *Vishaka*'s particular significance is its emphasis on the link between constitutional guarantees of gender equality and international human rights to respond to women's experience of sexual assault and sexual harassment in the workplace. In response to the gap in domestic legislation on this issue, the Supreme Court recognized its normative role to "fulfill this felt and urgent social need" (*Vishaka* 1997). Looking to CEDAW, the Supreme Court incorporated these legal provisions into Indian domestic law and entrenched international norms into Indian constitutional law to enlarge and interpret widely the guarantee of gender equality (*Vishaka* 1997).

Apparel Export Promotion Council v. A K Chopra (1999) concerned, once again, sexual harassment. The Supreme Court turned to CEDAW and other international agreements and directed the state to take appropriate steps to prevent all forms of discrimination against women. Relying on *Vishaka*, the Court held that international agreements must be applied when there is no inconsistency between international human rights law and domestic law. Although not dealing specifically with questions of gender equality, another landmark decision incorporating international law into domestic law in India is *Vellore Citizens' Welfare Forum v. Union of India* (1996), which concerned the compensation of victims of water pollution caused by tanneries.[10] In this case, the Supreme Court specifically incorporated norms from customary international law, the "Polluter Pays Principle," and the "Precautionary Principle," as integral aspects of domestic environmental law (*Vellore* 1996, 11-14). *Vellore* emphasizes the Supreme Court's commitment to considering and incorporating critical aspects of international law to strengthen national law.

In *Municipal Corporation of Delhi v. Female Workers (Muster Roll)* (2000), the question before the Court was whether the Maternity Benefits Act of 1961 applied to women who were employed on daily wages and not permanent employees. Asserting the fundamental rights to equality and non-discrimination to support these workers, the Supreme Court highlighted social and economic justice as fundamental organizing principles of the Indian Constitution. The Court once again supported its constitutional argument extending maternity benefits to female daily wage workers, relying upon the doctrine of social justice as embodied in the Universal Declaration of Human Rights (UDHR) and Article 11 of CEDAW, which calls on the state to eliminate discrimination against women in employment and the right to work. In its decision, the Court set out in detail the provisions of CEDAW's Article 11, ruling that these provisions must be read into the Maternity Benefits Act and upholding the right of female workers to maternity leave benefits (*Vellore* 2000).

In *John Vallamattom v. Union of India* (2003), which concerned the conflict between religious personal law and constitutionally guaranteed rights, the Court noted that the Declaration on the Right to Development and Article 18 of the International Covenant on Civil and Political Rights held that religious personal laws must conform to principles of gender equality and non-discrimination. The Court emphasized the normative role of the judiciary in ending inequality under religious laws. Drawing upon the interpretation of the Constitution as a living organ, it held that constitutional law must evolve in keeping with changing social contexts. International human rights law arguments were heard by the Supreme Court in *Sakshi* v. *Union of India* (2004). After an increase in violence against women, this writ petition was filed by way of public interest litigation by an NGO, calling for an expanded re-definition of sexual assault provisions in the Indian Penal Code (1860, §375). Although the Supreme Court did not agree to strike down the provision, this case is nonetheless significant as the appellants' arguments relied heavily on inter-national human rights law and India's obligations under the various treaties and conventions it had ratified. Referring specifically to the United Nations Convention on the Rights of the Child (1989) and to CEDAW, the appellants argued that the state "has created a legitimate expectation that it shall adhere to its International commitments as set out under the respective Conventions."

Clearly, the Supreme Court is acutely conscious of the importance of international law, not only as a persuasive tool, but also as a practical response to questions of inequality and discrimination. These cases are remarkable as the Supreme Court explicitly links constitutional guarantees of equality with women's human rights. The cases demonstrate the transformative potential of using international human rights norms to hold the state accountable to vulnerable groups where domestic legislation falls short. Nevertheless, the Supreme Court has generally approached the incorporation of international law into the domestic legal arena with caution, taking care in both *Vishaka* and *Vellore Welfare* to note that in the case of any conflict between municipal law and international law, municipal law would prevail (Hedge 2010). Upendra Baxi notes that the Indian Supreme Court, through its activism and acceptance of social action litigation, has demonstrated a willingness to embrace universal notions of human rights. The Indian judiciary has become "an institutionalized movement for the protection and promotion of human rights" (Baxi 1998, 125, 161). However, with regard to Muslim personal law, despite this progressive jurisprudence, the state has done little to enforce judicial decisions or to initiate domestic legislation to bring it into conformity with India's international law obligations. The *Vishaka* decision culminated in the Protection of Women Against Sexual Harassment at Workplace Bill, 2010. The Bill incorporates the guidelines laid out in *Vishaka,* explicitly linking constitutional rights to equality, life and liberty with universal human rights norms. It demonstrates the successful use of international human rights law to forward women's rights. Through this legislative initiative, Parliament has responded to the Supreme Court's insistence on incorporating international human rights law to enforce women's rights, where national legislation is inadequate. Yet, as the culmination of the struggle for recognition of sexual harassment begun with the *Vishaka* case, the Bill is an ambivalent victory. It has certain problematic provisions, specifically with regard to false and malicious complaints that might deter women from coming forward to report harassment. Second, there are certain groups of women who are excluded from the purview of the Bill, such as agricultural workers. Finally, enforcement mechanisms provided for in the Bill may not be particularly effective. Indeed enforcement might remain the biggest challenge as acknowledged by the Supreme Court in *Medha Kotwal*, decided on 4 October 2012, wherein it decried the lack of enforcement of the *Vishaka* guidelines. Nevertheless, acknowledging the Bill's limitations, it is a critical step forward. Its importance lies in the recognition that women's rights are human rights, and that India's ratification of CEDAW obliges the state to ensure the prevention of sexual harassment in the workplace. The Bill was approved by the lower house of Parliament in September 2012 and is currently awaiting ratification by the upper house before it is enacted as law. Notwithstanding constitutional mandates and judicial injunctions, Muslim women continue to be disadvantaged in all aspects of family law.

Universalism and Cultural Relativism

Invariably the framing of the debate about women, religion, and human rights focuses on misleading oppositional constructions of public/private, westernized feminist/true Muslim woman, east/west, modernity/tradition, and cultural relativism/universalism. These simplistic oppositions tend to abstract the material realities of the everyday lives of Muslim women and to perpetuate gender inequalities. Drawing from the insights of Sally Engle Merry (2006a), I suggest that in order to move beyond the universalism versus relativism debate, it is necessary to focus instead on how best to translate universal norms of women's human rights to local contexts. It is also important to close the gap between the religious and secular and to understand that it might not be realistic to draw too sharp an opposition between the two.

While the courts have been enthusiastic about enforcing gender equality using norms of international law, this has been restricted to the public sphere. Courts have been far less enthusiastic about extending these principles to the private sphere of the family, particularly regarding the constitutionality of Muslim personal law. This area of discrimination against women within the family, based on religious specificity and cultural particularism, is precisely what might provide the potential for an argument based on the notion of human rights. The public-private dichotomy reveals the way in which the private subjugation of Muslim women is an explicit part of the public agenda. Catharine MacKinnon notes that, "As a legal doctrine, privacy has become the affirmative triumph of the state's abdication of women" (1993, 117-18). These arrangements serve to exclude Muslim women from the enjoyment of equal rights, buttressing patriarchal structures of authority. Women experience the sharpest discrimination within the family sphere. As MacKinnon points out,

> Family law keeps a lot of women in place and in line, fearful of altering their lives because of how it could be made to look in court . . . The realm in which women's everyday life is lived, the setting for many of these daily atrocities, is termed the private. Law defines the private as where the law is not, that into which the law does not intrude, where no harm is done other than by law's presence (2003, 116-117).

The state, for its part, is reluctant to reform Muslim personal law, arguing that the initiative for change must come from within, and that religious personal law is a part of the protection of minority rights that the state will not interfere with as part of its commitment to protect minority rights.[11] Conservative religious leaders argue that family law cannot be reformed, as it is divine and immutable. Yet, religious law is not static: it is fluid and changes over time, even within religious traditions that insist on the immutability of the divine law. The need to formulate law and policy approaches to resolve such conflicts is imperative because of the substantial impact these religious laws have on women's equality and their full enjoyment and exercise of human rights. Reformists such as Abdullahi An-Na'im (1992) approach the relativism versus universalism question in a nuanced manner, seeking to integrate human rights within local cultural norms rather than positing them as oppositional. He argues that defenses of cultural relativism and even shari'a are limited by minimum standards of human dignity and universal norms of human rights. An-Na'im (2004) insists that the dichotomy created between the religious and the secular is misleading, and that it is used by elites to deny rights to women and to non-Muslims.

Interestingly, Jack Donnelly (2007) argues that universal notions of human rights, when properly understood and applied, allow for particular cultural and national interpretations that are specific to the local context. Insisting on the "relative universalism" of human rights offers the possibility of refuting arguments of "Westoxification," and breaks down the pejorative anti-Muslim Western feminism label that is so often used to delegitimize internal claims for equality. The appeal to the universality of human rights and the appeal of them is that all human beings can lay claim to the ideals of equality and freedom from discrimination (Baxi 1998).

Yet, as Donnelly (2007) readily acknowledges, the high level of abstraction renders these ideas of little consequence practically, and this is a difficulty with which human rights advocates must contend. Certainly, the implementation and enforcement of human rights remains dependent on national will (Donnelly 2007). Practically speaking, as the Supreme Court of India has shown, universal norms of human rights provide the normative framework within which to craft national legislation and formulate public policy. In the particular case of Indian Muslim women, the human rights framework is essential to establish the legitimacy of their claims, and provides a means to insist on state accountability.

Indeed, India has accepted the authority of the UDHR and CEDAW. Although this acceptance is at the elite interstate level, it does have significance for the equality struggle in India where movements for social justice have increasingly used the discourse of human rights to forward their claims (Donnelly 2007).

As Donnelly convincingly argues, rather than a universal ontological truth, human rights notions are based on varying cultural ontological foundations. Indeed there are multiple and diverse ontological foundations on which the claims to human rights are based (Donnelly 2007). This insight supports the argument that rather than reinforcing the oppositional argument between universality and particularism, in fact, human rights norms are more effectively justified when recognized as being relatively universal in that they are based on a plurality of ontological bases leading to "ontological universality" (Donnelly 2007, 282). This is extremely helpful in refuting the oppositions constructed between East and West, true Muslim woman and Westernized feminist, and tradition versus modernity.

Such a flexible stance and the accompanying acknowledgment of legal pluralism within the concept of universal norms of human rights help articulate and implement women's equality where cultural relativism and arguments of religion are used as a defense against granting women more equitable rights within the family. Further, it is helpful as a framework within which states can balance seemingly competing rights such as gender equality and religious freedom and minority rights (Donnelly 2007, 302).

Applying a human rights framework

Today, the concern that universal notions of human rights may serve politically to reinforce a neo-imperialism on developing nations threatens the legitimacy of human rights. Arguably, human rights were based on exclusion: "heathens," "slaves," "barbarians," colonized peoples, women, among others, and these exclusions justified imperialism and colonialism (Baxi 1998, 133-34). Indeed, the legacy of colonialism cannot be ignored in the argument regarding universal norms of human rights, which are often seen as a method or tool of coercion by those countries with differing cultural value systems (Donnelly 2007).

The proliferation and subsequent overproduction of human rights norms and laws have resulted in the bureaucratization of human rights, together with the creation of human rights entrepreneurs. Consequently, human rights have become state-bound. A significant impact of this focus on the state has been that human rights and social justice movements have been de-radicalized and depoliticized. As Baxi points out, the overproduction of "soft" human rights law resolutions declarations codes has resulted in very little hard law that is enforceable (2007, 139).

The contemporary discourse of human rights engenders identity politics that are not just liberating, but can also be repressive. Indeed, postmodern critics of universal discourses of human rights worry that the re-emergence of the idea of universality will result in a totalizing essentialism regarding human nature (Baxi 2007). Not surprisingly, the dangers of globalization and the impact on human rights give rise to anxieties about reinforcing homogenizing meta-narratives.

Baxi (2007), however, resists this fear of the big story, pointing out that human suffering is a concrete reality to which the theorizing of multiple identities and the fluidity of identities may have little relevance. For example, for those actually engaged in human rights struggles, the reality of oppression of caste and untouchability in India make it difficult to reconcile with theoretical discursive notions of multiple, fluid, and contingent identities (Baxi 2007). He also questions whether the postmodern account of identity actually empowers those who suffer massive and flagrant violations of their human rights (Baxi 2007).

Human rights discourse, despite charges of essentialism and universalism, still contains an emancipatory possibility and the potential for struggle that postmodern discourses of identity do not as yet (Baxi 2007). Human rights matter only if they can ameliorate suffering and give voice to human suffering (Baxi 2007). Most important, the claim to the universality of human rights has been central to equality-seeking groups who have fought for recognition of their rights using the language of human rights both in the domestic arena and internationally.

Ratna Kapur (2006) argues that human rights discourse and the resort to human rights strategies have been successful in many ways, empowering women particularly in the area of violence against women. Yet, the use of human rights law has certain serious limitations (Kapur 2006). First, human rights law places too much emphasis on legal strategies and thus encourages the idea that human rights instruments are themselves a sign of women's improved status (Kapur 2006). A related difficulty is that legal strategies emphasize the homogeneity of women as an undifferentiated group (Kapur 2006). Finally, this focus on law as a means to ameliorate women's status can result in reinforcing cultural essentialism. This is particularly problematic as invariably it is the customs and cultures of the third world that Western liberal feminists strongly criticize. Too often, third world women are portrayed as victims of their own cultures, necessitating rescue by their liberated Western sisters, and the dark side of human rights is exposed in these interventions.

Liberal feminists, such as Susan Moller Okin (1998), locate women's inequality in cultural tradition invariably in the global south and in minority racialized communities.[12] Such attitudes demonstrate the persistence of colonial discourse and the justification for imperialist interventions to save native women from barbaric customs and traditions, as well as from native men (Kapur 2006). The legalization of human rights reinforces the notion of third world women as victims, while simultaneously reinforcing the first world and third world divide (Kapur 2006).

As Radhika Coomaraswamy writes, "The colonial legacy of western powers championing the cause of third world women conditions the debate on women's equality in many parts of the world . . . Any movements for women's international human rights must recognize this historical colonial legacy" (2002-2003, 483, 487). It is necessary always to be mindful of the liberal assumptions on which the universal project of human rights is based and how it has been based on assumptions about difference and the cultural "Other," produced partly in and through the colonial encounter, which continues to discursively inform the postcolonial present. We need to pay attention to how universalist claims of human rights and the rational subject have justified political exclusions in practice, and have also set out the terms for political inclusion. The assimilative urge informing the legal responses, such as perceived sub- ordination by culture, is premised on shedding culture and on conformity (Volpp 2001).

This recognition signifies the need to begin by thinking critically about the terms in which the opposition between religion and women's human rights has been framed before jumping to conclusions like Susan Okin (1997), who suggests that women in "patriarchal" minority cultures

> *may* be much better off if the culture into which they were born were either to become extinct (so that its members would become integrated into the less sexist surrounding culture) or, preferably, to be encouraged to alter itself so as to reinforce the equality of women—at least to the degree to which this is upheld in the majority culture.

The human rights community needs to think harder about the liberal construction of the opposition between religion and rights. Rather than a unitary focus on culture, attention should be given to structural inequalities of wealth and power: access to education, employment, and racialized, gendered poverty. The notion of culture must be unpacked and demystified to gain recognition that it is not monolithic.[13] Culture is in fact deeply contested, politically contingent, and fraught with tension as it is actively negotiated, discursively created, and selectively reinvented.

Scholars like Baxi refute the notion that human rights ignore cultural diversity (Baxi 2007). He asserts that it is disingenuous to suggest that contemporary human rights are monologically produced. On the contrary, much of the production of human rights today is dialogical, mediated by diplomatic and political forces (Baxi 2007). The enactment of human rights norms into domestic legislation is even more culturally specific; however, a critique could be drawn that these states are not in equal relations of power. Nonetheless, Baxi (2007) rejects strong cultural relativism, though he respects cultural diversity and recognizes the fact of cultural diversity. He sees dialogic human rights as a part of the struggle and underscores the importance of dialogic engagement as a way to mediate the tension between universalism and relativism. The larger concern is that human rights should be used to forward the rights of the worst-off.

It is critical to pay attention to the political context when seeking to draw upon human rights norms to forward particular equality claims that are seen as being in tension with cultural practices or religious beliefs.[14] It is necessary to recognize that in some contexts, fundamentalisms, as well as political movements on the far right, manipulate religion in order to achieve their political aims. Arguably, the logic of the universality of human rights is better able to protect the cultural specificities of women and minorities by opening up the space for the interrogation of received notions of culture and tradition that culturally specific norms do not. Universal notions of human rights bring a transformative vision, a form of struggle, and engender a truth of resistance that challenges the truths of power. It is this aspect of universal human rights that we must highlight (Baxi 2007).

It is necessary to question the state as a site of struggle, to consider the appropriate role of the state, and to reflect on its duty to enforce women's equality rights. In accommodating Muslim groups' rights, women's rights were ignored. For the state, Muslim women have a prior religious and gendered identity. Arguably, using the notion of human rights allows for the possibility of inserting the notion of gender equality into this conversation. Inserting the language of human rights norms here can help move the focus back to the refusal of the state and community leaders to grant Muslim women equal rights within the family, invariably framing the issue as one of religious freedom, rather than of gender equality. Muslim women must be included in the dialogue between the state and the community regarding the balancing of seemingly opposing rights of gender equality and religious freedom. A certain tension exists between the notion of gender equality and religious freedom. The discourse of human rights can be used to mediate the tensions between the recognition of group interests, and women's equality. Ultimately, any solution must consider the rights of communities, individuals, and the common rights that reflect the universal principles of equality and freedom from discrimination.

Baxi contends that human rights have emerged as "the only universal ideology in the making, enabling both the legitimation of power and the *praxis* of emancipatory politics" (Baxi 2007, 126). Although human rights law has not radically ameliorated the situation of women, these norms and standards have served to empower social justice movements and also to question political practices, and Baxi (2007) counts this as a remarkable contribution of human rights. The demand for human rights has been a critical part of movements to empower disadvantaged groups, and women's groups in India have used the notion of human rights in the domestic arena.[15] The campaign in India could be seen as successful through the Indian Supreme Court's receptiveness to incorporate human rights norms in its decisions.[16] It is significant that laws have been made and changed in response to the demand from the human rights community for change in India and across the world (Kapur 2006). Despite this success, there has been some anxiety and ambivalence expressed over the efficacy of human rights to respond to disadvantage and suffering, and whether it can in fact bring about effective social change (Kapur 2006). Some argue that the difficulties with realizing human rights norms on the ground and the conceptual-practical divide result from lack of enforcement and lack of access (Kapur 2006). Others argue that human rights cannot dismantle structural disadvantage as they are a product of this structural inequality and also replicate it (Kapur 2006).

Certainly, we need to take a closer look at the assumptions on which these laws are based. We must subject human rights norms to a deeper interrogation so that we can understand the role of the law not simplistically as an agent of social change, but rather as a "complex and contradictory force" (Kapur 2006, 102). Human rights are constituted in a way that is premised on certain exclusions and inclusions (Baxi 2007). In addition, the proliferation of human rights norms calls into question their enforceability.

Arguably, the postmodern rejection of the meta-narrative may not be conducive to setting up a contextual narrative of discrimination and disadvantage (Baxi 2007). We need to have an understanding of the big picture so that we can situate and contextualize individual narratives of disadvantage. It is important to be careful not to reinforce or reify the sharp opposition constructed between cultural relativism and universalism, but to focus instead on how best to translate universal norms with emancipatory potential, such as equality and freedom from discrimination, to local cultural contexts. The more critical task at hand is how best to translate these universal norms to local contexts to make them meaningful and able to provide a liberatory praxis of human rights for disempowered groups.

Human rights decisions and international human rights conventions can provide helpful insights for domestic interpretation of the constitution and can greatly impact women's constitutional position. International human rights law impacts women's status through the acceptance and incorporation of these standards by national constitutional courts. This raises interesting issues for women's rights activists as to the transformative potential of international human rights law as a normative framework to hold the state accountable. Human rights are transnational ideas, used in the struggle to fight oppression, discrimination, and violence in countries across the globe. Yet, a common argument against the use of international human rights to promote women's rights has been that of cultural specificity: that human rights are Western and cannot easily be translated and applied to other contexts (Merry 2006; Bunting 1993). Arguably, the more useful focus is an inquiry into how human rights norms are translated locally and what impact they have on people's daily lives (Merry 2006a, 2006b). Rather than engaging solely in the theoretical debate on the perceived opposition between culture and rights, as Merry (2006b) asserts, a more fruitful focus would be instead on how human rights institutions help combat inequality in different contexts. While there can be no easy answers to these questions, it is helpful to establish the framework in which transnational ideas can forward the emancipatory struggles of marginalized groups and to examine how human rights discourse circulates and changes life in local contexts.

It is often the sentiment that third world societies are measured by universal standards of human rights that have no relevance to their particular local context (Merry 2006b). We must not overplay the binary distinction between global and local, but at the same time, we have to be wary of drawing too simplistic an assessment of the divide between local and transnational and to be aware of any value judgment that might stem from naming something as local in contrast to global. There can be no claim to a pure cultural authenticity, and indeed we must acknowledge both the hybridity of culture and the modernity of tradition. Clearly, this is a complex issue, to which there are no easy answers: how far should one go to adapt universal norms to specific norms in order to retain legitimacy, but also to be able to address inequality? What is the responsibility of the translator? It is crucial to consider how human rights are translated into the vernacular. How do societies adapt their use to suit their particular campaigns and agendas? This translation must be recognized as a two-way process that not only acknowledges the influence of global on local, but local on global as well. Such an understanding allows for the reality of the hybridity of culture, the normative influence of both local and global, and the two-way cultural traffic that Stuart Hall notes (Hall 2003). This insight is valuable both to refute assertions of a claim to a pure cultural authenticity, as well as to reject the use of cultural relativism to justify the subordination of women.

We need to remain mindful that the imposition of universal norms framed outside the particular context might in fact reproduce a neocolonialist difference. One of the dangers of a non-reflexive imposition of transnational concepts onto local contexts, however inadvertent, might be the value judgment implied and the fear of replicating neocolonialism through recreating categories of us and them with respect to transnational global progressive versus local parochial and unprogressive norms and values. Such an approach posits a recalcitrant particularity opposed to the progressive forces of global, transnational values (Merry 2003).

The translation of transnational norms to local contexts is a complex and nuanced issue. There can be no simplistic transplanting, but rather a considered contextualized application of norms and values that have a certain legitimacy within the cultural framework of a particular society. Tying together these theoretical themes, the question becomes: how can we use international human rights norms as transnational values to promote national constitutional rights and enforce them in local cultural contexts? What is the impact, if any, of transnational human rights laws on the constitutional jurisprudence of a particular state?

Sally Merry emphasizes the process of vernacularization, whereby ideas from transnational sources are adapted to local cultural institutions' conditions, within the cultural framework of a local context (Merry 2006b). Related to this is the notion of indigenization, which frames new ideas of international human rights in terms of existing cultural norms (Merry 2006b). Equally important is hybridity, whereby local activists use international human rights ideas combined with a local narrative to give it a new meaning and to produce a hybrid discourse that combines aspects of both the local cultural framework and norms, as well as concepts and ideas from international human rights (Merry 2006a). Translators or local human rights activists are central to this process. Merry notes their importance as they move between worlds, playing a critical role in connecting global transnational discourse with local contexts (Merry 2006a).

Indeed, the role of human rights activists at the grass roots level is of great importance. At the very least, such local grassroots activists pose a challenge to the received binary categories such as local versus global and Western versus traditional. Madhavi Sunder (2003) argues that human rights activism on the ground challenges received notions of religion and culture. Questioning the opposition constructed between culture and rights, Sunder suggests that rather than seeing culture as an obstacle to women's human rights, culture can be used strategically to forward women's rights campaigns (Sunder 2003). At the same time, as Hester Lessard (2011) cautions, romanticizing the local can be dangerous. Ultimately, the discursive creation of culture is a two-way process — the transnational is informed by the local, and the local is impacted by the global. This recognition raises many important questions about the discourse of human rights, most importantly in assessing its emancipatory potential. Can it indeed be transformative? How can women and other marginalized groups use international human rights discourse as a tool for social change?

Cultural translation, understood as a two-way reciprocal process, is a significant aspect of critical human rights. Cultural translation radically challenges the dominant discourse of human rights as it "works to resignify what it is to be human (ontologically, socially and politically)" (Lloyd 2007). The expansion of human rights norms to include previously excluded groups is a challenge at the ontological level, forcing a re-articulation of human rights within the dominant discourse (Lloyd 2007). This does not signify a rejection of universal norms of human rights, but on the contrary, a challenge for the inclusion of disempowered groups and recognition that rights have an importance. Patricia Williams notes, "For the historically disempowered, the conferring of rights is symbolic of all the denied aspects of their humanity" (1987, 401). Moya Lloyd (2007) argues that the very receptiveness of human rights to re-articulation and re-appropriation is pertinent, demonstrating the emancipatory spaces and possibilities within to challenge normative conceptions of inclusion and exclusion and who counts as the legitimate bearer of rights.

Indeed, "engaged human rights discourse makes possible a deeper understanding of the politics of difference insofar as it is an act of suffering rather than sanitized thought" (Baxi 2007, 145). Baxi (2007) advocates engaged human rights discourse, arguing that such engagement provides the possibility of a deeper understanding not only of the politics of difference, but more importantly, a deeper understanding of human suffering that a sanitized intellectual exercise on the politics of essentialism might not. Baxi (2007) does acknowledge that states co-opt human rights language and discourses for repressive agendas and that postmodern critics may be right when they argue that the classic notion of human rights as embodied in the UDHR contains certain contradictory elements. Furthermore, the links between statist human rights and policies of neoliberalism and globalization are evident across the globe.

Baxi (2007) convincingly questions the postmodern linking of meta-narratives with governmentality. Feminist legal scholar Martha Minow (1993) has noted that we need the meta and personal narratives if we are to have a context within which we can set the personal stories so that they have a systemic impact, rather than resulting in an individualized response to individual discrimination. What we need is a feminization of human rights so that we can better negotiate the conflict between the meta and micro narratives in a way that is more empowering for women (Baxi 2007). At the same time, we do not need cautions about meta-theory to remind us to be always mindful of the limitations of a human rights discourse and its claims to universality (Baxi 2007). The normative aspirational value and framework, rather than the reality of attainment, is what makes human rights universal (Baxi 2007).

Yash Ghai (2009) adopts the position of pragmatic engagement with human rights. Although he is skeptical of claims to universality, he finds in his practical work of postcolonial constitution-making that the framework and discourse of human rights offers a workable structure for negotiating political and constitutional settlements among politicians and sectarian leaders (Ghai 2009). Indeed, law has played a very important part in women's equality struggles. The critical question is not whether to engage with the law, but rather how best to apply this complicated understanding of the law and legal discourse to forward women's human rights.[17] We need to be mindful of the ways in which the women's movement could be de-radicalized and depoliticized by this emphasis on the role of the state in human rights struggles. States should be "[constantly attentive] to the dark side of human rights law" (Kapur 2006, 11). In the case of women's human rights, we need to analyze the ambivalent nature of human rights law, to understand and acknowledge that until now human rights law strategies have not always proved to be emancipatory for women, and we need to understand the paradoxical implications for women's equality struggles. Understanding the contradictory nature of law as a site of social transformation allows us to better craft legal responses and remedies to exclusion, inequality and discrimination (Kapur 2006).

Conclusion

The framework of human rights arguably allows Muslim women to reclaim a selfhood free from essentialist definitions of gender identity and what constitutes a group's interests. Certainly, we must be mindful of political uses of universalism that promote a neo-imperialist agenda and be wary of powerful developed nations extending their political authority under the guise of respect for human rights, especially women's rights. The critique of human rights universal claim is well taken as a caution against neocolonialism and the reproduction of imperial agendas. In the context of globalization and neoliberalism, these critiques are important and serve as a caution, as well as a reminder of the need to remain mindful of context and to favor cross cultural dialogue (Donnelly 2007). While remaining mindful of the limitations and political dangers of neo-imperialist agendas, arguably the "relative universality of those rights is a powerful resource that can be used to help to build more just and humane national and international societies" (Donnelly 2007, 306). We cannot abandon the project of translating universal norms of human equality and dignity to local contexts as they are a vital aspect of building a more just society.

In conclusion, how we understand human rights and their purpose is critical to engaging the emancipatory potential of human rights and to what makes it an enabling regime. In assessing what a human rights framework can contribute and what the limitations are when using such a framework, this article recognizes that the notion of human rights is currently "a common language of humanity (Baxi 2007, 127). Nevertheless, human rights can be both an emancipatory ally as well as an emissary of the state (Baxi 1992). It is necessary to acknowledge that there are several limitations to such a universal discourse and that reality on the ground is often not matched by the lofty aspirational norms of the UDHR.

The important insight that Baxi offers is that "Human rights languages are all that we have to interrogate the barbarism of power" (Baxi 2007, 127). Using this insight in the context of Muslim women's exclusion from equality, it is useful to relate the language of human rights to the suffering and continued disadvantage of Muslim women in India. Furthermore, it is necessary to reinsert gender equality and universal norms of human rights into the dialogue that currently focuses on religious freedom of the group rather than on the gender equality of women. Moving away from the argument of universal versus specific human rights, regardless of the postmodern questioning of the universality of human rights norms, there is a just anxiety about their universality (Baxi 2007). Yet arguably, what we should be concerned about instead is the universality of aspirations that human rights signify. As Baxi eloquently puts it, "Thus, the universality of human rights symbolizes the universality of collective human aspiration to make power more accountable, governance progressively just, and state incrementally more ethical" (Baxi 2007, 151).

References

An-Na'im, Abdullahi. 'Introduction'. In *Human Rights in Cross-Cultural Perspective : A Quest for Consensus.* 1-6. University of Pennsylvania Press, 1992.

—. "The Best of Times' and 'the Worst of Times': Human Agency and Human Rights in Islamic Societies'. *Muslim World Journal of Human Rights* 1 (2004) : 11-12.

Baxi, Upendra. 'The State's Emissary': The Place of Law'. In *Subaltern Studies Vii : Writings on Asian History and Society*, edited by Partha Chatterjee, and Gyanen. Oxford University Press, 1992.

—. 'Voices of Suffering and the Future of Human Rights'. *Transnational and Contemporary Problems* 8 (1998:125,161).

Bunting, Annie. 'Theorizing Women's Cultural Diversity in Feminist International Human Right's Strategies'. *Journal of International Society* 20 (1993) :6, 8.

C. Masilamani Mudaliar v. The Idol of Sri Swaminathaswami Thirukoil, A.I.R. 1996 S.C. 1697 (India), *available at* http://www.indiankanoon.org/doc/1999938/.

Convention on the Elimination of All Forms of Discrimination Against Women, *adopted* 18 Dec. 1979, G.A. Res. 34/180, U.N. GAOR, 34th Sess., U.N. Doc. A/34/46 (1980), 1249 U.N.T.S. 13 (*entered into force* 3 Sept. 1981).

Convention on the Rights of the Child, *adopted* 20 Nov. 1989, G.A. Res. 44/25, U.N. GAOR, 44th Sess., U.N. Doc. A/44/49 (1989), 1577 U.N.T.S. 3 (*entered into force* 2 Sept. 1990).

Coomaraswamy, Radhika. 'Identity Within: Cultural Relativism, Minority Rights and the Empowerment of Women'. *George Washington International Law Review* 34 (2002) : 483, 487.

Cossman, Brenda. 'Turning the Gaze Back on Itself: Comparative Law, Feminist Legal Studies, and the Postcolonial Project'. In *Feminist Legal Theory : An Anti-essientialist Reader*, edited by Nancy E. Dowd, and Michelle S. Jacobs , 89–90. New York : New York University Press, 2003.

Daly, Mary. *Gyn/Ecology : The Metaethics of Radical Feminism.* Boston : Beacon Press, 1978.

Declaration on the Right to Development, *adopted* 4 Dec. 1986, G.A. Res.
41/128, U.N. GAOR, 41st Sess., Annex U.N. Doc. A/RES/41/128
(1986).

Donnelly, Jack. 'The Relative Universality of Human Rights'. *Human
Rights Quarterly* 29 (2007) : 281-306.

Ghai, Yash. 'Universalism and Relativism: Human Rights as a Framework
for Negotiating Interethnic Claims'. In *Human Rights, Southern
Voices. Edited by William Twining*, 109-50. Law, Social Justice and
Global Development Journal, 2007.

Hall, Stuart. 'The Spectacle of the 'Other'. In *Representation : Cultural
Representation and Signifying Practices*. Edited by Stuart Hall, 223-
90. London : Sage, 2003.

Hegde, V G. 'Indian Courts and International Law'. *Leiden J. Int'l L.* 23
(2010 : 53, 60-61).

Indian Penal Code, Act No. 45 (1860).

International Covenant on Civil and Political Rights, *adopted* 16 Dec.
1966, G.A. Res. 2200 (XXI), U.N. GAOR, 21st Sess., art. 18, U.N.
Doc. A/6316 (1966), 999 U.N.T.S. 171 (*entered into force* 23 Mar.
1976) [hereinafter ICCPR].

Jiva, Vedna and Christine Forster. 'What Would Gandhi Say? Reconciling
Universalism, Cultural Relativism and Feminism Through Women's
Use of CEDAW'. *Singapore Year Book of International Law and
Contributors.* 9 (2005) : 103-123.

John Vallamattom v. Union of India, A.I.R. 2003 S.C. 2902 (India).

Kapur, Ratna. 'Revisioning the Role of Law Rights in Women's Human
Rights Struggles'. In *The Legalization of Human Rights :
Multidisciplinary Perspectives on Human Rights and Human Rights
Law*, edited by Saladin Meckled-García, and Bas¸ak Çali, 101-
116.New York : Routledge,2006.

Lessard, Hester. 'Jurisdictional Justice, Democracy and the Story of
Insite'. Constitutional Forum 19 (2011): 93.

Lloyd, Moya. '(Women's) Human Rights: Paradoxes and Possibilities'.
Review of International Studies 33 (2007) : 91, 97.

MacKinnon, Catharine A. 'Reflections on Law in the Everyday Life of
Women'. In *Law in Everyday Life,* edited by Austin Sarat, and Thomas
R. Kearns. 109-122. University Press of Michigan, 1993.

Madhu Kishwar v. State of Bihar, A.I.R. 1996 S.C. 1864 (India).

McCalla Vickers, Jill. 'Memoirs of an Ontological Exile : The
Methodological Rebellions of Feminist Research. In *Feminism : From
Pressure to Politics*, edited by Angela Miles, and Geraldine Finn. 43-
46. Blackrose books, 1989.

Merry, Sally Engle. 'Constructing a Global Law-Violence against Women and the Human Rights System'. *International & Social Inquiry* 28 (2003) : 941-979.

—. *Human Rights and Gender Violence : Translating International Law Into Local Justice.* Chicago : University of Chicago Press, 2006a.

—. 'Transnational Human Rights and Local Activism: Mapping the Middle'. *American Anthropologist.* 108 (2006b :38-51).

Minow, Martha. 'Surviving Victim Talk'. *UCLA Law Review* 40 (1993): 1411, 1437.

Mohammed Ahmed Khan v. Shah Bano Begum, (1985) 2 S.C.C. 556 (India), *available at* http://www.cscsarchive.org/dataarchive/textfiles/textfile.2008–07–22.2150472804/file [hereinafter Shah Bano].

Moller Okin, Susan. Is Multiculturalism Bad for Women?. *Boston Review* (Oct./Nov. 1997), http://bostonreview.net/BR22.5/okin.html.

Municipal Corporation of Delhi v. Female Workers (Muster Roll), A.I.R. 2000 S.C. 1274 (India).

Narain, Vrinda. *Gender and Community : Muslim Women's Rights in India.*Toronto: University of Toronto Press, 2001.

—. *Reclaiming the Nation: Muslim Women and the Law in India.* Toronto: Toronto University Press, 2008.

Pathak, Zakia, and Rajeswari Sunder Rajan. 'Shahbano'. *Signs* 14 (1989: 558-582).

Sakshi v. Union of India, A.I.R. 2004 S.C. 3566, ¶ 8 (India).

Sunder, Madhavi. '(Un)disciplined'. *Political and Legal Anthropology Review* 26 (2003) : 277, 80.

The Muslim Women's (Protection of Rights of Divorce) Act, No.25 of 1986, Gazette of India, Extraordinary, section I(2) (19 May 1986).

The Protection of Human Rights Act, 1993, No. 10 of 1994, INDIA CODE (1994), amended by the Protection of Human Rights (Amendment) Act, 2006, No. 43, Acts of Parliament, 2006 (India), *available at* http://nhrc.nic.in/documents/Publications/HRActEng. pdf.

Universal Declaration of Human Rights, G.A. res. 217A (III), U.N. Doc A/810 (1948).

Valsamma Paul v. Cochin University, A.I.R. 1996 S.C. 1011 ¶ 3–4, 6 (India).

Vellore Citizens Welfare Forum v. Union of India, A.I.R. 1996 S.C. 2715 (India).

Vishka v. State of Rajasthan, (1997) 6 S.C.C. 241 (India).

Volpp, Leti. 'Feminism Versus Multiculturalism'. *Columbia Law Review* 101 (2001) : 1181-1218.

Williams, Patricia J. 'Alchemical Notes: Reconstructed Ideals from Deconstructed Rights'.*Harvard CR-CL Rev*, 22 (1987): 401, 416.

Wishik, Heather Ruth. 'To Question Everything : The Inquiries of Feminist Jurisprudence.' *Berkley Women's Law Journal* 1 (1985 : 64-75).

Notes

[1] *See* Said, Edward. *Orientalism.* Vintage Books, 1979.

[2] India Constitution arts. 14–16(2).

[Article] 14. Equality before law—The State shall not deny to any person equality before the law or the equal protection of the laws within the territory of India.

[Article] 15. Prohibition of discrimination on grounds of religion, race, caste, sex or place of birth—(1) The State shall not discriminate against any citizen on grounds only of religion, race, caste, sex, place of birth or any of them. (2) No citizen shall, on grounds only of religion, race, caste, sex, place of birth or any of them, be subject to any disability, liability, restriction or condition with regard to—(a) access to shops, public restaurants, hotels and places of public entertainment; or (b) the use of wells, tanks, bathing ghats, roads and places of public resort maintained wholly or partly out of State funds or dedicated to the use of the general public. (3) Nothing in this article shall prevent the State from making any special provision for women and children. (4) Nothing in this article or in clause (2) of article 29 shall prevent the State from making any special provision for the advancement of any socially and educationally backward classes of citizens or for the Scheduled Castes and the Scheduled Tribes. (5) Nothing in this article or in sub-clause (g) of clause (1) of article 19 shall prevent the State from making any special provision, by law, for the advancement of any socially and educationally backward classes of citizens or for the Scheduled Castes or the Scheduled Tribes in so far as such special provisions relate to their admission to educational institutions including private educational institutions, whether aided or unaided by the State, other than the minority educational institutions referred to in clause (1) of article 30.

[Article] 16. Equality of opportunity in matters of public employment—(1) There shall be equality of opportunity for all citizens in matters relating to employment or appointment to any office under the State. (2) No citizen shall, on grounds only of religion, race, caste, sex, descent, place of birth, residence or any of them, be ineligible for, or discriminated against in respect of, any employment or office under the State.

[3] *Id.* arts. 25, 29.

> [Article] 25. Freedom of conscience and free profession, practice and propagation of religion—(1) Subject to public order, morality and health and to the other provisions of this Part, all persons are equally entitled to freedom of conscience and the right freely to profess, practise and propagate religion.
>
> [Article] 29. Protection of interests of minorities—(1) Any section of the citizens residing in the territory of India or any part thereof having a distinct language, script or culture of its own shall have the right to conserve the same. (2) No citizen shall be denied admission into any educational institution maintained by the State or receiving aid out of State funds on grounds only of religion, race, caste, language or any of them.

[4] Under Indian Muslim Personal Law, women do not have equal rights with men in family law, including: marriage, divorce, custody, guardianship, inheritance, and succession. *See Asaf A. A. Flyzee, Outlines of Muhammadam Law,* (4th ed. 1999).

[5] *See* Vrinda Narain, Reclaiming the nation 78, 93, 97 (2008).

[6] Shah Bano, 2 S.C.C. 556 (India). For a full discussion of the *Shah Bano* case. *See* Narain (2001).

[7] Indian Constitution. art. 51(c). "The State shall endeavour to . . . foster respect for international law and treaty obligations in the dealings of organized peoples with one another."

[8] *Id. art. 253.*

> Legislation for giving effect to international agreements- Notwithstanding anything in the foregoing provisions of this Chapter, Parliament has power to make any law for the whole of any part of the territory of India for implementing any treaty, agreement or convention with any other country or countries or any decision made at any international conference, association or any other body.

[9] Other notable cases are All India Democratic Women's Association v. Union of India, (1989) 2 S.C.R. (2) 66 (India); Apparel Export Promotion Council v. A. K. Chopra, A.I.R. 1999 S.C. 625 (India) [hereinafter AEPC]; The Chairman, Railway Board v. Mrs. Chandrima Das, A.I.R. 2000 S.C. 988 (India); Delhi Domestic Working Women's Forum v. Union of India, (1995) 1 S.C.C. 14, [1994] JT (7) 1983 (India).

[10] *See* Vrinda Narain, *Water as a Fundamental Right: A Perspective from India,* 34 vl, 1 Rev. 917, 921 (2009).

[11] *See* Zoya Hasan, *Minority Identity, State Policy and Political Process, in forging identities: gender, communities and the State in India,* 59 (Zoya Hasan ed, 1994).

[12] *See* Susan Moller Okin, *Feminism and Multiculturalism: Some Tensions,* 108 Ethics 661, 661 (1998).

[13] *See* Iris Marion Young, Justice and the politics of difference (1990).

---

[14] In that political moment, India was experiencing a sharp rise in politicized religious identity and the rise of the Hindu rights, which threatened postcolonial India's secular democratic consensus seeking assimilation of minorities and erasure of their rights.

[15] *See* Vishka v. State of Rajasthan, (1997) 6 S.C.C. 241 (India).

[16] *See* Kapur (2006) at 101.

[17] *Ibid* at 110-12.

PART III

CHANGING SOCIETIES, STATE INSTITUTIONS AND HUMAN RIGHTS

CHAPTER SEVEN

CANADA'S CLASH OF CULTURALISMS

PEARL ELIADIS

The management of pluralism and diversity is a matter of longstanding importance in Canada. In Europe, however, multiculturalism has been deemed a "failure" at least in some circles, while in Canada, it remains popular and has played a role in successfully integrating a relatively diverse population (Kymlicka, 2011). Multiculturalism reached middle age in Canada in October 2011, the 40th anniversary of its introduction in 1971 as a major social policy plank by the federal Liberals. Multiculturalism was then entrenched as an interpretive policy in the *Constitution Act, 1982*. It became law in the *Canadian Multiculturalism Act* in 1985 and was designed to "encourage and assist" full participation in Canadian society of individuals of all origins and to:

> (...) promote the full and equitable participation of individuals and communities of all origins in the continuing evolution and shaping of all aspects of Canadian society and assist them in the elimination of any barrier to that participation (1985, s 3).

Interculturalism, a second and Quebec-based approach to managing diversity, has attracted some visibility and momentum in recent years. This was partially the result of the 2008 report of the Commission on Accommodation Practices Related to Cultural Differences (the "Bouchard-Taylor Commission") which endorsed interculturalism to preserve Quebec's specificity and offer an alternative to the Canadian multicultural model.

In 2011, Quebec academic Gérard Bouchard spearheaded the International Symposium on Interculturalism in Montreal (May 2011). The Symposium provided a forum for participants from Quebec and Europe to explore the idea of interculturalism further and to respond to what the conference organizers described as a "growing interest" in this idea in Europe.[1]

Interculturalists are skeptical about whether multiculturalism can respond to Quebec's social realities or address the legitimate goal of protecting the French language.[2] Predictably, multiculturalists tend to minimize the differences between the two forms of "culturalism." A majority of Quebecers supports the promotion of "multicultural" values in Quebec,[3] but interculturalism is *de rigueur* among Quebec's political classes.

There is no single definition of interculturalism, but the Bouchard-Taylor Commission focused on integrating groups into the "core" of Quebec society, namely the French Canadian majority. The Commission's report did emphasize that this integration or assimilation should not create a hierarchy of citizens (Bouchard-Taylor Report, 118).

This essay considers the two Canadian "culturalisms" from the perspective of human rights. Interculturalism offers a distinct approach to social cohesion and to managing diversity, but it also attracts an ethnocentric approach to public policy that has been adopted enthusiastically by nationalists, at the expense of Anglophones, allophones and, increasingly, religious minorities. The resulting social and legal conflicts have triggered human rights cases under the *Canadian Charter of Rights and Freedoms* (the *Charter*) and the Quebec *Charter of human rights and freedoms* (the Quebec *Charter*). Interculturalism does not have sole responsibility for the developments discussed in article, but it has provided fertile ground.

Interculturalism has nurtured efforts to enhance differences with the rest of Canada and to push distinct "Quebec values" and "Quebec heritage." These include the protection of the French language, the imposition of *laïcité,* an extreme form of secularism (similar to the French policy by the same name), and the pre-eminence of a particular conception of gender equality. The politicization of these "super-values" has had increasingly negative implications for minority rights, including civil and political rights, that are discussed later in the paper.

Interculturalism's preoccupation with the preservation of the majority culture has made it resistant to acknowledging the minority status of Anglophones or of religious minorities.[4] This is in part because French-Canadian Quebecers view themselves as minorities within Canada and in North America. It is also because of a deliberate break with a staunchly Roman Catholic tradition that dominated much of French Canadian life until well into the 20th century. Quebecers draw their political identity from this national minority status and from secularism. This response is understandable, first because of the multiple and repeated efforts to marginalize and assimilate French speakers, both inside and outside

Quebec since the late 18th century, and because of the iron grip that the clergy had over all aspects of life, and especially women's lives. At the same time, this history has made it difficult to acknowledge and legitimize the minority status of other groups, especially English speakers in Quebec and religious minorities.[5]

The government of Quebec divides its citizens into three groups: the French Canadian majority, the dwindling historic Anglophone community, and the growing group of "others" who are called "cultural communities." The nomenclature is not trivial and it has legal implications aimed at the assimilation of the latter group into the first one.[6] In international law, linguistic, ethnic and religious minorities have established rights under the *International Covenant on Civil and Political Rights*. "Cultural communities" do not have rights and the term does not reflect or follow accepted international usage. By identifying minority groups as "cultural," the government promotes terminology, language and bureaucracy that set minorities apart largely on the basis of immigrant status, ethnic and racial origin, and language. Its policies aim not at supporting these groups but at integrating them to the core majority group and treating them as clienteles to be integrated and "francisized."

The avoidance of the term "minorities" is not arbitrary. In 1989, a group of Anglophones filed an international complaint about Quebec language laws. In 1993, the United Nations Human Rights Committee (the UN Committee) issued its views on the case. The complainants won on the ground of freedom of expression, but lost on the claim for minority status. The UN Committee took the position at that time that the Anglophones in Quebec are not a "minority" because that term meant 'national minorities' (*Ballantyne*, 1993).

Two decades later, things have changed. In 2010, the United Nations have issued guidelines on minority rights, specifying that a group that constitutes a majority at the national level may nonetheless comprise a minority in a sub-region. The definition of "minority" is thus more inclusive today than it was in 1993. The 2010 Guidelines say, "It is now commonly accepted that recognition of minority status is not solely for the State to decide, but should be based on both objective and subjective criteria" (UN OHCHR 2010, 3). Canada recognized Quebec as a "nation" within Canada, and this recognition should bring responsibilities to minorities within its borders. Today, based on the UN Guidelines, Anglophones would likely be considered as a minority in Quebec under the *International Covenant on Civil and Political Rights*.

Rights and "Culturalisms"

Human rights laws in Canada offer legal protections and remedies against discrimination and seek to eliminate barriers to full and equal participation in society. Multiculturalism provides an interpretive lens through which those rights are both understood and enforced. Within the bounds of established human rights law, new immigrants have, or should have, just as much right to hold onto their religions, cultures and identities as more settled groups and not to be "integrated" into any culture, beyond the political or legal requirements of Canadian citizenship and the Canadian Constitution.

With a few notable exceptions, the relationship between "culturalisms" and rights has not been central to debates about interculturalism in Quebec, at least not until recently. In multiculturalism, on the other hand, rights are central to understanding how multiculturalism should be interpreted.[7] Passing, *pro forma* references to the Quebec *Charter* (RSQ c C-12) are made from time to time in the literature, but there is little sustained analysis of the role of the *Charter* in discussions about interculturalism.[8] The Bouchard-Taylor Report, in its section on discrimination "The Fight against Discrimination," does not refer once to Quebec's human rights commission, nor does it make any reference whatsoever to decisions of the Quebec Human Rights Tribunal.

Instead, the interculturalism debate emphasizes terms like harmonization, integration and social cohesion. *Charter* rights tend to emerge only when people challenge assimilationist policies and laws before the courts. Because neither *laïcité* nor social cohesion has any legal foundation, they generally fail when confronted by established constitutional rights (*e.g.*, *Syndicat Northcrest v. Amselem* 2004; *Multani v. Commission scolaire Marguerite-Bourgeoys* 2006). As discussed below, the Quebec government has responded by attempting to legislate these values.

The "inter" in "interculturalism" indicates, or should indicate, a degree of reciprocity, mutuality and even equality between two or more things (Soans and Stevenson 2006). However, a closer examination of its deployment in "interculturalism" in Quebec points instead to an increasingly ethnocentric form of "super-culturalism." It aspires to integrate minorities and newcomers into the "core" group of French Canadian Quebecers who claim "ad hoc" precedence (Bouchard 2011, 251). Interculturalism is described as a "cultural integration model" (Bouchard and Taylor 2008, 118). It emphasizes a different sort of values, elevating the "interests of the majority culture" above others [.]" (Bouchard 2011, 451).This feature underpins a fundamental difference between the "culturalisms." Multiculturalism aims to support the participation of individuals and communities into Canadian society without integrating or assimilating then into another ethnic group or culture. Fundamental questions arise as to what values matter, beyond human rights, Canadian citizenship, and the rule of law.

It was foreseeable and perhaps inevitable that politicians would use interculturalism and the *ad hoc* precedence of the majority to push for *de jure* precedence and for political leverage with an increasingly fearful French Canadian community, raising important questions about the consequences for equality rights.

***

The Charter guarantees equality rights. Section 15 of the Charter provides:

> S. 15. (1) every individual is equal before and under the law and has the right to the equal protection many will benefit of the law without discrimination and, in particular, without discrimination based on race, national or ethnic origin, color, religion, sex, age or mental or physical disability.

Equality rights are enforceable and strong norms that have been defined in Supreme Court of Canada decisions of *R v. Kapp* (2008) and *Withler v. Canada (Attorney General)* (2011).[9]

Section 15 explicitly prohibits discrimination on the grounds of, among other things, national or ethnic origin and religion. Cultural policies must comply with equality rights, not the other way around. It is true that equality rights do not apply to distinct legal regimes in the Constitution that carve out special rights, for example for English and French as official languages and for Aboriginal peoples. These exceptions aside, section 15's equality rights operate in combination with section 27 of the *Charter* which interprets the Constitution in a way that supports multiculturalism. Together, these provisions promote rather than suppress the cultural diversity of Canadians. These ideas have been central to how the courts approach equality rights and other rights or freedoms such as religious rights.

Two cases illustrate the point, starting with the Supreme Court of Canada's 2006 decision in *Multani*. Most Canadians know that the case sparked the current opposition to multiculturalism in Quebec. The decision was about whether a Sikh boy could wear his kirpan to school. The school board commissioners had refused permission. Although the Quebec Superior Court overturned that decision, the Quebec Court of Appeal restored the commissioners' original refusal. The Supreme Court of Canada allowed the appeal, and affirmed the scope of religious freedoms of the *Charter* and the *Quebec Charter*. The Supreme Court relied on principles of reasonable accommodation of religious rights to find that the kirpan, a key element of faith for Sikh men, could be worn provided it was securely sewn into a sheath and hidden from view.

Multani imposed on schools the legal obligation to accommodate the religious needs of children. Reasonable accommodation is a direct requirement of equality law. It requires that rights claims and the adequacy of responses to them must be weighed on a case-by-case basis and not through a pre-ordained hierarchy of rights or absolute bans on religious practices.

Multani did not create much of a stir in the rest of Canada: kirpans had been permitted in schools, courtrooms and legislatures since at least the early 1990s in Ontario where there is a large Sikh community. However, *Multani* provoked an outcry in Quebec. The religious claims were seen as antithetical to the "values" of a hyper-secularized Quebec. *Multani* was not a one-off case: a delegation of Sikh men was rejected from the National Assembly in Quebec City in 2011 for wearing kirpans. The occasion of their visit was an invitation to the Sikh community to present a brief on reasonable accommodation. Two years later, Quebec's soccer federation barred young Sikh boys from playing while wearing religious head coverings until FIFA, the international soccer federation, intervened.

The second case started Ontario and was the 2012 decision of the Supreme Court of Canada in *R. v. N.S.* The accused were two family members alleged to have committed sexual assaults against the complainant when she was a young girl. The complainant had sought to testify at a preliminary inquiry while wearing a niqab. She was ordered at the preliminary inquiry to remove the niqab because of the rights of the accused to face his accuser.

She refused, and the matter was appealed. The Court of Appeal determined that the preliminary inquiry judge had not assessed adequately the complainant's right to religious freedom. The right of the accused to a fair trial is a fundamental common law right. The Supreme Court of Canada dismissed the appeal and sent it back to the preliminary inquiry judge to render a decision based on these principles. The interesting point is not the final outcome (the preliminary court judge again ordered her to remove the niqab, and the decision was going back up on appeal at the time of writing), but rather the extent to which a multicultural approach to religious rights introduced a lens to the courts' approach to fundamental legal rights of the accused that took seriously her religious claims.[10]

In Quebec, however, religious freedom to display one's conviction through apparel or through other symbols has been receiving short shrift in the public sphere, in circumstances where the opposing right is far less serious than *R. v. N.S.* In 2010, two women wearing niqabs were in the news when officials expelled them from French-language classes designed to welcome immigrants.[11] The argument in favour of their expulsion was simply that it was hard for the teachers to see their mouths or confirm that they were speaking properly. In another move designed to control Muslims, the government of Quebec sought to legislate a blanket rule prohibiting a covered face when seeking public services in Bill 94, which is discussed below.

Equality is not an absolute right, but rather a modulated and contextualized norm. The subtlety of and differences in human identity and personal characteristics need to be weighed in the balance, along with other factors to determine their significance in a legal balance. Formulaic assertions of the precedence of any given "value," be it in the form of culture, language or secularism, must be carefully examined. Human rights have precedence over other forms of laws let alone social values, because of their constitutional status.[12] However, this principle is being steadily eroded.

Developments in Quebec

Quebec is moving toward a more diverse society especially in Montreal where most minority groups in Quebec live. This is the product of higher levels of immigration from non-European source countries. It has also generated considerable anxiety about the future of the French language and of Quebec's ability to maintain its traditional culture and heritage.

Recent immigrants tend to fare poorly in Canada overall as compared to those immigrants who arrived in previous generations. Discrimination is at least part of the reason.[13] This is not news. Nor is it news that Quebec has even worse employment outcomes for recent immigrants (who have been in Canada five years or less) and somewhat worse outcomes for immigrants (who have been here for five to ten years as compared to the Canadian average), as compared to Ontario and the Atlantic provinces.[14]

The *Multani* case and the Bouchard-Taylor Commission brought these issues into higher relief. Whether the Bouchard-Taylor Commission laid bare existing intolerance or whether it actually heightened it is a matter of some debate.[15] It does appear that human rights complaints based on the combined grounds of race, colour, national and ethnic origin increased in the aftermath of the Bouchard-Taylor Commission. In 2006-2007, the year the Bouchard-Taylor Commission was created, Quebec's human rights commission reported that such complaints numbered 22 percent. In 2011-2012, the figure had risen to 26 percent (*Commission des droits de la personne et droits de la jeunesse* 2006, 38; 2012, 45). Comparing Quebec to Ontario, complaints based on race-related grounds dropped over the same period from about 35 percent in 2006-2007 to about 30 percent of complaints in 2011-2012 (Ontario Human Rights Commission, 2007; HRTO, 2012). Ontario's level of diversity is more than twice as high as Quebec's when comparing the two largest cities' populations.[16]

A spate of incidents related to racial profiling in Quebec has raised concerns about the "normalization" of intolerance of difference. In 2011, Quebec's human rights commission issued a major report on racial profiling, not only in the context of law enforcement, but also the public service more broadly. Racial profiling is not unique to Quebec, but the strategies adopted by police to counter claims of racial profiling have been highly adversarial and litigious in Quebec. Police services have blocked access to data in racial profiling cases (*Commission des droits de la personne et des droits de la jeunesse* 2011).[17]

As noted earlier, the exclusion of kirpan-bearing Sikhs from the National Assembly in Quebec in January 2011 was a powerful public symbol of the politics and policies of secularism (Dougherty 2011, 10). The supposed "neutrality" of Quebec secularism has meant that public displays of non-Christian religion are more likely to be suppressed while aspects and symbols of its Catholic tradition are preserved, including the cross that is hanging in the Quebec National Assembly and the recital of Christian prayers in some municipal meetings.[18] Studies have shown negative perceptions of certain immigrants in Quebec, racial minorities (Blacks, Hispanics) and religious minorities (Jews and Muslims) (Jedwab 2011).

Jumps in discrimination numbers, negative media treatment of multicultural issues, and inadequate responses to racial profiling in Quebec are not necessarily indicative of intolerance that is worse than the rest of Canada. But they do suggest differences in approach that have coincided with attempts to implement interculturalism, or at least its main planks, in the years following the Bouchard-Taylor Commission.

***

The first was on November 24, 2009 when Parti québécois leader (and now Premier) Pauline Marois tabled Bill 391, *An Act to assert the fundamental values of the Quebec nation* (2009). Clause 2 of the Bill would amend the Quebec *Charter of Human Right and Freedoms* as follows:

> The Charter shall be so interpreted as to take into account Quebec's historical heritage and the fundamental values of the Quebec nation, including equality of women and men, the primacy of French and the separation of state and religion.

It was a boldfaced bid to occupy the nationalistic territory abandoned by a nationalistic party, the *Action démocratique du Quebec*, a populist party that was in the process of imploding at the time, but that had previously made tremendous gains at the polls on the back of nationalist sentiment. Bill 391 would have created hierarchies of rights, with gender equality taking precedence over other rights, and the language rights of the Francophone majority trumping those of the Anglophone minority. Human rights would be interpreted in a way that would "take into account Quebec's historical heritage." It was not a government bill, and it never passed.

The second example of interculturalism gone sideways was Quebec Minister Kathleen Weil's 2011 policy proposal to create quotas or caps on immigrants based on region of origin. The idea was a response to the dilution of the "core culture" by non-traditional and especially non-French speaking source countries. The proposal was roundly and instantly condemned by Quebec academics and practitioners (Anctil et al. 2011). Restricting admission to Canada based on region of origin is overtly discriminatory. It was unprecedented in more recent Canadian immigration history, but echoed the more distant past when restrictions on Asian immigration were introduced in the late 19th century (see *Mack et al. v. Attorney General (Ontario)* 2001). The 2011 proposal was quickly dropped.

In 2010, Bill 94, *An Act to establish guidelines governing accommodation requests within the Administration and certain institutions* (2010) was tabled. A cursory reading the bill made it immediately obvious that Bill 94 would have made Quebec the least progressive of any Canadian jurisdiction on the issue of equality rights and accommodation. It is worth reproducing the relevant provisions that are at the heart of the Bill.

> **4.** An accommodation must comply with the Charter of human rights and freedoms (R.S.Q., chapter C-12), in particular as concerns the right to gender equality and the principle of religious neutrality of the State whereby the State shows neither favour nor disfavour towards any particular religion or belief.

5. An accommodation may only be made if it is reasonable, that is, if it does not impose on the department, body or institution any undue hardship with regard to, among other considerations, related costs or the impact on the proper operation of the department, body or institution or on the rights of others.

6. The practice whereby a personnel member of the Administration or an institution and a person to whom services are being provided by the Administration or the institution show their face during the delivery of services is a general practice.

If an accommodation involves an adaptation of that practice and reasons of security, communication or identification warrant it, the accommodation must be denied.

Normally, the obligation to accommodate is situated as an integral part of human rights law, creating a positive obligation on employers and service providers. Bill 94 was drafted quite differently. It was not a positive amendment to the Quebec *Charter*. Rather, it was a standalone bill, designed to limit rights rather than to take a broad and purposive approach. Clause 4 created a hierarchy of rights in favour of gender equality through the words "in particular." The legislator is never deemed to speak for nothing, and so the words "in particular" in Clause 4 had normative implications for the balance of the statute. While gender equality is a crosscutting right that has to be integrated into all law, the idea of a hierarchy of rights has been rejected at the international law level since at least 1993 by member nations of the United Nations in the following terms:

> (...) all human rights are universal, indivisible and interdependent and interrelated. The international community must treat human rights globally in a fair and equal manner, on the same footing, and with the same emphasis" (Vienna Declaration and Programme of Action 1993, s 5).

Similarly, placing religious "neutrality" as a State-sponsored "value," used to trump individual religious rights in the name of gender equality suggests a weak understanding of both rights. Religious freedom protects individuals and communities against state intrusion or interference. Bill 94 would have created a formal state power to suppress religious freedoms in the name of neutrality. No democratic nation can allow the deployment of religious freedoms to violate democratic rights, legal rights, equality or the rule of law. And that is precisely the point: there is no basis in Canadian law for using state neutrality as a sword against individual rights instead of a shield to protect them. By explicitly preventing the provision of public services to a person who chooses to cover her face under Clause 6 of Bill 94 – a practice clearly directed at Muslims – the Bill distorted human rights legislation and emphasized the right of the state to preserve homogeneity.

Bill 94 also created a strong defence for failing to respond to a request for accommodation based on interference with the operations of an organization, which is neither defined nor limited. Most human rights statutes in Canada require much more stringent justifications for refusing an accommodation request, such as excessive cost or demonstrable health and safety concerns.

These concerns were raised in 2010 by the Bâtonnier of Quebec (the head of Quebec's Bar Association) in an open letter (Chagnon 2010). The bill went nowhere, but elements of it resurfaced in two subsequent bills.

Bill 14 was tabled in December 2012, entitled *An act to amend the Charter of the French language, the Charter of human rights and freedoms and other legislative provisions*. It targeted employment, schooling and health care rights of English speakers and allophones. Business groups, minority and Anglophones opposed the Bill. The Quebec Bar Association (Plourde, 2013) again spoke against the Bill, as did the Quebec Human Rights and Youth Rights Commission (*Commission des droits de la personne et des droits de la jeunesse*, 2013). The Parti québécois was a minority government at the time, and the premier, Pauline Marois, announced in September 2013 that the Bill would likely die on the order paper.

In 2013, the Quebec government took another run at legislating the main planks of interculturalims by releasing a policy paper entitled *A firm belief in our values* which announced the government's intention to assert a "charter" of Quebec values (Quebec, 2013). Once again, the neutrality of the state was asserted, but this time with a new provision that would ban public servants from wearing "ostentatious" religious symbols like head scarves and kippahs. One public sector union immediately objected to the proposal, noting its impact on gender equality because many of its members were women who would be forced to leave the workforce.

Mind the Gaps: Culturalisms v. Rights

Multiculturalism is criticized for many things by interculturalists. Most of them are features that multiculturalism does not actually possess or aspire to. The first is that multiculturalism is designed for "Canada anglais," not for Quebec. This assertion is simply ahistorical. Multiculturalism was an outcome of the Royal Commission on Bilingualism and

Biculturalism. It evolved as a policy, a constitutional principle and then a law to recognize and affirm the contributions of groups *other than* the English and French settler groups, as well as their participation and role in Canadian society. It was never about asserting English language dominance (Yalden 2009).

Multiculturalism is also accused of being empty and lacking a vision for Canadian society. The result, critics argue, is a form of cultural relativism that is incapable of opposing harmful traditional or cultural practices that are illegal, sexist or contrary to public policy.

I am aware of no empirical support for any of these claims. Harmful gender-specific practices such as female genital mutilation – as well as far less dramatic acts of violence and assault – are prohibited in Canada by criminal law and have been for many years. Sexist and discriminatory behaviour is illegal in Canada and has been for decades.

The problem is not that multiculturalism encourages relativism: the problem is when multiculturalism is severed from its roots in human rights law, the result is precisely the one about which critics complain. When "culturalisms" are cut off from their normative roots in human rights, they lose both their normative ballast and their legitimacy (Eliadis, 2008). Accusations of cultural relativism nonetheless have had resonance in Quebec, making the claim for undefined "values" and "heritage" more attractive.

This has implications that extend far beyond Quebec. At the international level, culture-based claims are often used to shield human rights violations. A few states fend off human rights through arguments that their practices are or should be shielded by traditional culture and by their heritage.[19] They agree that certain harmful practices may be illegal, but heritage, culture or religion (or combinations of these) make it difficult to eradicate them. When a society seeks to use its own "heritage" as a lawful shield, it is essentially protecting human rights violations. Given that many culture-based claims are directed specifically against women in other countries, it would be ironic indeed if Quebec, such a strong supporter of women's equality, would choose to adopt a heritage-based policy that provides ammunition to religious extremists who use the same argument (namely ignoring rights in order to promote cultural values) against women's rights.

Interculturalists go so far as to claim that multiculturalism encourages ghettoization, but multiculturalism is better understood not as a refuge for those who would retreat to ghettos, but as a refusal to place a single culture at the apex of Canadian society. That is a long way from encouraging ghettoization. Quebec, like every other region of the world that has experienced significant immigration, has areas of greater or lesser concentrations of particular populations, and this has always been so. There is no reason to suppose that large numbers of Jews in Montreal's Côte-St-Luc or Greeks in Park Extension necessarily reflect social policy failures or ghettoization any more than the concentration of French Canadians in the Saguenay region.

Although most Anglophones in Quebec support the importance of promoting and protecting French as the common language, interculturalism as currently articulated in Quebec fails to recognize, let alone affirm, the historic and contemporary realities of English-speakers in relation to their rights and is part of the foundational identity of the province (Eliadis, 2012). An explicit affirmation of both the historic and the contemporary rights of Anglophone communities in Quebec, a signal that English is actively welcomed in the province and on the streets of its towns and cities, would go a long way to addressing this gap, without threatening French. To the extent that interculturalism can be redeployed in this direction, some of the past damage could be remedied.

***

A final gap in both forms of culturalism is the exclusion of Aboriginal peoples. Neither Canadian nor Quebec culturalism integrates Aboriginal rights and neither has really tried. Any satisfactory account of a cultural policy in Canada must include Aboriginal peoples. The Royal Commission on Bilingualism and Biculturalism explicitly but reluctantly excluded First Nations peoples from its work, because the issue was not included in its terms of reference. Interculturalism also declines to take on this question, for the reason that First Nations insist upon being dealt with as "nations" and not as "cultures" or racial minorities. This is true, but integrating Aboriginal perspectives into an open society through an inclusive approach should be especially acceptable to Quebec, of all Canadian provinces, given its own struggles to successfully assert its right to be treated as a nation.

Conclusion

Canada has a relatively successful record of accomplishment in building societies that are open, pluralistic and positive. It is perfectly understandable why some European countries have chosen interculturalism because of its focus on integration, but that does not mean that Canada should follow suit. Quebecers have much more in common with the rest of Canada than with Europe. Canada is a relatively young country, and its openness to pluralism is part of who we are and not a new lesson that we are struggling to learn.

Canada's exceptionalism is to some extent a matter of circumstance and plain luck: Canada is geographically isolated from immigration source countries in the developing world. We have had a relatively short history within which ethnic divisions and animosities could proliferate. Multiculturalism builds on this natural advantage and does not encourage divisions that have proved so damaging elsewhere.

Even within particular national identities, it is easy to see how different Canada's approach is: it is difficult if not impossible for me to consider my own ethnic background and citizenship as a Greek, without thinking and even insisting on the Greek language and to a lesser extent, the Greek Orthodox religion. The heritage and values of an ancient culture continue to inform modern life.

On the other hand, it is very easy for me to conceive of being Canadian without considering, let alone insisting on, my own ethnic background, or my parents' language or any other language that I happen to speak. The ability to create one's own identity and not to be integrated or assimilated to the majority "core" identity is a gift and not a curse. There is little reason for Canada to turn to a European model in order to acquire tensions that the Europeans are struggling to manage for reasons of their own particular circumstances, geographies and histories.

This does not mean that specificities cannot be acknowledged, recognized or nurtured. Nor does it preclude, and indeed has not precluded, Quebec from developing its own distinct society. Beyond that, though, the examples discussed above show that interculturalism and its constitutive elements are being used to diminish minority rights, language rights, and individual civil and political rights. These trends, even if they are unintended consequences, are worrying. The bills discussed in this essay may not yet be law, but they show a trend of increasingly regressive legislation aimed at preserving Quebec "values," heritage and other constituent elements of interculturalism that are divorced from and even opposed to human rights. Neither multiculturalism nor interculturalism as currently formulated provides an adequate answer to the concerns raised in Quebec: there has to be another way.

The social sciences tend to be preoccupied with ideas like social cohesion and harmonization of values, but, at the end of the day, a social policy must be consistent with human rights law. Section 1 of the *Charter* provides for the flexibility and equilibrium that should prevail in any public policy that distinguishes between groups of people based on their social differences:

The *Canadian Charter of Rights and Freedoms* guarantees the rights and freedoms set out in it subject only to such reasonable limits prescribed by law as can be demonstrably justified in a free and democratic society.

Getting the balance right is not an easy business. Section 1 is one of the most frequently interpreted provisions of the Charter and for good reason. It introduces the notion of reasonableness and is based on flexibility and tolerance. This uniquely Canadian sense of reasonableness should inform the spirit and the letter of any legislative initiatives that aim to preserve a range of diverse cultures and ensure the respect, protection and fulfillment of human rights.

References

Anctil, Pierre, Françoise Armand, Mireille Baillargeon, Alain Bélanger, André Boisclair, Gérard Bouchard, François Crépeau, Micheline Dumont, Madeleine Gagné, Élisabeth Garant, Micheline Labelle, Annick Lenoir, Guillaume Marois, Marie McAndrew, Victor Piché, Gérard Pinsonneault, Maryse Potvin, Stephan Reichhold, Jean Renaud, Gisèle Ste-Marie, Michèle Vatz, Bilkis Vissandjee and Daniel Weinstock. 2011. "Immigration: No to quotas by geographic origin." *[Montreal] Gazette*, May 10. http://oppenheimer.mcgill.ca/Immigration-No-to-quotas-by.

Assemblée Nationale du Québec. 2012. *Bill 14: An act amend the Charter of the French language, the Charter of human rights and freedoms and other legislative provisions.* 1st Sess, 40th Leg, Quebec.

—. 2009. *Bill 391: An Act to assert the fundamental values of the Quebec nation.* 1st Sess, 39th Leg, Quebec.

—. 2010. *Bill 94: An Act to establish guidelines governing accommodation requests within the administration and certain institutions.* 1st Sess, 39th Leg, Quebec.

—. 2008. *Bill 63: An Act to amend the Charter of human rights and freedoms.* 1st Sess, 38th Leg, Quebec.

Association for Canadian Studies. 2011. "Multiculturalism versus Interculturalism: majority of Quebecers unclear about the difference." Last modified May 23. Online: <http://www.acs-aec.ca/en/social-research/multiculturalism-diversity/>.

Authier, Philip. 2008. "Distorted reports fueled 'crisis' ", [Montreal] *Gazette*, May 23, A6.

*Ballantyne, Davidson, McIntyre v. Canada, Communications Nos.
359/1989 and 385/1989,* U.N. Doc. CCPR/C/47/D/359/1989 and
385/1989/Rev.1 (1993).

Bouchard, Gérard and Taylor, Charles, *Building the Future: A Time for
Reconciliation, Report of the Consultation Commission on
Accommodation Practices Related to Cultural Differences* (Quebec:
Gouvernement du Québec, 2008).

Bouchard, Gérard. 2011. "What Is Interculturalism?" *McGill Law Journal*
56: 395-468.

Canadian Charter of Rights and Freedoms. 1982. Part I of the
Constitution Act, 1982, being Schedule B to the *Canada Act 1982*
(UK).

Canadian Multiculturalism Act, RSC 1985, c 24 (4th Supp.).

Chagnon, Pierre. 2010. "Projet de loi 94 intitulé 'Loi établissant les balises
encadrant les demandes d'accommodement dans l'Administration
gouvernementale et dans certains établissements.'" *Cabinet du
bâtonnier*, April 30. Online:
<http://www.barreau.qc.ca/export/sites/newsite/pdf/medias/positions/2
010/20100430-projet-loi-94.pdf>.

Charter of human rights and freedoms, RSQ c C-12.

Charter of the French Language, RSQ c C-11.

Commission des droits de la personne et droits de la jeunesse. 2007.
Rapport d'activités et de gestion 2006-2007. Quebec:
Government of Quebec. Online <http://www.cdpdj.qc.ca>.

—. 2011. "Racial profiling and systemic discrimination of racialized
youth." . Quebec: Government of Quebec. Online
<http://www2.cdpdj.qc.ca>.

—. 2010. *Rapport d'activités et de gestion 2009-2010*. Online:
<http://www2.cdpdj.qc.ca>.

—. 2012. *Rapport d'activités et de gestion 2011-2012.* Quebec:
Government of Quebec. Online:
<http://www.cdpdj.qc.ca/Publications/RA_2011_2012.pdf>.

Dougherty, Kevin. 2011. "National assembly turns away Sikhs."
[Montreal] *Gazette*, January 19, A10.

Eisenberg, Avigail and Jeff Spinner-Halev, eds. 2005. *Minorities within
minorities; Equality, Rights and Diversity*. Cambridge: Cambridge
University Press.

Eliadis. Pearl. 2012. "Bill 14 chips away at English minority rights" [Montreal] *Gazette,* December 11, online: <http://www.montrealgazette.com/news/Opinion+Bill+chips+away+English+minority+rights/7676733/story.html>.

Gallardo v. Bergeron. 2010. CanL a II, QCTDP 5.

Human Rights Tribunal of Ontario. 2012. *Annual Statistics,* 2011-2012, New applications, online: <http://www.hrto.ca/hrto/index.php?q=en/node/150>.

Insurance Corp. of British Columbia v. Heerspink, [1982] 2 SCR 145

Jedwab, Jack. 2011. "Groups and Intergroup Relations: Canadian Perceptions" *Association for Canadian Studies,* October 17. Online, <http://www.acs-aec.ca/en/social-research/multiculturalism-diversity/>.

Kymlicka, Will. 2011. "The Evolving Canadian Experiment with Multiculturalism." Paper delivered at the International Symposium on Multiculturalism, Montreal May 25 to 27. Online <http://www.symposium-interculturalisme.com/11/english/fr>.

Mack et al. v. Attorney General (Ontario), (2001), 55 OR (3d) 113 aff'd (2002), 60 OR (3d) 737 (Ont. C.A.). Leave to appeal to SCC refused (April 2003).

Marissal, Vincent. 2010. "*Une musulmane : Femme d'origine égyptienne explusée d'un cours*", *La Presse,* March 2, A2-A3.

Montréal (Ville de) (Service de police de la Ville de Montréal/SPVM) c. Tribunal des droits de la personne 2009) QCCA 22, leave to appeal to SCC refused (March 5, 2009). http://www.cdpdj.qc.ca/Documents/Rezko_Milad_TDP_18_avril_2012_MTL018560.pdf

Multani v. Commission scolaire Marguerite-Bourgeoys, 2006 SCC 6, [2006] 1 SCR 256.

Ontario Human Rights Commission. 2007. *Annual Report 2006-2007.* Toronto.

Plourde, Nicolas. 2013. *Projet de loi n°14 : Loi modifiant la Charte de la langue française, la Charte des droits et libertés de la personne et d'autres dispositions législative, Cabinet du bâtonnier,* online: http://www.barreau.qc.ca/pdf/medias/positions/2013/20130215-pl-14.pdf.

Quebec. 2006. Ministry of Immigration and Cultural Communities. *Towards a government policy to fight against racism and discrimination*: Summary of the Consultation Document. Government of Quebec. Online

<http://www.micc.gouv.qc.ca/publications/en/dossiers/SYN-ANG-RacismeDiscrimination-INT.pdf>.

Quebec. 2013. Ministry reponsible for Democratic Insitutions and Active Citizenship, *A firm belief in our values*. Online, <http://www.nosvaleurs.gouv.qc.ca/en#minister>.

R v. Kapp, 2008 SCC 41, [2008] 2 S.C.R. 483.

R. v. N.S., 2010 ONCA 670.

R. v. N.S., 2012 SCC 72.

Reitz, Jeffrey G. and Rupa Banerjee. 2007. "Racial Inequality, Social Cohesion, and Policy Issues in Canada." In *Belonging? Diversity, Recognition and Shared Citizenship in Canada*, edited by Keith Banting, Thomas J. Courchene and F. Leslie Seidle, 489-545. Montreal: Institute for Research on Public Policy.

Soanes, Catherine and Angus Stevenson, eds. 2006. *The Concise Oxford English Dictionary*. Oxford: Oxford University Press.

Statistics Canada. 2010. *Projections of the Diversity of the Canadian Population: 2006 to 2031*. Catalogue no. 91-551-X. Canada: Minister of Industry.

—. 2011a. "Labour force characteristics by immigrant status of population aged 25 to 54, by province (Atlantic, Quebec, Ontario)." Last modified January 6. http://www.statcan.gc.ca/tables-tableaux/sum-som/l01/cst01/labor89a-eng.htm.

—. 2011b. "The Daily." June 7. Online: <http://www.statcan.gc.ca/daily-quotidien/110607/dq110607-eng.pdf>.

Symposium international sur l'interculturalisme. 2012. "Un symposium international sur l'interculturalisme a eu lieu à Montréal en mai 2011." Online, <http://www.symposium-interculturalisme.com/11/english/fr.>

Syndicat Northcrest v. Amselem, 2004 SCC 47, [2004] 2 SCR 551.

United Nations. 1993. "Vienna Declaration and Programme of Action." *World Conference on Human Rights* A/CONF.157/23, July 12. http://www.unhchr.ch/huridocda/huridoca.nsf/%28symbol%29/a.conf.157.23.en.

—. 2010. Office of the High Commissioner for Human Rights. *Minority Rights: International Standards and Guidance for Implementation*, online: <http://www.ohchr.org/Documents/Publications/MinorityRights_en.pdf>.

Withler v. Canada (Attorney General), 2011 SCC 12, [2011] 1 SCR 396.

Yalden, Maxwell. 2009. *Transforming Rights: Reflections from the Front Lines*. Toronto: University of Toronto Press.

Zurich Insurance Co. v. Ontario (Human Rights Commission), [1992] 2 SCR 321 at 339.

Notes

[1] The author was a member of the Steering Committee (*Conseil de direction*) of the International Symposium on Interculturalism (Symposium 2011) (Montreal, 25-27 May 2011). This article revises and updates the text prepared for the Symposium, Pearl Eliadis, "Canada's Clash of Culturalisms", online. <http://www.symposium-interculturalisme.com/11/english/fr>.

[2] Whether or not multiculturalism should do either of these things is a different question. From the perspective of the federal government, there is no particular reason to support the specificity of any particular province, given that multiculturalism is about people and communities, not provinces. Multiculturalism does not attempt to force English as a common language, but it must also be acknowledged that it does not need to since English is not a threatened language outside Quebec.

[3] "Multiculturalism versus Interculturalism: majority of Quebecers unclear about the difference" (Association for Canadian Studies 2011).

[4] There are multiple examples of the resistance to using the term "minorities" in the intercultural literature. In his lengthy article, "What Is Interculturalism" (2011), Gérard Bouchard does not refer once to English-speaking Quebecers as a minority, despite the obvious reality that, within Quebec as a "nation", English speakers are a minority. This minority status is obvious from the minority fraction of the English-speaking population in Quebec, legal restrictions on education, health services and other public services in English, and a lack of control over a broad legislative agenda that systematically has sought to restrain the use of English.

[5] Pierre Curzi, a former Parti Québec member of the National Assembly, stated on May 1 2013 that Anglophones are not a linguistic minority at a conference held at McGill University on bilingualism. See Marian Scott, "Bilingualism panel civil" [Montreal] *Gazette* May 2, 2013 A6.

[6] Quebec officialdom uses "cultural communities" to refer to "immigrants, visible minorities, and individuals born in Quebec with neither French nor British origins" (Quebec, 2006). The term first appeared in the early 1980s in official Quebec documentation.

[7] *Multiculturalism Turns 40: Reflections on the Canadian Policy.* 2011. Association for Canadian Studies. ASC Annual Conference. September 30 to October 1. Online, <http://www.acs-aec.ca/en/events/acs-annual-conference/multiculturalism-turns-40-reflections-on-the-canadian-policy-/>. A key reflection during the conference was the relationship between multiculturalism and human rights.

[8] The Bouchard-Taylor report makes passing reference to the Charter. Gérard Bouchard (2011) does not refer to s. 15 of the Charter. Other writers have looked at these issues in recent years (Symposium 2012).

[9] In *Kapp*, the Supreme Court reverted to an earlier version of its equality "test" namely (1) does the law create a distinction based on an enumerated or analogous ground? (2) Does the distinction create a disadvantage by perpetuating prejudice or stereotyping?

[10] In 2013, a preliminary court judge decided that when balancing the two rights, the right of the accused to see the complainant's face and assess her demeanor outweighed her religious rights. The matter will likely be appealed again.

[11] One of the cases is discussed in Vincent Marissal, "Une musulmane : Femme d'origine égyptienne explusée d'un cours" *La Presse* 2 March 2010. A2-3.

[12] *Insurance Corp. of British Columbia v. Heerspink*, [1982] 2 SCR 145. Human rights laws are described as the last protection of the most vulnerable members of society and also embodying fundamental Canadian values (at p. 157-158); see also Zurich Insurance Co. v. Ontario (Human Rights Commission), [1992] 2 SCR 321 at 339.

[13] See (Reitz and Banerjee 2007), especially as regards the outcomes for ethnic and racial minorities.

[14] Statistics Canada reports lower employment rates for immigrants, including permanent residents, immigrants in Canada for under five years and immigrants over five years as compared to both Atlantic Canada and Ontario (Statistics Canada 2011a).

[15] See Philip Authier, "Distorted reports fueled 'crisis' ", [Montreal] *Gazette*, May 23, 2008 at A 6.

[16] The 2006 ethnic diversity statistics at a national level in Canada showed that Canada's largest and most diverse city, the Toronto Census Metropolitan Area (CMA), had almost 43 percent visible minorities. The Montreal CMA had about 16 percent visible minorities (Statistics Canada, 2010).

[17] In Quebec, human rights proceedings have been blocked by the Montreal police services (SPVM) by a lack of cooperation (*Montréal (Ville de) (Service de police de la Ville de Montréal/SPVM) c. Tribunal des droits de la personne* 2009). Allegations of police misconduct are not investigated by independent civil oversight bodies, but by other Quebec law enforcement officials, raising concerns of independence and apprehension of bias.

[18] *Commission des droits de la personne et des droits de la jeunesse c. Laval (Ville de)*, 2006 QCTDP 17 (CanLII). The *Mouvement laïque québécois* has brought other complaints in the Quebec towns of Saguenay and Trois-Rivières.

[19] Several countries, mostly Muslim ones, have made significant reservations to the *Convention on the Elimination of Discrimination against Women* on religious grounds. Harmful traditional practices that do not have a religious basis, like FGM, are often supported on the grounds of culture and local values.

Chapter Eight

Russia's Evolution and Human Rights Changes since 1991

Anna Sevortian

Over the past 20 years in Russia, we have witnessed many achievements and failures in terms of democracy, building of new institutions and new civil identity. Paradoxically, though Russians love to talk about the past of their land (especially glorious episodes in the past), the state that emerged in 1991 is to a great extent principally a new one. It is struggling, not only with the common hardships of the Post-Soviet transition, but also to adapt to a new self, with a new form of governance, different economic and political systems and a new territory and composition. This new self is also about heterogeneity of society – Russia as we know it today is more diverse than Soviet society ever was. In this article, we aim to touch on several dimensions of diversity – growing ethnic diversity and migration, economic diversity, diversity of personal life choices – and their connection to major human rights challenges. In this chapter, we examine the past two decades of Russian history through the lens of human rights.

Twenty years since 1991

The past two decades have been enormously turbulent politically, economically and culturally. The chaotic events since the collapse of the USSR never provided a respite in which Russians could "dream about the end of history," as Jeffrey Mankoff puts it in the opening article to the Journal of International Affairs' Volume "Rethinking Russia":

> With the passing of the optimism that characterized the era of perestroika and the first days of Russian independence, the scope of the challenges facing Russia became apparent. The early 1990s were characterized by a degree of upheaval scarcely imaginable in the West. In percentage terms,

Russia's economy shrank by a larger amount in the 1990s than the American economy during the Great Depression (Mankoff 2010).

After the dissolution of the regime and the world they were accustomed to, millions of people struggled to adapt to fast and vast changes. Certainly, the past years have been busy and eventful for Russians and have brought enormous diversity in terms of incomes and lifestyles as well as growing vulnerability to economic turbulence. This naturally made people less responsive to political challenges and inevitably decreased political participation.

One of the most respectful Russian political scientists, Liliya Shevtsova, analyses how Gorbachev's glasnost and opportunities to introduce real institutional political pluralism unfolded in the 90s:

> For a long time we continued to perceive the remaining freedoms (freedom of the media, freedom to criticize powers-that-be and to fight for the monopoly of power) as evidence of being a path to democracy. In fact these freedoms went hand in hand with a turn in the opposite direction. What Yeltsin did was not only creating a new autocracy. (...) Putin became the stabilizer and first manager of the system Yeltsin created (2011).

Although one may question whether the changes could have been less stressful and deplorable, history professor Stephen Kotkin in his provocative work, "Armageddon Averted," (2003) argues that the changes that occurred could have been a lot worse. The scale and speed of change were so overwhelming in the 1990s that Russia could have found itself up against a real disaster. According to Kotkin, the Soviet collapse went on for the decade, distorting, slowing down and discrediting Yeltsin-era reforms while leaving some of the old Soviet institutions almost intact (Thornhill 2011). This is a most profound observation. The risk of a large-scale catastrophe may have past, but many other negative factors soon got to work: hyperinflation, hasty privatization, growth of criminality, the Chechen war, proliferating social inequality and a growing distrust in institutions.

For many in Russia, the tumult of the early 1990s became associated with "liberal Western democracy." Disillusionment in stalling reforms, together with a feeling of total social insecurity, prepared a "mass audience" for readiness to compromise some of the proclaimed rights in exchange to proclaimed stability. The manipulated 1996 election and Yeltsin's handing of power to a successor in 1999 further added to the corrosion of standards and triggered Russia's sliding down to a more authoritarian system (Shevtsova, 2011). It all had far-reaching societal consequences.

Years of political apathy bore strong effect on people's attitudes and political behavior. A pragmatic approach and a certain extent of cynicism spread in all spheres of life. People often stopped trusting such concepts as rule of law, human rights or democracy while experiencing corruption, abuse from law enforcement agencies' representatives or the dysfunction of state institutions. At the same time, new economic opportunities were there as well as positive economic dynamics. Loyalty was offered in exchange for economic opportunities – younger generations seem to have internalized this bargain with the regime probably better than any other (Mankoff 2010).

By the late 2000s, these changes resulted in making Russia the country with the world's largest number of dollar billionaires and one boasting the highest profits it had made from oil revenues in a long time. The society witnessed the emergence of a middle class and a new consumerism, as well the development of a huge class of newly poor and underprivileged people. In the midst of the current economic crisis, Russia, in a certain sense, did a "full circle" and found itself in an era comparable to pre-Gorbachev years, struggling to modernize technologically, politically and economically and even having political prisoners. At this point, Liliya Shevtsova thinks it is time for a re-set and a new start.

In our view, the events of 1991 and their consequences can (and should) be continuously studied, discussed and interpreted to allow modernization and avoid possible missteps. There is no doubt that Russia has by and large succeeded in adjusting to a market economy, that it became much more interconnected with the world and that its society in fact became even more diverse. Many other facts and tendencies could be mentioned; we shall therefore allow ourselves to take a closer look at some of the realities of today's Russia, albeit not in historical or economical perspective, but through a human rights and societal lens.

Vox pop and diverse self-perceptions

In the Soviet times, ideology was a core element of nation-building and functioning of the state and society. After 1991, the situation changed dramatically – the "market supply" for nation-building ideas turned out to be unexpectedly poor. The place previously occupied by ideology could not technically be filled with either "market values" or "democratic values." The latter got distorted over the 90s and the building of democratic institutions was only partially successful. Experiments with "stronger Russia rising to its feet" or "modernized Russia" have so far not exactly succeeded either.

Finding a unifying idea that resonates constructively with people and that could drive modernization remains one of Russia's challenges today. These thoughts are echoed by Konstantin Eggert, analyst and media observer, in his column on the anniversary of 1991:

> Twenty years on, Russia is in search of its way from Soviet totalitarianism to becoming a normal nation-state... Defining national interests for a transient entity that Russia is today is a difficult task, to say the least. With a political class that is largely unable and uninterested in formulating ideas that would take Russia forward, this becomes nearly impossible (2011).

In the run-up to the election campaign of 2011-2012, Russia's Prime Minister Vladimir Putin, while addressing a motorcyclists' community, suggested that historical memory can become an idea: "Historical memory is a perfect cement that creates a united and indivisible Russian nation, that builds and strengthens a united and indivisible Russia."[1] No doubt, historical memory is one of the core narratives in the nation-building process, but the Russian society is perhaps not the best example of one that managed to come to terms with its own history, whether recent or more ancient. Along with some victorious episodes in the 20th century, there are many darker sides and corners that the nation should reflect upon and live through before moving on.

The diversity of opinion about history in Russian society is quite perceptible. Russians have strongly varying views on major historical events. To an extent, these controversies reveal the lack of informed discussion on all points where the traditional Soviet historical narrative collides with later disclosed facts. The Katyn massacre is probably one of the most obvious examples of the kind. Likewise, if we examine the events of 1991, we would immediately discover the same dispersion in people's perceptions (possibly, the only consensus that exists would be in relation to 1945 and the victory over fascism in World War II).

What do Russians think of 1991? According to the Levada Center, Russia's independent pollster, several social groups tend to assess these events as "tragic." Pensioners, public sector employees, housewives, women, people aged over 55, poorly educated with modest income, living in rural areas are prone to "lament" the breakdown of the Soviet world.[2] Another popular explanation of those events is that it was a banal "fight for power" between political forces. This version appeals most to the unemployed, workers, men, people in their 40s, the college-educated, people with the poorest incomes and small towns dwellers. The third alternative is equating 1991 to the victory over communism; this view is shared by many managers, entrepreneurs, high income earners and Muscovites.

Diversity of opinion is almost always a positive thing and it differentiates modern Russia from the Soviet state. Dissimilar perceptions of self, of the state and of the past and present prove that freedom of personal speech became a natural habit adopted over the perestroika years and beyond. In the meantime, Russians' interest and involvement in politics has been dying down ever since. The Levada Center's study in October 2010 revealed that only 32% of respondents retained such interest against 64% that lacked it (the percentage ratio for Moscow is 19% and 74% respectively).

Surprisingly or not, what ordinary people care about today is price growth and poverty, corruption and threats to their security such as potential terrorist acts.[3] History and state-building are reflected in rather simple black-and-white formats and dichotomies. For example, when questioned "What is currently more important for Russia: order and a "strong hand" or observance of human rights?" 53% chose order and 42% favored human rights.[4] When given a choice between "trustworthy nation leadership" and "firm, well-working laws," the majority of 58% preferred the laws to 37% prioritized leadership.

As a part of their regular observation, in August 2011, Levada sociologists studied the nation's views on the quality of freedom.[5] How much freedom is there in Russia now? Generally, half of the respondents believed there was "just enough freedom," ratings for "too little" and "too much" were comparable (18% and 23% respectively), 8% had no view. At the same time, 39% of Russians trust their homeland is advancing towards democracy or believe that "democratic society" yet exists; youth under 24 and people with higher incomes are more likely to support this statement. 47% take a more restrained position and disagree. Perception of a democratic society of those asked is primarily linked to freedoms (speech, conscience, movement), equal opportunities and responsibility of those in power to their electorate.

Finally, when elaborating on a type of democracy Russia requires, 23% preferred one "like in Europe and America," 16% sympathize with one "like in the USSR" and 45% insist on "Russia's own unique form of democracy," others see no need in any form of democracy or fail to answer.

Indeed, many interpretations can be offered of the somewhat sketchy statistics above. What the Levada Center data helps us to observe is the explicit heterogeneity of the Russian society, the lack of universally shared values and reference points for development.

Migration and migrants

Rapid increase of migration flows greatly added to the heterogeneity of society, which also has not been consistently officially interpreted. Historically, multiethnic Russia is the second-largest country after the US receiving migrants. Officially, Russia has between 4 and 9 million migrant workers, over 80% of whom come from the region of the former Soviet Union (World Report 2012). Other estimates say that up to 15% of Russia's population is migrants and their families.

The majority nonetheless keeps a low profile; in Russia, one can find migrant workers not only in big cities, but almost anywhere, occupying all sorts of low-paid positions like those of janitors, cleaners, nannies, salespeople in small kiosks. Many come to the country illegally to earn money and send back to their families in the CIS, many have very little knowledge of Russian and no knowledge of Russia's laws. They often face abuses that include the confiscation of their passports, denial of contracts, non-payment or delayed payment of wages and unsafe working conditions (World Report 2012). Experts say that before this huge "shadow" layer of workforce in Russia's labor market and society comes into the open, the system for the legal employment of migrant workers needs to get simplified, transparent and must provide effective options to redress abuses.

According to HRW research, 40% of migrant workers labor in construction. Not long ago, I witnessed good proof of this figure, being deep in the heart of traditional rural Russia. After a series of research interviews in the village of Usoliye (Perm region), we were brought to feast our eyes on the renovated 17th century cathedral and estate. A brigade of Central Asian workers were at the site painting one of the buildings nearby... Today Russia uses thousands of such brigades. Ambitious large-scale construction projects within the 2014 Winter Olympic Games in Sochi, perhaps, could not be completed without hiring large numbers of migrant workers from all parts of Russia and other countries.

A paradox of modern diversity and migration, these people are at the same time visible but unseen. They are a part of contemporary Russian life and economy and yet on the margins of it. Thousands and millions of people remain in the shadows, in a parallel reality, and yet they are intertwined with the "official" Russia that we know.

In 20 years, there has only been one migrant worker with a positive story. Better known as "Tajik Jimmy," Baimurat Allaberiyev is a migrant worker and an amateur musician and singer from Tajikistan. He moved to a provincial Russian town and worked in a stockroom. His talent was discovered thanks to a co-worker's cell phone video of Baimurat's extraordinary performance from the Bollywood movie "Disco Dancer." The video got posted online and soon made Mr. Allaberiyev famous. He was offered a contact from a production company and moved to St. Petersburg to perform in theaters and nightclubs. He is probably the only Russian migrant worker with thousands of fans.

This first sign of recognition stands a long way from the nation accepting migration, labor mobility and diversity as a norm. Baimurat's exceptional story highlights how difficult the migration process is without a comprehensive plan of integration into society. Sadly, this story can only partially be called one with a happy ending: the city Baimurat moved to is known for violent racist attacks.

Though attacks are often targeted at "immigrants" originating from the Caucasus and Central Asia, many big cities in Russia can in fact be unsafe for anybody that visually looks different, even if they are Russian citizens.

Xenophobia

Some form of ethnic-based nationalism, to a certain extent, was deemed to have emerged after 1991. Remains of the Soviet identity were largely replaced with ethnic or national identities in all the new independent states. Each of them got their own issues with ethnic minorities. This was Russia's way as well – it took a long time before the first Russian president Boris Yeltsin's words "let them get as much sovereignty as they want" were comprehended by the new Russia.

By the way, Boris Yeltsin tried to shape and to expedite the process of nation-building by introducing a special word "rossiyane" (which stands for citizens of the Russian Federation as opposed to "russkiye", or ethnic Russians). This important process of distinguishing ethnic and civic identities hasn't come anywhere close to fruition in 20 years. Today many "nationalisms" exist within this multiethnic country, some of them moderate, some harsh.[6]

Economic hardships and challenges of Post-Soviet transformation and globalization, growing economic divide, disintegration – all of these factors fed xenophobia in the past. However, it is doubtful that xenophobia – which manifests itself in many ways, from derision to violence – can be explained and excused solely by Russia's transition. The late and insufficient official response to the problem also played this role so that post-Soviet changes have been given negative interpretations.

In the early 2000s, xenophobia was largely overlooked and perceived as a minor problem when compared to other "emergencies" such as the war in Chechnya.[7] In this favorable climate of rare public condemnation and prosecution of ethnic violence xenophobic sentiments, activities by far-right groups grew steadily. By 2005, the issue could no longer be ignored. Racist attacks were framed as "extremist crimes" that constituted a threat to Russia's security, as Russian President Vladimir Putin addressed the issue at the internet-conference session.[8]

The mid-2000s were years when another trend gained prominence: people started lacking interest in public life and concentrating on non-political and personal lives. This could have been a purely reactive thing, some analysts say, as the space for political discussion had been shrinking along with the growth of Russia's resurgence discourse. NGOs and party and electoral legislation were altered to become more restrictive and bureaucratic, while new regulations on public meetings, rallies and demonstrations were enacted.[9]

These changes (probably introduced for political reasons to bring "greater stability") have clogged some important ways of political communication between citizens and the state for speaking out their discontent. It led to further "atomization" of the society and underground nationalism breeding.

Because of the late recognition of xenophobia's detrimental potential and strands of aggressive nationalism, it took the whole system a while to start responding appropriately to an identified threat. Actions differed significantly on the level of political rhetoric, law enforcement agencies' actions, the educational system and the media. Mixed signals continued to be sent to the Russian society about xenophobia and racism.

This inconsistency came at a price – nationalism and xenophobia are now boiling beneath the surface of society and can break through even in case of a minor inter-ethnic clash.

Recently, the level of racial violence has noticeably declined as criminal prosecution for hate crimes continued its rapid increase in scope and improvement in quality.[10] The number of convictions almost doubled, so did the share of suspended sentences. Sadly, experts in interpretation say these numbers show that while the law enforcement efforts affect more aggressive groups, they can no longer keep under control the entire mass of violence-prone ultra-right activists (Verkhovsky and Kozhevnikova 2011).

Manezh, new generation and violence[11]

On December 11, 2010, many people gathered in Manezhnaya Square to advocate for a speedy investigation into the murder of Yegor Sviridov.

This young man, a Spartak football club fan, was killed a few days before in a fight by a group of young Caucasian men. Protesters believed that the police were bribed to release the men and demanded that law enforcement agencies investigate the murder and that the offenders be charged. This was a non-sanctioned and, to an extent, spontaneous demonstration that brought up to 5,000 people next to the Kremlin walls.

The protest quickly spiraled out of control when a group of young men who appeared to be from the North Caucasus walked by. The crowd started violently rioting, and their protest overtly took on a racist tone. Some photos taken of the riots show young men and women – many of them teenagers – raising their hands in Nazi salutes. Some threw bottles, ice and rocks at minorities and the police. When the police successfully broke up the rally, the protestors dispersed to the metro stations and other districts of Moscow. There were instances throughout the city in which a group of young men entered metro carriages yelling, "White carriage," and started beating or pushing out any person who did not look Slavic.

In the week following the December 11 riots, the police were on heightened alert. According to law enforcement, there were many discussions of similar nationalist protests or "response protests" by Caucasian groups, the biggest of them on December 15, 2010 around "Evropeisky" shopping mall, near one the main railway stations.[12]

The official reaction to the riots unfortunately was a clear example of "mixed signals." On December 16, 2010, Prime Minister Vladimir Putin addressed the riots on a live television broadcast. He said that he believed the reason for the demonstrations was alleged inaction of law enforcement agencies to Sviridov's death. He added that the protesters' motive did not give the right to break the law and advanced an "inflexible response" by the authorities to further violence.[13] However, a few days later Vladimir Putin attended a memorial service for Sviridov at his gravesite.

President Dmitry Medvedev condemned the violence only three days after the demonstration: "Our reaction to any nationalist intolerance, riots or incitement to hatred or enmity will be the same."[14]

Human rights activists and observers were critical of the way national leadership reacted to the events on Manezhnaya. Galina Kozhevnikova, a leading expert on xenophobia, interpreted these actions as an indication of the Kremlin's uncertainty in responding to the xenophobic violence and failure to realize the rise of the ultra-right movement and growing nationalist sentiments among Russia's youth.[15]

In a series of interviews, Kozhevnikova criticized the police for failing to treat these demonstrations as extremist protests rather than football fan gatherings. She insisted that by ignoring the connection between the riots and the activities of ultra-right groups, the police remain ineffective at controlling the violence and the tone of the gatherings.

Lessons of Manezhnaya

The 11 December 2010 riots on Manezhnaya Square dramatically raised the profile of issues of nationalism and racism in Russian society, thinks Alexander Verkhovsky, director of the SOVA Center (Verkhovsky and Kozhevnikova 2011). The events on Manezhnaya square constitute a most disturbing call coming from a specific part of society. Altogether, they reveal many fault lines of today's Russia transition.

First of all, though attackers' concerns had very little in common with the situation and human rights abuses in the North Caucasus, the protestors on Manezhnaya Square directly and indirectly reflected on Russia's continued entanglement with that region. What was clearly shown was common disintegration and alienation of the North Caucasus, typical for most parts of Russia. Another issue that has arisen after December 11 is the possibility of the quick emergence and mobilization of racist anti-Russian groups.

According to SOVA Center analysis, the greatest ongoing threat, however, is ultra-right violence. The complex events of 2010 allowed the learning of new lessons in tactical handling of clashes between the ultra-right, the radical anti-fascists and the police, but the main lesson remained underestimated.

The morphology of the nationalist movement visibly changed after 2005 and became increasingly complex. New coalitions and units are now being established, after the two biggest ultra-right organizations – the DPNI (the Movement against Illegal Immigration) and the Slavic Union – were banned (Yudina and Alperovich 2011).[16] Violence-prone ultra-right activists are building small autonomous ultra-right groups, increasingly hostile toward the authorities and regarding their daily activities as a "guerrilla war." The December riots were an unambiguous statement about the preparedness of these groups to indiscriminate violence.[17] That's the second observed trend.

Third, perhaps even more disturbing than the revelation that nationalist groups are easily able to wreak havoc on the center of Moscow, is that many of those suspected of racially motivated attacks were young – some as young as 14-years-old. The years these youths were growing up coincided with the authorities' indifference to hate crimes and flirting with nationalism.

Finally, the events on Manezhnaya illuminated the ineffectiveness of the Russian anti-extremism legislation (Rozalskaya 2011). When written, these laws were designed to combat nationalism and growing xenophobia in Russia and to imitate similar laws in Europe that criminalize Holocaust denial, Nazi ideology and forms of extremist speech. However, vague legal definitions led to inappropriate enforcement of the anti-extremism actions by the state agencies, and in many instances laws were used to silence dissent and punish disagreement. Perception of this legislation and law enforcement practice as repressive was fully formed in 2010, and even Russia's Foreign Ministry admitted that the definition of extremism in Russia is "too broad," in its testimony before the European Commission.

On the bright side, the most significant step to changing the pattern was made with the Supreme Court's Resolution N11 "On judicial practice in criminal cases involving crimes of an extremist nature." Passed in June 2011, the Resolution contains several ground-breaking points welcomed by human rights community.[18] Nevertheless, the issue of application of this document raises concerns. Besides, general misuse of the anti-extremist legislation cannot be fully discontinued through the Supreme Court's resolutions while the law remains active. Just as it often happens, right steps are made but are not sufficient to counter the scale of the problem.

There hasn't been a lot of profound thinking around the evolution of nationalism in Russia recently (and it has never been a subject of full-scale national debate). The most controversial metaphor about it was used from Alexander Auzan, Moscow State University's professor and a member of the governmental commission on modernization. He compared nationalism to a fever, a symptom of an infantile disease. Professor Auzan believed that this "fever" is a natural state for the body that fights a disease. If the "body" is strong, it will recuperate – that's the moment when a healthy "civic" nation is born.

Taking on this theory, the Manezhnaya events prove that both the disease and fever are growing more dangerous... Part of the first truly Post-Soviet generations seem not to be immune to the virus of xenophobia, and these generations are definitely of crucial importance for Russia's further development.

In February 2011, the President Dmitry Medvedev gave a speech in the city of Ufa on measures to improve the harmonization of intercultural relations. He proposed a six-point plan that focuses on education reform and changes within the government structure.[19] To his credit, the president emphasized the need for greater diversity and suggested targeting schools and the youth. The President's bill also proposed to strip convicted extremists of the right to teach in public schools. Other proposed steps sounded relatively vague and lacking concrete timeframes. It seems as if overcoming vagueness, building up consistency and reacting in a more expedited manner are the most pressing goals – without these, any plan of action is difficult to realize.

Is there justice?

In the 2000s, turning to the rhetoric of Russia's special way of democracy and unique democracy resulted in obfuscation about the way decisions were being made: tactical solutions got priority over strategic ones in many spheres of Russian life. Adherence to substantial reforms was weakening with time, so many important reforms ended up being completed half-way or being rescinded, causing understandable public disappointment and at times undermining their whole idea. Though trust and understanding of democratic institutions were compromised in the 90s, we dare think that Russians have no less demanded their underlying principles. One of the core words with great transformative potential is justice.

There has been a lot of fair criticism of the Russian judicial reform and the failure to create a system of independent courts throughout the country. These concerns were pointed out by both Russians and international institutions, e.g. in the massive report by the presidential think tank Center for the Strategic Projects in 2009. Are people disillusioned with respect to the hope for justice when the judicial system is not independent and deeply flawed? This question is frequently asked and the argument is purely commonsensical. No matter what people expect or get, they nonetheless demand justice.

According to the Levada data, some 63% of Russians still believe that in a dispute between the state and a simple individual, a court will always decide in favor of the former. 17 % believe bribes decide everything. Only 11% of Russians currently believe the judicial system in Russia is free and fair (Sevortian 2010). Indeed, the figures look at least frustrating, but when speaking of the weaknesses of democratic institutions, the non-independent judiciary system and the frozen judicial reform in Russia, we should not underestimate the changes that have taken place over the past 20 years. Russia's accession to the European Convention on Human Rights and the accepting of the jurisdiction of the European Court of Human Rights (ECtHR) in 1998 are probably the most important of them. The significance of these steps, to certain extent, are comparable to the

Helsinki Accords. After the accession, Russia's justice system was no longer locked within the national borders.

Since the very first European Court of Human Rights judgement on a Russian case delivered in 2002, "Strasbourg" has become a synonym for international justice in the eyes of many Russians. Today, the European Court receives tens of thousands of applications from Russia each year (Sevortian 2011).

Even with Russia's problematic record on implementing the court's judgments (over 1,000 by now) many in Russia – the authorities and the public alike – seem to recognize the court's transformative potential (Letter to President Medvedev 2011).

Despite the appearance since 2010 of several recent revisionist initiatives to limit or block the court's rulings on the national level, the proposed amendments cannot reverse the system completely. Backlashes are possible, of course: even leaving aside the numerous judgments involving the North Caucasus and holding Russia responsible for the human rights violations in Chechnya, the number of judgments that require fundamental change in Russia is increasing.

Most importantly, this pressure doesn't simply come from the international community and the court in the first place. It is in fact growing from the ground, from Russian citizens that seek justice, a fairer organisation of life and the state's commitment to human rights obligations.[20] Though Russians who file complaints with the European Court of Human Rights are very unlikely to use words such as "human rights," the idea of justice resonates well with the Russian people.

Civil society

Civil society development in Russia is often overlooked within the scope of changes of last 20 years. Despite inefficient regulation, lack of recognition and support, Russian civil society has grown unprecedentedly which also signifies a shift in thinking and a triumph of individual initiative.

Although few mass membership NGOs organised or supervised by the state existed in Soviet times, what we might consider modern NGOs came into being in the late 80s, with the *glasnost* times (Shevtsova 2011). The major piece of frame-setting legislation on NGOs appeared later on in 1995. For a decade beginning in the early 90s, Russia was also the focus of numerous international donors, with giving support to civic initiatives and NGOs being high on their agenda (Sevortian 2009). Today, some 219,668 NGOs are registered to work for the public good.[21]

Over the last 20 years, the non-profit sector (also referred to as the "third sector") in Russia has become an effective vehicle of civil society development. Impressively diverse in terms of scale, field of operation and other specificities, NGOs are involved in the delivery of social, philanthropic, cultural, educational, scientific and managerial services. Much social change would not have happened without the NGOs' active participation, as they have been influencing Russia's economic, political and social development. In terms of its contribution to GDP, NGOs in 2004 made up 1.2% of Russia's GDP, a figure growing surely since then (Institute for Urban Economics 2012).

Facing fast and expansive development in Russia, NGOs have, however, been affected and impaired by a number of objective and subjective factors typical for many transitional societies, whether "open," "opening" or "closing," to use the Open Society's approach. Pressures on NGOs first took verbal and then – in some instances – administrative and legal form. This became a growing challenge to NGOs, particularly those engaged in the human rights and environmental sectors, and those working to influence government policies.

Recently, one of the most respected national daily newspapers published an editorial suggesting that individuals with their non-profit projects replace state institutions (bloggers and anti-corruption web-projects replace the Prosecutor's office, etc). Well, with all ridicule of this suggestion, we cannot deny it as an acknowledgement of NGOs and civil society. Of course, we shouldn't oversimplify – many people in Russia have never heard about NGOs or thought about civil society.[22]

This recent account on the growing civil society might look contradictory to some of our previous points – aggressive ultra-right nationalism, apathy, lack of participation and widespread human rights abuses. But there is no controversy: all these are faces of modern Russia, along with many more, with more stereotypical or unusual images one can imagine.

Sarah Lindemann, a researcher who observed NGOs in Siberia for these 20 years, warns western students of Russia to treat each dimension of its political space independently and not to allow distaste for a particular political figure to lead to the caricature of the country:

It is reasonable to be horrified at atrocities in Chechnya and still objectively report public activism and government responsiveness on other issues. It is reasonable to suspect electoral manipulation and still objectively report the creation of a new legislative base to support citizen participation in government. It is reasonable to worry that new NGO laws will curtail NGO activities and then report that the anticipated negative effects did not materialize whereas increased funding did (Javeline and Lindemann-Komarova 2010).

Lindemann encourages attempts to understand the true situation in the country, with all of its blemishes and beauty marks. After all, as Russian grass-roots activists say, with all the imperfections, problematic human rights record, unfinished reforms and regressive trends, life in Russia since 1991 has never been monotonous, uneventful, failed to bring new challenges nor to surprise and inspire.

Russia today is a new state and a new society still struggling to refine its trajectory after a long Soviet experiment and 20 years of transition. Through these transitional years, Russia has become more connected than ever to the rest of the world. This gives us hope that the situation with human rights and diversity will remain issues topical not just for local, but global community. Though not many will dare to say with certainty how Russia will evolve, there is a diversity of tools to watch it, interpret it and relate to the on-going change.

References

Eggert, Konstantin, "Due West: Moscow's tortuous foreign policy," accessed August 17, 2011,
   http://en.rian.ru/columnists/20110817/165862371.html.
Human Rights Watch, "Letter to President Medvedev regarding ECHR legislation," last modified August 12, 2011,
   http://www.hrw.org/en/world-report-2011/russia.
—. "World Report 2010: Russia," accessed July 30, 2012,
   http://www.hrw.org/en/world-report-2011/russia.
Javeline, Debra, and Sarah Lindemann-Komarova. "Rethinking Russia: A Balanced Assessment of Russian Civil Society." *Journal of International Affairs* 63(2010): 171-188.
Kotkin, Stephen. *Armageddon Averted: The Soviet Collapse 1970-2000.* New York: Oxford University Press, 2003.
Mankoff, Jeffrey. "Rethinking Russia: Generational Change and the Future of U.S.-Russian Relations." *Journal of International Affairs* 63 (2010): 1-18.
Rozalskaya, Maria. "Inappropriate enforcement of anti-extremist legislation in Russia in 2010." *SOVA Center for Information and Analysis.* Accessed April 11, 2011. http://www.sova-center.ru/en/ misuse/reports-analyses/2011/04/d21360/.
Sevortian, Anna. "Russian NGOs and their relationship with the state, 1995-2007: Identifying models and mechanisms for the retention of

independence". Manuscript presented at "Supporting human rights in today's Russia: the role of NGOs", Multicultural Center Prague, March 30, 2009.

—. "Many problems, but one purpose: human rights in Russia." Open Democracy. Accessed December 10, 2010. http://www.opendemocracy.net/od-russia/anna-sevortian/many-problems-but-one-purpose-human-rights-in-russia.

—. "Moscow attempts to elbow Strasbourg aside." Open Democracy. Accessed September 5, 2011. http://www.opendemocracy.net/od-russia/anna-sevortian/moscow-attempts-to-elbow-strasbourg-aside.

Shevtsova, Liliya. "Gorbachev: history will be a fairer judge." Open Democracy. Access February 26, 2011. http://www.opendemocracy.net/od-russia/lilia-shevtsova/gorbachev-history-will-be-fairer-judge.

The Institute for Urban Economics. "Role of Non-Profit Sector in Economic Development of Russia." Accessed July 30, 2012. www.urbaneconomics.ru/eng/publications.php?folder_id=4&mat_id=31.

Thornhill, John. "Russia's Past is No Sign of its Future." *Financial Times*, August 25, 2011. http://www.ft.com/cms/s/0/f73a9f2c-ca8c-11e0-94d0-00144feabdc0.html#ixzz1WFRqT7Ij.

Verkhovsky, Alexander, and Galina Kozhevnikova. "The Phantom of Manezhnaya Square: Radical Nationalism and Efforts to Counteract It in 2010." *SOVA Center for Information and Analysis*. Accessed May 5, 2011.http://www.sova-center.ru/en/xenophobia/reports-analyses/2011/05/d21561/.

Yudina, Natalia and Vera Alperovich."Spring 2011: Causes celebres and New Ultra-right Formations." *SOVA Center for Information and Analysis*.fjoris Accessed July 12, 2011. http://www.sova-center.ru/en/xenophobia/reports-analyses/2011/07/d22101/.

Notes

[1] "Putin na Harleye pokhvalil baikerov za ikh patriotism". *BBCRussian.com, August 30, 2011.* http://www.bbc.co.uk/russian/russia/2011/08/110830_putin_bikers.shtml [accessed May 10, 2013].

[2] "Rossiyane o sobytiyakh avgusta 1991 goda". *Levada Center*, August 16, 2011. http://www.levada.ru/press/2011081601.html [accessed May 10, 2013].

[3] "Ostrye obstchestvennye problemy". *Levada Center*, March 11, 2011. http://www.levada.ru/press/2011031101.html [accessed May 10, 2013].

[4] Notably, the first variable hasn't changed considerably since August 1994, but the human rights variable has seen growth from 25% to 42% over 17 years.

[5] "O blagopoluchii naseleniya o demokratii v strane". *Levada Center*, August 10, 2011. http://www.levada.ru/press/2011081003.html [accessed May 10, 2013].

[6] A rather unifying role is played by the Russian language spoken by absolute majority of the population.

[7] Anna Sevortian, "Xenophobia in Post-Soviet Russia". *Equal Rights Trust Bulletin, Vol.Three, 2009.* http://www.equalrightstrust.org/ertdocumentbank/anna%20sevortian.pdf [accessed May 10, 2013].

[8] "Stenogramma internet-konferentsii prezidenta Rossii". The official website of the Russian President*Kremlin.ru*, July 06, 2006. http://archive.kremlin.ru/text/appears/2006/07/108326.shtml [accessed May 10, 2013].

[9] The majority of activities of this kind now require official permission from the authorities complying with a special procedure, and failure to obtain permission renders them illegal.

[10] For example, in spring of 2011, 34 people became victims of racist and neo-Nazi-motivated attacks; three of them were killed, compared to 97 people suffered and 14 of them killed over the same period in 2010.

[11] The author thanks HRW intern Colleen Fitzharris for gathering material for this section of the article.

[12] "Besporyadki v Moskve 15 dekabrya: ofitsialnaya khronologiya", *RBK*, December 16, 2010. http://top.rbc.ru/incidents/16/12/2010/515990.shtml [accessed May 10, 2013].

[13] "Premier RF o besporyadkakh v Moskve I drugikh gorodakh", *SOVA Center*, December 17, 2010. http://www.sova-center.ru/racism-xenophobia/news/counteraction/2010/12/d20546/ [accessed May 10, 2013].

[14] Medvedev also set the FSB with the task of exposing the organizers of racial provocation and suppressing future violent acts.

[15] *Id.*

[16] The most important banning action during the period under report was the ruling of the Moscow City Court that deemed the DPNI extremist.

[17] Once it spread to the underground, it was directed not to Caucasians, but to any foreigners, mainly Central Asians.

[18] Such as criticism of political, ideological, and religious organizations in and of itself cannot be considered hate speech; the limits of permissible criticism of public officials and politicians should be wider than similar criticism of private individuals; expert examination should be appointed only when necessary, etc.

[19] The president suggested implementing a curriculum of inter-ethnic and multi-cultural understanding to the Russian school curriculum. He also announced that he plans to introduce legislation in the state Duma to ban anyone who has been convicted of extremist activity from teaching in Russian schools. The president said that the Kremlin and Duma should sponsor a public service announcement campaign that emphasizes the benefits of international, inter-religious, inter-cultural, and inter-ethnic cooperation and tolerance, and create multi-media program that educates Russian citizens about different ethnicities. Finally, he

condemned the lack of diversity in federal offices and proposed introducing programs that support increasing departmental religious and ethnic diversity.
[20] According to Levada Centre's figures from December 2009, some 11% of Russians believed the interests of the state should usurp the rights of the individual (12% think the opposite). Almost a fifth – 18% – were "in certain circumstances" prepared to surrender their rights to the state. 49% of those surveyed felt people had a right to "defend their rights, even if that goes against the interests of the state." 10% had no view.
[21] "Annual report on execution of the governmental supervision in the sphere of non-profit organisations – 2013". *Ministry of Justice of the Russian Federation,* 2013. http://minjust.ru/ru/node/4851 [accessed May 10, 2013].
[22] "Otnoshenie rossiyan k blagotvoritelnosti. Obzor rezultatov issledovaniya". *Donor's Forum,* 2006. http://www.donorsforum.ru/materials/otnoshenie-k-blagotvoritelnosti-v-rossii/ [accessed May 10, 2013].

CHAPTER NINE

BETWEEN COMPLIANCE AND RESISTANCE: EDUCATION FOR PEACE IN ISRAELI PUBLIC SCHOOLS

YOSSI YONAH

On the 20th of September, 2010, the daily Haaretz reported that Zvi Zameret, the head of the pedagogical secretariat in the ministry of education, decided to cut the earmarked budget to citizenship education and to re-channel the money to programs promoting Jewish heritage and history. Two weeks later, on 27th of September 2010, Haaretz also informed its readers that "The ministry of education was ordered to stop teaching the Arab version of the conflict alongside the Zionist one." This version of the conflict appeared in a book entitled *To teach the historical narrative of the other: Israelis and Palestinians*. The book is banned. This is not the only book banned. During the year 2009 the book entitled *Nationality: Building a state in the Middle East*, was also banned. The reason–it recounts the Palestinian refugee problem from a Palestinian point of view. And again, during September of 2010, the head of the pedagogical secretariat decided to shelve yet another book, entitled *To be Citizens in the State of Israel*. The reason–the book included the assertion that "since its inception, the state of Israel carried out discriminatory policies against its Arab citizens." These steps receive now the seal of the legislator. The Israeli Parliament passed a law, last March 2010, banning activities commemorating the Palestinian Nakba on Israel's Independence Day.

These developments reflect a culmination of systematic and official efforts made recently to infuse the school-climate with national values. They aim, as Zameret bluntly put it "to strengthen national patriotism." And as part of the efforts to achieve this goal, children are now required to sing the anthem at the beginning of the school day, and army officers are allowed to instruct teachers how to promote the motivation of youngsters to serve in the Army. Many other initiatives, as the minister of Education, Gideon Saar, declared, are on the way.[1]

This jingoistic *Zeitgeist* is also translated into public campaigns run by independent organizations such as "This is Our Land" and "The Institute for Zionist Strategy." The campaigns are directed both against various NGOs accused of supporting anti-Zionist activities and against the academia for showing "anti-Zionist biases." Thus, we currently witness growing claims that Israeli academic institutions seemingly maintain hiring procedures that favor leftist candidates and that the faculties of social sciences and humanities promote a scholastic agenda that undermines Zionist ideology. And there is also the emergence of a new phenomenon. University syllabuses are circulated and minutely scrutinized in daily newspapers. Thus prominent columnists, self-appointed censors, embark upon a mission to uncover traitors in the academia. And some academics themselves jumped on this eerie wagon: Haifa University held an academic conference in June of this year devoted to the subject of "New Anti-Semitism." Special attention was given to manifestations of Anti-Semitism within the Israeli left. The latter – the Israel left – who are regularly described as "self-hating Jews" (The New Anti-Semitism: Program X).

The outburst of these initiatives aims to silence leftist criticism against the national narrative as it is transpired in recent policies of Israel's right-wing government. Here is a random example, gleaned from an op-ed page of the daily "Israel Today," of how the Israeli left is depicted in mainstream media. Commenting on the launch of another flotilla trying to break the blockade on Gaza, a flotilla manned by Jewish activists, the column reads:

> The [Israeli] radical left is not interested in humanism but in the unraveling of Israel, in the defamation of Israel, in the besmirching of Israel. These Jews broke away from the public; broke away from their own people…The provocation of these Jews, like the rest of the flotillas, aims at undermining the authority of Israel and its legitimacy to protect itself and to fight Islamo-fascistic terror (Idar 2010, 5).

The initiatives that aim "to strengthen national patriotism" and the rationale behind them are nothing but a logical conclusion – though not by any means inevitable – of recent challenges with which Israel's basic structure has to grapple. This paper aspires to examine these challenges, especially in view of major political developments emerging in the last two decades. It also aims to examine these challenges vis-à-vis the possible roles the education system may play in either promoting unbridled national patriotism or in curbing it.

Social inclusion versus social exclusion: the role of education

Before embarking directly on the aims of the paper, here is a brief theoretical framework of the possible roles that education may play in either the inclusion or exclusion of children in a society which aspires to be liberal and democratic. There are three contrasting, but not mutually exclusive, roles that education may play in this regard. First, there is the ideal case. Education may promote complementary practices that *reinforce inclusion*. That is, on top of a political system that provides political, social, and cultural rights, the education system may provide, as Amy Gutmann writes, "the ability to participate effectively in the democratic process" (1987, 136). This participation requires a mastery of relevant information, critical reasoning skills, and specific character traits and virtues (Dewey 1988, 365). It seems that Rawls, through his partially-articulated role of education in liberal democracy, provides a good example of the role of education under ideal conditions. Rawls restricts his discussion of this role to what he coins "a well-ordered society," which is effectively regulated by a public conception of justice (1993). As to be expected, he finds the role of education crucial in a well-ordered society to ensure its survival and prosperity by developing an effective sense of justice among its future citizens. This sense of justice actually provides an efficacious motivational force to comply with the conception of justice guiding it. Rawls's main interest, though, is in a well-ordered society guided by a liberal conception of justice that reflects its beliefs, values, and principles. This concept's three components are: the basic beliefs and values characterizing the public culture of liberal democracy, the principles of justice derived from them, and the justification of these principles (Rawls 1993, 70). Predicated on a liberal conception of justice, the effective sense of justice then leads individuals in their social interactions and reverberates within a social and political system that guarantees them civic, political, and social rights.

Critics of Rawls find his conception of liberal education seriously wanting. One major reason is that his list of rights leaves no room for the cultural component owed to individuals in a liberal society. Thus, for instance, Bruce Ackerman argues that the educational system should provide children with "cultural coherence" (Ackerman 1980, 141) and inculcate in them a sense of belonging to the community, and not foreclose its common cultural heritage and values. In a similar vein, Will Kymlicka emphasizes the crucial role that community plays in the formation of personal identity. The community, he argues, provides the meaningful context for choice for human beings, a context without which personal autonomy – which is of paramount importance to the liberal worldview – loses all meaning (1995, 93). Adding a social twist to this criticism, Hirsch emphasizes the connection between the mastery of cultural heritage – manifested through cultural literacy – and equal opportunities. "Cultural literacy," he argues,

> (...) constitutes the only sure avenue of opportunity for disadvantaged children, the only reliable way of combating the social determinism that now condemns them to remain in the same social and educational condition as their parents (Hirsch 1987, xiii; Gellner 1983).

Adding the cultural component to the list of rights owed to individuals in an upgraded "well-ordered society" then assures individuals equal and full inclusion in society. That is, all the inclusion they can hope for in a well-ordered society. This includes a substantive array of claims that the individual may make against the body politic to which he or she belongs. In the field of education, the social rights necessitate material goods (e.g., schools and teachers); the political rights entail cultivation of the skills necessary for effective participation in the democratic process; and the cultural rights require that the curriculum promoted by the school incorporate sufficient elements of the cultural and national heritage of all children. Thus, enjoying the various rights and benefiting from educational practices that render them reflexive, critical, and embedded selves, individuals are assured equal and full inclusion in society.

The second role that education may play vis-à-vis the interplay between citizenship and inclusion is essentially detrimental to the inclusion of children in society. It actually reinforces forms of exclusion or partial inclusion manifested in the social reality that exist outside the education system and deprives individuals and communities of political, social, and cultural rights. The vast Marxist, neo-Marxist and multicultural literature in this regard provides some of the finest and most nuanced articulation of how the education system fulfills this appalling role in modern and postmodern eras (Suoranta, McLaren and Jarmillo 2011; Kivisto 2002).

The third role that education may play vis-à-vis the inclusion/exclusion dialectics is subversive, understood constructively (Rorty 1989). That is, given the existence of forms of exclusion or partial inclusion manifested in the social reality existing outside the educational system, it may nonetheless function as a subversive site in which meaningful resistance and contestation of this social reality may occur (Giroux 1981). It may compensate for practices of exclusion occurring outside the educational system and promote empowerment of disenfranchised and oppressed social groups in society and encourage their inclusion within it. As Rorty asks,

> Is the socioeconomic setup in accordance, more or less, with nature? Is it, on the whole, a realization of human potentialities or rather a way of frustrating those potentialities? Will acculturation to the norms of our society produce freedom or frustration? (1989, 199).

These questions, however, are part and parcel of the curricular agenda of critical pedagogy to be applied *mutatis mutandis* in various societies (Giroux 1981, 1994).

To recap, there are three roles that education may play regarding the inclusion/exclusion dialectics, taking into account the analytical distinction between the normative and the descriptive. First, it may operate in an ideally just and fair society reinforcing the conception of justice underlying its social order; it may act as an accomplice to the advancement and normalization of exclusionary practices existing in society; third, it may act as a social agent in challenging the exclusionary practices existing within or without the educational system.

The Role of Education and the Israeli-Palestinian Conflict: Historical Overview

Although assuming material and curricular responsibility for Arab children enrolled in Israeli schools, the Israeli educational system is flawed with structural and systematic exclusion of them since the inception of the state of Israel. It would be difficult to contest, therefore, the claim that the role played by the educational system vis-à-vis Arab children is consistent to a large extent with the second role attributed to public education in general. That is, Israel's educational system actually reinforces forms of exclusion or partial inclusion of Arab children in lieu of systematic discrimination exercised against Arab minority at large, a discrimination that deprives them of full political, social, and cultural rights. These forms of exclusion or partial inclusion have been manifested in unequal distribution of material resources as well as in misrecognition of the Palestinian cultural heritage in Israel's school curriculum.

Actually, practices of misrecognition in this regard have always displayed an ambivalence and vicissitude. On the one hand, it has acknowledged this heritage and recognized Arabic as the official language used in schools and it has left room for an Arabic literary legacy in the school curriculum (Tzartzur 1985; Gabizon 1999). This has been facilitated by residential segregation between Jews and Arabs, supported and authorized by school registration (especially at the elementary school level) according to place of residence. On the other hand, the Ministry of Education's policy regarding the Arab minority in Israel throughout the years has been characterized by an adamant refusal to include the national-Palestinian narrative in the curriculum of either Arab or Jewish pupils.

Reports dealing with "The Goals of Arab Education" reflect this ambivalent attitude. For example, a report drafted by Deputy Education Minister, Aharon Yadlin, and submitted to the Education Minister Yigal Alon in 1972, states the following educational goals for Palestinian pupils:

> Education grounded in peace values; identification with democracy and social morality; education for loyalty to the State of Israel, while emphasizing the common interests of all its citizens and cultivating the uniqueness of Israeli Arabs; bequeathing programs intended to alleviate social and economic integration; and educating girls towards independence and improvement of their social status (Tzartzur 1985, 499).

Even though later reports placed greater emphasis on the need to express the cultural uniqueness of Israel's Palestinian minority, none of them proposed acknowledging their national cultural uniqueness. For instance, a report prepared by Elad Peled, former Director General of the Ministry of Education, to establish principles to guide the future of Arab education in the 1980s essentially repeated the previous report's recommendations. It stated that "the goal of public education in the Arab sector in Israel is to ground education on the foundations of the Arab culture," and the education of Arab students should be based "on a love of the homeland shared by all the state citizens and on loyalty to the State of Israel – while emphasizing their common interests and reference to the distinctiveness that Israeli Arabs have" (Peled 1976, 421).

The 1990s began with big hopes, but ended with deep disillusionments in Israeli society. In 1992, Prime Minister Yitzhak Rabin formed a left-wing coalition government, and in the next two years Israel signed the Oslo agreements with the Palestinian authority and a peace treaty with Jordan. The decade also saw intensified globalization, gleefully embraced by Israel's political and economic elites. So it seemed that the combination of a new era, in terms of Israel's Arab/Israeli relationship and escalated entry into the global order, created a political atmosphere favoring the formal accommodation of Israeli Arabs as a national minority within

Israeli society. The hope was that these developments would encourage a transition from Israeli society being consumed with existential fears and absorbed with tasks of nation-building to the stage where it emerged as a confident and self-assured society, free of existential anxieties, and a comfortable agent in the new global order (Shafir and Peled 2002). But these hopes were cruelly dashed, in part by the deadlocked peace negotiations with the Palestinian Authority, and in part by the nationalism and neo-liberal ideology of the last decades in Israel, as well as in other societies throughout the world. Dialectical processes weaken the state in certain spheres while strengthening it in others, giving rise to the re-emergence of a fervent national discourse and to the role of the state in promoting it (Yonah, Dahan and Markovitch 2008). These dialectical processes receive ample expression in the field of education, especially as it reiterates the aims of Arab education in Israel.

A few months before the outbreak of the second Intifada (October 2000), the Israeli parliament accepted an amendment to the 1953 Compulsory Public Education Law revising its basic aims. The law states that one of the goals of public education in Israel is to provide pupils with the option of "getting to know the language, culture, history, heritage, and the unique tradition of the Arab population and of other population groups in the State of Israel and to acknowledge the equal rights of all the citizens of Israel" (section 2.11). Although signaling some positive changes towards the legal status of Israeli Palestinians in the Israeli educational system, this amendment did not recognize Israeli Arabs as a national minority, but only as a distinct cultural group, as if they constituted a mere ethnic minority.

If Israeli Arabs anticipated further auspicious developments in this regard, the year's ensuing events forestalled their expectations. Israel witnessed the collapse of the Oslo agreements, leading to the second Palestinian uprising, the Intifada of 2000. Protesting in support of their Palestinian brethren, Israeli Palestinians were engulfed in a circle of violence leading to the killing of 13 Arab protesters. Following this tragic event, a group of Israeli academics, composed of Jews and Palestinians alike, wrote an emergency report in which they demanded that the Israeli government initiate large-scale programs to integrate Israeli Palestinians in Israeli society while recognizing their unique national heritage. As to education, the report stated:

> An analysis of the professed goals of education and an examination of the Arab education's curriculum illustrate that there is no acknowledgement of the Arabs in Israel being a national minority and in their being an inseparable part of the Palestinian nation. Instead, it is evident that the

system is governed by the aim of creating a subservient Arab, lacking any clear identity (Al-Haj et al. 2000, 33).

Andre Mazawi argues that leaders of the educational system view education as a political and ideological instrument of control over the Palestinian population in Israel (Mazawi 1999, 388). The educational system dedicates resources to blurring the national identity of Israeli Palestinian citizens while continuing to reinforce the national-Zionist character of education in frameworks that serve Jewish pupils (Al-Haj 1998, 705). Moreover, the schools serving Arab pupils "put pressure on the [Arab-Palestinian] minority towards unilateral bilingualism and biculturalism" (Saban 2002, 269). Arab pupils must learn the Hebrew language and Jewish culture and history, while Jewish pupils are not required to learn about Palestinian language, culture, or history.

The year 2005 seemed to herald a political atmosphere ripe again for new initiatives to accommodate Israeli Palestinians within Israeli society as a national minority deserving collective rights. As to education, it seemed that cultural misrecognition of Israeli Arabs and discrimination as to the allocation of material resources was about to finally reach an end with the publication of the Dovrat Report – "The National Task Force on Education" (Ministry of Education 2005). Written within the strictures of neo-liberalism with the support of the Israeli government and the Ministry of Education, the Dovrat Report is the most comprehensive educational reform proposed in Israel in the last four decades.

As to Arab education in Israel, the Report suggests the beginning of a new era in the relationship between the state of Israel and its Arab citizens. It "recommends turning over a new leaf… despite the existence of a national conflict," which should not prevent the educational system from "giving expression to the Arab heritage" (2005, 218). As part of this new dawn, the Report proposes adding the following clauses to the Public Education Law:

> (A) Developing and cultivating the personal and collective Arab identity as a psychosocial educational anchor, complete integration in Israeli society and in the State of Israel as a Jewish and democratic state; (B) Knowledge and cultivation of the Arabic language, and introduction to Arab culture and heritage; (C) Introduction to Jewish culture, the Hebrew language and the history of the Jewish nation (The Ministry of Education 2005, 219).

However, even though former Education Minister Amnon Rubinstein called it a "historical document," and even though the Report determined that "the right for a separate education system to exist is correct in the case of [groups belonging] to separate nation and language" (2005, 215), it still does not recognize the right of Israel's Palestinian minority to a separate stream of education.[2]

This denial looms large when we consider that the Report recommends legally grounding the special status of four educational communities in Israel: religious, ultra-Orthodox, Arab, and Druze. The Report makes this recommendation based on "the existence of a separate nationality and language, or a distinct and separate lifestyle" (2005, 215). But even though the Arab minority fully satisfies this requirement, the Report does not recognize its right to a separate educational stream.

While the Zionist-religious and ultra-Orthodox communities are entitled to express their cultural and educational autonomy via independent education administrations under their control, the Arab and Druze communities are not granted independent administrations that can express their autonomy and facilitate collective control over the Arab schools. Institutional support for Arab community autonomy is mainly symbolic – general recommendations regarding the appointment of representatives and advisors in the Ministry of education's various units; the continued existence of an advisory council established in 1995; and a recommendation that a regional education administration with more than 50 per cent Arab pupils appoint an Arab as its Director or Deputy Director.

We see then that despite the promise to "turn a new leaf" in the relationship between the state of Israel and its Arab minority in the field of education, the Dovrat Report does not significantly improve on previous reports. Its vision of Arab education does not challenge the definition of the state of Israel as Jewish and democratic. The Arab pupil still must adopt the State of Israel's goals and values as a Jewish state, even though the very character of the state produces central institutional arrangements that openly discriminate against her. A provision drafted by the Ministry of Education and endorsed by the Report requiring an experimental core curriculum as a pre-condition for public funding of education poignantly illustrates the problem. One-third of the concepts appearing in this curriculum, the state-called "100 Foundation Concepts for Arab Education" (Ministry of Education 2003), relate to "Zionist Concepts for Arab Education." The Arab pupil must first learn about Jewish settlements in modern Palestine, such as Dgania and Nahalal, about the Jewish spy, Eli Cohen (who infiltrated into the highest circles of power in Syria), and about pre-state Jewish military organizations such as Etzel, the Lehi, and the Palmach. The second category, "Arab Sector Heritage," includes among other things, a list of terms from Arab folklore such as Al-diyafa (the culture of Arab hospitality), Aljhaha (a group of men with religious and cultural status who participate in important cultural events such as engagements, death, and marriage) and Al-hima (the Tent). While the Arab pupil is required to study and know concepts from the history of the Israeli nation and learn the words of the national anthem, the Jewish pupil is not exposed at all to the Israeli Arab heritage. This asymmetry reflects the ongoing policy of the state towards the national Palestinian minority, whose essence is "putting pressure [on it]… towards unilateral bilingualism and biculturalism" (Saban 2002, 269; Gabizon 1999, 14 and 18).

In conclusion, we should be able to see how the educational system functions as a state agency that institutionalizes marginality of social groups and compromises their inclusion in society. In this case, citizenship education, which makes no effort to resist the marginalization of Arab students, does not contribute to their inclusion in society but rather to their exclusion from it, at least in part.

Ethno-nationalism: Exclusion of Arabs and Israel's basic Structure

To acquire good understanding of the material and symbolic exclusion (or their partial inclusion in this regard) in Israeli society at large, the traditional distinction between civic and ethnic nationalism ought to be brought to the fore of the discussion. Bearing in mind that this distinction, like many other distinctions, is inherently blurry, it helps nonetheless to get a good understanding of these practices.

Opposed to civic nationalism, *jus solis* nationalism, that confers equal status upon all individuals residing within the territorial boundaries of the nation and irrespective of any "primordial ethnic affiliation," ethnic nationalism, *jus singuinis* nationalism, reserves the status of full national membership only to those displaying specific affiliation of this sort. Israel's declared national identity subscribes to the latter, which informs the very essence of the "basic structure" of its political system.

Israel does not constitute a sui generis case. Ethno-nationalism provides the main organizing principle that dominates political reality in Central and Eastern Europe and Eurasia, a space that was under the control of the Habsburg, Ottoman, and Romanov Empires (Brubaker 1996). Emerging in a political space that encompasses poly-ethnic, poly-religious, and poly-linguistic populations, ethno-nationalism manifests a "triadic nexus" that includes "nationalizing nationalism," where dominant groups aim to consolidate their political and economic hegemony in the nation-state, "external national homelands" of social groups that reside outside the state's borders but allegedly constitute an integral part of the dominant groups, and "national minorities" residing in the nation-state and perceived as a constant threat to the dominant groups (Brubaker 1996, 4). This nexus has typically given rise to nation-states that often defy, as stated, the logic of civic nationalism displayed by the West European nation-states and espouse a territorial principle of citizenship (jus solis).

Israel seems to present a *locus classicus* for Brubaker's triadic nexus of nationalism. Zionism, the national ideology that ushered in the establishment of Israel, fits Brubaker's logic of nationalizing nationalism. It is defined along ethno-cultural, not civic, categories and it expresses the desire of the core national group (i.e., Jews) to have their own independent state, which they view both as a form of restitution for past suffering and as a means to forestall future threats to their existence. Led then by a perceived threat and by a sense of cultural, economic, and demographic weakness, this group employs various means to consolidate its grip over the country and its resources. Thus, the core national group maintains a large army, runs a land policy that secures control over all territorial reservoirs that lie within its borders (and only there), and provides special economic benefits to its members. Furthermore, through the state's agencies, it exercises an immigration policy designed to secure its majority in the country. Nationalizing nationalism assumes, then, that the institution of the nation-state and the need to protect it is an ongoing project – a mission that has not been yet sufficiently accomplished – since the members of the core national group believe they continue to face an existential threat. One can easily see how ethnic nationalism imposes structural limitations on the inclusion of individuals and groups who do not belong to the core national group in the nation-state.

Ethno-nationalism, it ought to be stressed, often operates under the assumption that national conflicts are zero-sum games. This is definitely true in the case of Israel, and public education is one of the main discursive sites in which this assumption appears most abrasively. Reuven Rivlin, currently the chairperson of the Israeli parliament, gave a succinct expression to this assumption. Following a modest initiative of the minister of Education in the year 2000 to include poems of Mahmud Darwish, the Palestinian national poet, in Israeli school curriculum, he said:

> If we allow the teaching of a Palestinian national poet who denies our right for self-determination we actually renounce any claim to moral justice. If we allow this we actually instill in our children the thought that maybe the Zionist movement was not a moral movement after all.

And he continued to ask sarcastically: "Maybe there is no justice in the wish of the Jewish people to return to its homeland after 2000 years of exile? Maybe we should get out of here." The Poet Aharon Amir – Israel prize laureate – expressed a similar opinion. "Before we are completely swept away to the shore of the 'Other,' we should first be sure of our own identity. We should remember the dictum of our sages: 'he who hears many voices will never hear his own voice.'"

Although indicating a firm feature of the basic structure of Israeli political system, ethno-nationalism, it should be stressed, is itself negotiable; it is itself malleable. This desperately sanguine conviction on my part draws credence from political events unfolded in the past. Let me explain: The regretful statements of the politician and the poet cited above were launched, paradoxically, during an epoch when a window of opportunity was meagrely, scantily, ajar: It was the year 2000. It was the year when peace talks were held between Arafat and Barak under the auspices of the Clinton administration. There was a glimmer of hope. And when the ringing of the bells of peace was heard, no matter how feebly, the education system began to inculcate, somewhat tentatively, the Palestinian heritage and national narrative. This situation happened twice: in the year 2000 and previously in the year 1994, following the Oslo agreements signed between Israel and the Palestinian Authority. It is during these moments that efforts were made to reshape the basic structure of Israel, nudging it away from ethno-national ethos and bringing it closer to liberal constitutional democracies.

Circumstances have changed since then radically, for the worst. The Likud-led government coalition, enjoying the support of the Labor party headed by Ehud Barak, is not really interested in reaching a peace treaty with the Palestinian Authority. We should remember that the legacy left by Ehud Barak, following the failure of the 2000 peace talks, is that there is no Palestinian partner to peace in the years to come. And thus all tragic events occurring since then – the second intifada of 2000, "Defense Wall Operation" of 2002, the second Lebanon war of 2006 and "The Cast Lead Operation" of 2008 – are interpreted by many Israelis in light of this dubious legacy. Many of them are former leftists who have become, so to speak, "disillusioned." And thus they unwittingly echo the position provocatively promoted by Israel's pugnacious minister of foreign affairs, Avigdor Liberman. All Israel should aspire to do, he believes, is to effectively manage the conflict – not to solve it. And the Israeli Media – public and commercial alike – is obsequiously promoting the "official line."

Given this political climate, one cannot expect that public education operates as an independent agent in the service of moral and political agenda inconsistent with the one endorsed and promoted by the government. Here is an example of a self-drafted credo of an Israeli school: "We see ourselves as emissaries of the state of Israel; we are committed to deepen and consolidate the pupil's roots in Jewish-Zionist tradition and heritage while deepening the commitment to democracy."

This is not surprising. Public education has always assumed a submissive role; it has always been an obedient servant of governments, of hegemonic worldviews and of the swaying mood of the public. One can hardly bring a single example in modern history showing the opposite. This claim should not be understood as an apologetic gesture but rather as part of my assessment as to the meager potential of public education as an independent agent of great moral and ideological change. This regrettable fact was recognized by the great philosopher John Dewey who lamented the appropriation of the humanist moral agenda of 18th century Enlightenment by the modern nation state and the infusion of particularistic and nationalistic ingredients within this agenda. Public schools, he added, have always been the main agent entrusted with this unholy task. And in times of protracted and violent national conflicts, we may add, schools embark upon this task zealously. In such times, the educational system promotes perseverance, steadfastness and strong conviction in "our cause." In brief, it promotes the personal dispositions of children needed to effectively confront "unyielding enemy and future existential threats." Here comes again Zvi Zameret, the head of the pedagogical secretariat. When asked what is wrong with citizenship education, he said: "I felt that there is not sufficient emphasis on the topic of the Jewish state. I assumed the job so I can accomplish this goal."

Public Education becomes an awesome agent of moral and ideological change – taking on board high moral values and ideals – only when governments decide to bring about a radical change in their policies consistent with these values and ideals. This is actually what began to emerge gingerly in Israel following the Oslo agreements in the year of 1994. But even then the education system did not immediately and unanimously comply with the decrees of the government. Schools affiliated with religious Zionism, objecting to the Oslo agreements, managed to find ways to avoid celebrating the cause of peace and reconciliation between the two peoples. They displayed tacit resistance to the new policies espoused by the government.

Paradoxically, this example indicates the possibility for resistance and defiance available to schools that resist current political climate and government's chauvinistic policies. This possibility, as indicated in the second section of the paper, is consistent with the third role that education may play vis-à-vis practices of social exclusion and marginalization. And they are developments occurring today in Israel's public education that allows the possibility for such resistance. In the last two decades, Israel has zealously embraced neoliberal ideology and initiated, accordingly, policies of privatization and decentralization of social services previously provided by the state, and this includes educational services. Indeed, these processes contribute to widening social gaps and undermining equal educational opportunity, yet they may open up the possibility for citizenship education that views critical pedagogy as an integral part. This is by no means an easy task, since these processes are accompanied by attempts to maintain curricular content consistent with neo-liberal philosophy and chauvinistic national ideology. Yet, they may leave some room for critical pedagogy which may be able to moderately contain efforts to promote narrow-minded national patriotism at the expense of democracy. As we know very well, hegemony is never complete, never hermetic; one may always detect cracks and fissures in it; one may always exploit the inconsistencies and multifarious voices of hegemony in order to forge counter hegemonic options in the service of high human values and ideals. True, aspirations under such circumstances ought to be limited. Acting dissentingly and defiantly, schools can bring changes only on the margins. But this has always been the destiny of critical pedagogy, especially when we witness regrettable closure of the mind.

References

Ackerman, Bruce A. 1980. *Social Justice in the Liberal State*. New Haven: Yale University Press.

Al-Haj, Majid, XX. 2000. "Education and Higher Education." In *After the Divide: new directions for government policy towards Arabs in Israel*, edited by D. Rabinowitz, Asad Ganem, and Oren Yiftachael, 33-7. Tel Aviv: Shatil.

Al-Haj, Majid. 1998. "Multicultural Education in Israel in Light of the Peace Process." In *Multiculturalism In a Democratic and Jewish State*, edited by Menachem Mautner , Avi Sagi and Ronen Shamir, 703-713. Tel Aviv: Tel Aviv University Press/Ramot.

Apple, Michael W. 1996. *Cultural Politics and Education*. Buckingham: Open University Press.

Bar-Tal, Daniel. 2006. "Socialization in the Service of the Conflict" (in Hebrew). In *I Know How to Speak Only About the Conflict: socialization in the service of the conflict in Israeli-Jewish society*, edited by Rachamim Yehezkel and Daniel Bar-Tal, 15-22. Tel Aviv:

Walter Lebach Institute for Jewish-Arab Coexistence Through Education.

Bowels, Sam. and Herb Gintis. 1976. *Schooling in Capitalist America*. New York: Basic Books.

Brubaker, Rogers. 1996. *Nationalism Reframed: nationhood and the national question in the New Europe*. Cambridge: Cambridge University Press.

Dewey, John. 1984. *The Public and its Problems*. Carbondale: University of Southern Illinois Press, 365.

Firer, Ruth. 2006. "Agents of Zionist Education: learning books in Hebrew language in Eretz Israel since the beginning of the 20th Century to present time" (in Hebrew). In *I Know How to Speak Only About the Conflict: socialization in the service of the conflict in Israeli-Jewish Society*, edited by Rachamim Yechezkel and Daniel Bar-Tal, 63-72. Tel Aviv: Walter Lebach Institute for Jewish-Arab Coexistence Through Education.

Gabizon, Ruth. 1999. *Does Equality Require Integration? The case of the education system in Jaffa*. Position Paper, Beit Berl: The Study of Arab Society in Israel Research. Beit Berl Press. (In Hebrew).

Gellner, Ernest. 1983. *Nations and Nationalism*. Ithaca: Cornell University Press.

Giroux, Henry. 1981. *Ideology, Culture and the Process of Schooling*. Philadelphia: Temple University Press.

—. 1994. "Insurgent Multiculturalism and the Promise of Pedagogy." In *Multiculturalism: A Critical Reader*, edited by David Theo Goldberg, 325-343. Cambridge: Blackwell.

Government of Israel. 2003. *The Or Commission* (in Hebrew). Jerusalem: The Government of Israel.

Gutmann, Amy. 1987. *Democratic Education*. New Jersey: Princeton University Press.

Hirsch, Emil. D. 1987. *Cultural Literacy: what every American needs to know*. Boston: Houghton Mifflin.

Idar, Dror. "Israel Hayom". *Israel* Today, September 28, 2010. http://www.edu.haifa.ac.il/~ilangz/antisemitism_conference/program.htm

Jabarin, H. 2000. "Israeli-ness that 'anticipates the future' of Arabs according to Jewish/Zionist temporality, in a space lacking Palestinian time". *Law and Government* 6: 53-86. (in Hebrew).

Kahan, S. and Yelnik, Y. (2000) "The Discrimination of the Arab Sector in the Allocation of Special Resources in Education its Scope and the Implications of its Cancellation," a working paper. Jerusalem: The Hebrew University of Jerusalem. (In Hebrew).

Kivisto, Peter. 2002. *Multiculturalism in A Global Society.* Blackwell, Oxford: UK.

Kymlicak, Will. 1995. *Multicultural Citizenship.* Oxford: Oxford University Press.

Maraai, A. I. 2006. *Hebraizing Names of Palestinian Towns and Sites: a reflection and extension to the Israeli-Palestinian conflict.* Tamra: Iban Haldun Center. (in Arabic).

Mazawi, André. 1999. "Concentrated Disadvantage and Access to Educational Credentials in Arab and Jewish Localities in Israel." *British Educational Research Journal* 25(3): 355-70.

Ministry of Education. 2003. *Concepts in Zionism for the Arab Sector.* Jerusalem: The Ministry of Education and Culture.

—. 2005. *The National Plan for Education (The Dovrat Report)* (in Hebrew). Jerusalem: The Ministry of Education and Culture.

Peled, Elad. 1976. *Education in Israel During the 1980's* (in Hebrew). Jerusalem: The Ministry of Education and Culture.

Rawls, John. 1993. *Political Liberalism.* New York: Columbia University Press.

Rorty, Richard, 1989. "Education Without Dogma." *Dissent* (Spring): 189-204.

Saban, Ilan. 2002. "The Collective Rights of the Arab-Palestinian Minority: what there is, what there is not and the taboo." *Lyune Mishpat* 26(1): 241-319.

Shafir, Gershon and Yoav Peled. 2002. *Being Israeli: the dynamics of multiple citizenship.* Cambridge: Cambridge University Press.

Suoranta, Juha, Peter McLaren and Nathalia Jaramillo. 2011. "Becoming a Critical Citizen: A Marxist-Humanist Critique." In *Citizenship, Education, and Social Conflict: Israeli Political Education in Global Perspective*, edited by Hanan A. Alexander, Halleli Pinson and Yossi Yonah, 39-60 London: Routledge.

"The New Anti-Semitism: Program X". Last modified July 10, 2013. http://construct.haifa.ac.il/~ilangz/new_antisemitism_rational.pdf

Tzartzur, Saad. 1985. "Regarding the Problem of Educating a Foreign Minority in his Country" (in Hebrew). In *Education in a Forming Country*, edited by Walter Ackerman, Eric Carmon and David Zucker, 473-526. Jerusalem: The Van Leer Institute and Hakibutz Hmeauchad Publishers.

Yonah, Yossi, Yossi Dahan and Dalya Markovitch. 2008. "Neo-Liberal Reforms in Israel's Education System: the Dialectics of the State." *International Studies in Sociology of Education* 18(4): 199-216.

Notes

[1] Sarr: We will continue to strengthen the heritage:
http://www.haaretz.co.il/hasite/spages/1186685.html
[2] Quoted by Yair Atinger, "This is how we became familiar with the collective Arab identity" (*Haaretz* February 10 2005, B3-B4)

CHAPTER TEN

NATIONAL HUMAN RIGHTS INSTITUTIONS AND DIVERSITY

JORIS DE BRES

National human rights institutions (NHRIs) are an increasingly common form of human rights body. They are internationally accredited, with strong links to the United Nations Office of the High Commissioner for Human Rights (OHCHR) as well as regional bodies. Increasingly, they are engaged with the United Nations Human Rights Council and human rights treaty bodies, having a voice in their own right in these forums. The Durban Review Conference in Geneva in 2009 reinforced the role of NHRIs in implementing the World Programme to Combat Racism. To achieve accreditation, NHRIs are required to comply with the Paris Principles for National Human Rights Institutions, which specify (*inter alia*) that they must be established by statute, be adequately funded by government and be able to act independently from government. NHRIs operate in the space between government and civil society. To the extent that they focus on diversity and race relations, they tend to do so from a discrimination and equality perspective. The New Zealand Human Rights Commission, being an amalgam of the previous Office of the Race Relations Conciliator and the Human Rights Commission, has a dual mandate for the promotion and protection of human rights and encouragement of the development and maintenance of harmonious relationships between diverse communities. This paper examines the growing role of NHRIs as a local partner for United Nations human rights bodies in promoting and monitoring compliance with international human rights standards. Using the New Zealand Human Rights Commission as an example, it then explores the potential of NHRIs to contribute to a broader goal of harmonious relations in diverse societies. The various roles of independent advocate, mediator, monitor, educator, networker, catalyst and facilitator are outlined and some conclusions drawn on what would assist NHRIs to engage effectively on issues of race relations, cultural diversity and indigeneity.

What are National Human Rights Institutions?

National human rights institutions (NHRIs) come in a variety of guises – ranging from Human Rights Commissions to Human Rights Institutes and Offices of the Ombudsman. The vast majority were established only in the past 20 years, but they have become an important part of the national and international human rights system. They are now a feature of states on all continents within a wide variety of cultures. They are internationally accredited by the International Coordinating Committee of National Human Rights Institutions (ICC) and recognized by the United Nations. They occupy a unique space between government and civil society and provide United Nations human rights bodies with a significant independent local partner in promoting and monitoring compliance with international human rights standards.

As Anna-Elina Pohjolainen has noted in her study of the evolution of NHRIs, in the 1990's they represented a new concept which in some respects was revolutionary:

> The idea that governments should establish and fund agencies, which would develop transnational connections and possess a certain scope of freedom of action at the international level must have appeared strange in the state-centered world which had only recently learned to accept the participation of non-governmental organisations... The fact that the institutions...did not fit easily in the traditional three-division of state powers but appeared to have a role in both the legislative, judicial and executive field, must have confused many governments. Despite these peculiar characteristics, national institutions have spread to many new places all over the world since the introduction of the Paris Principles in the early 1990s. (2006, 8).

The Paris Principles were drawn up by a workshop of NHRI's in Paris in 1991 and adopted by the United Nations General Assembly in 1993 (Paris Principles 1993). They continue to be the basis on which NHRIs are accredited by the ICC and recognized by the UN. They require NHRIs to be established by statute, with competence to promote and protect human rights and with the broadest possible mandate. Their roles should include advice to government and Parliament, human rights education, and publicizing human rights and efforts to combat all forms of discrimination, in particular racial discrimination. The provision of dispute resolution services is optional, although it is a feature of the mandate of many

NHRIs. They must be transparently funded, be plural in composition and independent of government.

Importantly for the purposes of today's discussion, NHRIs should promote compliance with international human rights instruments, encourage ratification, contribute to United Nations Treaty body reports and cooperate with UN bodies and regional institutions. NHRI's are increasingly engaging with the UN Committee on the Elimination of Racial Discrimination (CERD), providing input into government reports or producing independent reports, facilitating NGO involvement, directly advising the Committee at its examination of States and monitoring implementation of the Committee's recommendations. There are also calls for NHRIs to become more engaged with the Declaration on the Rights of Indigenous Peoples and the United Nations Expert Mechanism on the Rights of Indigenous Peoples.

The evolving role of NHRIs

Until recently, the focus of many NHRIs has been on human rights generally, particularly civil, political, social and economic rights. This includes racial discrimination as one form of discrimination, and racial inequality as one form of inequality. It has not necessarily extended to cultural rights and cultural and religious diversity in general, or to race relations and the distinct rights of indigenous peoples. Human rights advocates are not automatically engaged on issues relating to cultural diversity or indigeneity. That role is often left to other government or civil society organisations. In Canada, for example, there is a separate Race Relations Foundation. Nevertheless, greater cultural diversity, as a result of increased global migration, presents human rights challenges in many societies, and NHRIs are being challenged to respond.

The Durban Review Conference in Geneva in April 2009 was attended by some 40 NHRIs. Those attending committed themselves, and challenged other NHRIs, to engage more actively with the Committee on the Elimination of Racial Discrimination and other United Nations human rights bodies, to establish race relations focal points and to share good practice. They called on NHRIs to exercise their mandates more actively in relation to indigenous peoples, ethnic and religious minorities and vulnerable groups. They gave their support to the development of national plans of action to combat racism and the collection of data about racism, and undertook to monitor racism. There was a recognition that NHRIs need to do more about race relations and diversity, and that they have an important role to play. At its meeting in Marrakesh in March 2010, the

ICC Bureau resolved to establish a network of NHRI race relations focal points to implement these commitments. This is being coordinated by the New Zealand and Australian Human Rights Commissions.

At an OHCHR workshop for NHRIs held in Bangkok in November 2009 on the implementation of the United Nations Declaration on the Rights of Indigenous Peoples, the role of NHRIs was again emphasised. States were called on to establish NHRIs and enable them to address indigenous rights. Existing NHRIs were asked to pay particular attention to indigenous rights and engage with UN treaty bodies and the UN Expert Mechanism on the Rights of Indigenous Peoples (EMRIP). In response to a recommendation for further regional and national dialogue on the Declaration, an Asia Pacific workshop of NHRIs was hosted by the Office of the High Commissioner for Human Rights and the New Zealand Human Rights Commission in Auckland in November 2010. The recommendations from the Bangkok workshop again recognize the need for NHRIs to focus more on indigenous issues than they may have done in the past. The issue was raised in a joint statement by the Australian and New Zealand Human Rights Commissions at the annual EMRIP meeting in Geneva in July 2010, and is due to be considered by the UN Human Rights Council (Statement on the Rights of Indigenous Peoples 2010).

The UN Committee on the Elimination of Racial Discrimination has itself been a strong advocate of the role of NHRIs. In General Comment 17, as early as 1993 (Establishment of National Institutions), it called on States to establish NHRIs to facilitate implementation of the Convention. In 2009, in General Comment 33 (Follow-up to the Durban Review Conference) it called on States to cooperate with NHRIs in preparing reports to CERD and following up on recommendations (United Nations High Commissioner for Human Rights 2012). CERD has also amended its procedures to provide for NHRIs to speak in their own right at the Committee's examination of their State's report and provides informal opportunities for direct engagement with the Committee separately from government and NGOs.

Example: New Zealand

Because the New Zealand Human Rights Commission in its present form is the result of a merger with the Office of the Race Relations Conciliator, it provides an interesting example of a National Human Rights Institution with a specific mandate to foster harmonious relations. The Commission's principal objectives under the Human Rights Act are:

- to advocate and promote respect for, and an understanding and appreciation of, human rights in New Zealand society, and
- to encourage the maintenance and development of harmonious relations between individuals and among the diverse groups in New Zealand society.

The Act also provides for a dedicated position of Race Relations Commissioner, who is supported by a Principal Advisor, Senior Policy Analyst, three Community Advisors, and two Kaiwhakarite (Indigenous Relationship Managers). There is thus a specific capability, within a relatively small organization, to focus on race relations and indigenous rights. Further support is provided from generic human resources, external relations, communications, dispute resolution and strategic policy teams.

The Commission's race relations functions can be described as a combination of advocacy, mediation, strategy, monitoring, education, networking, and facilitation.

As an *advocate*, the Commission makes submissions to Parliament, engages with government policy development processes, produces reports and makes public statements. It provides input into CERD, the Universal Periodic Review and other UN treaty bodies and procedures (New Zealand Human Rights Commission 2012a).

As a *mediator*, it provides dispute resolution for complaints of discrimination on the grounds of race, colour, ethnic or national origins, religion, and racial harassment and incitement.

As a *strategist*, it produces a five-yearly review of human rights and a New Zealand Action Plan for Human Rights (including race relations), negotiating with government on implementation and encouraging civil society to contribute (New Zealand Human Rights Commission 2010).

As a *monitor*, it produces an annual review of race relations, the Race Relations Report (New Zealand Human Rights Commission 2012b), which identifies ten top priorities for action. It also produces an annual report on implementation of CERD recommendations and matters still to be addressed.

As an *educator*, it delivers a range of community human rights education programmes: Taku Manawa, developing community human rights leadership, Tuhonohono, human rights training for indigenous groups, and Te Mana i Waitangi, community forums on the Treaty of Waitangi and human rights.

As a *networker and catalyst*, it operates the New Zealand Diversity Action Programme (New Zealand Human Rights Commission 2013), a partnership with 250 government and civil society organisations, with networks for religious diversity, refugee issues, language policy, and media, as well as an annual New Zealand Diversity Forum, monthly and annual diversity awards, and a number of national diversity events (such as Race Relations Day on 21 March).

As a *facilitator*, it has engaged the government and civil society in developing national statements on religious diversity (New Zealand Human Rights Commission 2009), race relations (New Zealand Human Rights Commission 2008), and language policy (Languages in New Zealand 2008), and guidelines on religion in schools and in the workplace. It also cooperates with government to achieve civil society input into its UPR and CERD reports.

What the Commission has sought to do since it received its broader mandate in 2002 is develop a framework for race relations containing the above elements. Particularly strong features of the framework are the Diversity Action Programme, the annual Race Relations Report, the on-going Treaty of Waitangi dialogue, the five-yearly review of human rights and the ensuing Action Plan for Human Rights.

Challenges faced by the Commission include maintaining an appropriate relationship with government which is independent but engaged. The high profile of race issues in New Zealand and the polarisation of public opinion can mean the Commission attracts public hostility whichever way it acts. Public expectations can be based on misconceptions about the role of the Commission, particularly the erroneous perception that its role is to judge and penalise rather than provide alternative dispute resolution. Similarly there can be an expectation that the Commission should have a more strident anti-racist rather than pro-diversity orientation. The Commission's defence of freedom of speech when dealing with complaints about racially or religiously offensive comments is also challenged.

Other NHRI's

There are many other examples of national human rights institutions responding to the heightened profile of diversity and indigenous rights in the human rights landscape. The Australian Human Rights Commission, which maintains close relations with the New Zealand Commission through the Australasian Race Relations Round Table, has a Race Discrimination Commissioner and an Aboriginal and Torres Strait Islander Social Justice Commissioner. It was the Australian Commission that produced the report on the "stolen generations" which ultimately led to the celebrated government apology by Prime Minister Kevin Rudd to the Aboriginal people of Australia. The Commission is required to produce annual reports to Parliament on Aboriginal social justice and Aboriginal land title issues. It also has dedicated staff to support the role of the two Commissioners. Other recent race relations projects have included those on Muslim Australians, African Australians, race and sport, cyber-racism, and action on international student safety. Recently, the Commission made a major contribution to the concluding observations of CERD on their examination of Australia, including preparation of a Commission submission, an address to the Committee by the Race Discrimination Commissioner, and informal engagement with the Committee. The Commission plans to develop an implementation monitoring system for the CERD recommendations.

The South African Human Rights Commission has initiated a project, in partnership with the Office of the High Commissioner for Human Rights, to address the recent outbursts of xenophobia and violence against migrant workers. The Commission has also engaged actively with the CERD Committee and is committed to developing a National Plan of Action on Racism.

The Canadian Human Rights Commission, following the repeal of Section 67 of the Canadian Human Rights Act (which restricted the ability of First Nations people living on reserve to file a complaint against band councils or the federal government), has embarked on a National Aboriginal Initiative, the objective of which is,

> (...) to strengthen relations with Aboriginal groups and foster a dialogue on how to incorporate the unique context of First Nations communities into human rights protection mechanisms. Its focus is on making the Commission's programmes more accessible and culturally sensitive to First Nations people and communities, and on supporting First Nations human rights.

Conclusion

The number of national human rights institutions continues to increase, as do calls for them to play a greater role in race relations and indigenous rights. United Nations bodies have recognized the unique role that NHRIs can play in advocating for the implementation of international human rights standards and the recommendations of treaty bodies such as CERD, and are adjusting their procedures accordingly. There is a clear international agenda to establish NHRIs where they do not yet exist, and for them to receive or exercise the broadest possible mandate, extending to diversity, indigenous rights and race relations. They have an important role to play in developing action plans on human rights and racism. Because of the unique space they occupy between government and civil society, they are able to develop partnerships with both to achieve better diversity outcomes while guarding their independence. They need to monitor and regularly report on race relations, and perhaps most importantly, strengthen their relationship with United Nations bodies, in particular those with a specific mandate relating to race relations and indigenous peoples, so that they can work together to achieve harmonious race relations based on respect for human rights.

References

Pohjolainen, Anna-Elina. *The Evolution of National Human Rights Institutions: The Role of the United Nations.* Copenhagen: Danish Institute for Human Rights, 2006.

New Zealand Human Rights Commission for the New Zealand Diversity Action programme. "Languages in Aotearoa, New Zealand: Te waka reo: Statement on Language policy." Last modified in August 2008. http://www.hrc.co.nz/hrc_new/hrc/cms/files/documents/25-Aug-2008_11-45-14_Language_Policy_Aug_08.pdf.

New Zealand Human Rights Commission. 2008. Race Relations in Aotearoa New Zealand. http://www.hrc.co.nz/hrc_new/hrc/cms/files/documents/25-Aug-2008_11-45-29_Race_Relations_final_Aug_08.pdf

—. 2009. Religious Diversity in New Zealand. http://www.hrc.co.nz/hrc_new/hrc/cms/files/documents/27-Aug-2009_09-44-53_Religious_Diversity_09_Web.pdf

—. "Joint Statement by the Aboriginal and Torres Strait Islander Social Justice Commissioner Mick Gooda, Australian Human Rights Commission and Commissioner Karen Johansen, New Zealand Human Rights Commission to the Expert Mechanism on the Rights of Indigenous Peoples." Last modified 16 July. http://www.hrc.co.nz/hrc_new/hrc/cms/files/documents/06-Aug-2010_11-31-09_UNDRIP_KJ_and_MG_Aus.html.

—. 2010. Human Rights in New Zealand. http://www.hrc.co.nz/hrc_new/hrc/cms/files/documents/Human_Rights_Review_2010_Full.pdf

—. 2012a. Report to the United Nations Committee on the Elimination of Racial Discrimination. http://www.hrc.co.nz/wp-content/uploads/1999/11/Report-to-the-United-Nations-Committee-on-the-Elimination-of-Racial-Discrimination-July-20123.doc

—. 2012b. Tui, Tui, Tuituia: Race Relations in 2011, 2012.

http://www.hrc.co.nz/wp-content/uploads/2012/03/Race-relations-report-2011-for-web.pdf

—. 'The New Zealand Diversity Action Programme : Te Ngira'. Last modified 2013. http://www.hrc.co.nz/race-relations/te-ngira-the-nz-diversity-action-programme.

Office of the United Nations High Commissioner for Human Rights. "Principles relating to the Status of National Institutions (The Paris Principles) A/RES/48/134." Last modified 20 December 1993. http://www2.ohchr.org/english/law/parisprinciples.htm[accessed at X].

—. 2012. "Committee on the Elimination of Racial Discrimination: General Recommendations." Accessed 30 July. http://www2.ohchr.org/english/bodies/cerd/comments.htm.

PART IV

"OTHERING" AND EMERGING HUMAN RIGHTS CHALLENGES IN A GLOBAL AND INTERCONNECTED WORLD

CHAPTER ELEVEN

IS OTHERNESS A QUESTION OF SECURITY
OR A QUESTION OF FREEDOM?

DIDIER BIGO

This article will concentrate on how security policies deal with prevention regarding Otherness. The conceptualisation of the "Other" as a threat in the public discourse and public policies entails consequences. In the post-9/11 context, governments have given much leeway to their security services to define who and what constitute threats. Critics argue that the authorities have deliberately focused on minority and immigrant communities, prioritizing certain security threats over others, casting too wide a net and affecting the personal security of millions through racial profiling and severe invasions of privacy. How should we collectively deal with the resulting deprivation of civil liberties, exacerbation of ethnic tensions, and lack of accountability and transparency?

My answer to this challenging question is to avoid coming back to US policies, their transformations and continuities through the different administrations, even if it is a spontaneous answer, which has its merits. Instead, I have tried to think about how we, as academics, have framed not only our support or criticism to the different policies of counter-terrorism at the so-called global scale, but how we have framed the question itself. Is the question of Otherness a question of security? Is it a move of the government, in the name of security, to develop illiberal practices and to focus on some minorities, on national, ethnic or religious grounds, with the development of profiling (Agamben 2003; Bigo 2003; Bigo 2008b)? I have myself, in many articles and books, developed this line of thought, but I am less and less comfortable with this approach, and it seems to me that it needs to be at least complemented with two other important questions: firstly, is the image of the enemy conducting the strategy of security professionals, and in that case they just answer to new configurations of enmity, or is strategy justified by new narratives framing the enemy as a global enemy? Secondly, has counter-terrorism affected security strategies by developing an agenda of prevention, or has it even more profoundly altered the practices and conceptions of freedom, which are in no way eternal and guaranteed?

To try to answer these two problems, I will present in a first part the main assumptions of the dominant discourses about the value of security and its relation to global prevention. If security is seen as the protection of a certain category of population, the "free men of the world" against crime and violence, what happens to the "Others"? Are they all enemies, forms of "evil?" I will secondly address the way Otherness is constructed as enmity, and how enmity may be a practical regime of justification, more than a frame of understanding. In that case the relation between enmity and strategy is not a straightforward path. Thirdly, I will analyse why, in my opinion, critics of these discourses, when using the notion of balancing freedom and security, develop around a state of exception and a world permanently at risk. By doing so, they *de facto* share a great deal with the security doxa and do not sufficiently question our framing of liberty as a value. This is implied when we present liberty as universal and as the property of a collective group of civilised people (rational, free men anticipating the future through risk assessment).

The main narratives of the professionals of (in)security management: security, prevention and protection

Security as a core value - security as protection of humanity?

One of the main assumptions in liberal democracies shared both by experts and security professionals (such as police, intelligence services, customs, immigration services, border guards and the military) after 11 September 2001, has been that security is a core value threatened by "global terrorism." Security is about the protection of the individual, but also of the collective self, of the nation state, and even the protection of planet Earth itself. Security becomes intrinsically intertwined with survival in an even more intimate way than before, as it encompasses personal fears and everyday unease of individuals with the emancipation of humanity as the project. Of course, this was already the case during the Cold War, but in present times, these assumptions claim that it is even more critical because rationality has gone away and others are irrational, fanatics, or children-like. Many academics from the realist school have supported these views of the possibility that war and crime were more mixed than political science was saying before, and that rationality was always on the verge of collapse, deterrence being a bet on one side, more than a structure itself. They have tried to preserve the idea of national interest but they have changed their approach concerning what is war and what is crime. They have considered terrorism and global organised crime as "serious threats," even if they called them peripheral for years. They re-read Morgenthau and Raymond Aron and explained what these authors had already suggested back in the 1960s, that the relations between war and crime were merging, but it was nevertheless to each state to have its own national agenda and the coalition-alliance was secondary when national interests were at stake. They continue with this position. Nevertheless, nowadays, according to the current experts on counter-terrorism and the risk managers trying to predict the future, the world has changed radically because the state and the community of states no longer have the monopoly on organised violence. A small group of 'terrorists' with weapons of mass destruction might target a city or an entire country, and if all the states do not collaborate, then Armageddon is coming (Blair 2003; Blair 2004; Bush 2002; Coker 2002; Gips 2003; Harris 2002; Hoffman 2002; Lamm 2002; Shultz and Vogt 2003; Tenet 2002).

The logic of the narrative is to impose a *first* assumption which is that we have entered a *radically new era* in which the state cannot pretend anymore to have an effective monopoly on violence, in order to justify a *second* assumption according to which *security is first* and liberty is second, and a *third* assumption which is the central one: the assumption under which global insecurity justifies the goal of a global security agenda operated through a transnationalisation of the different professional guilds of security (of the Western world), their exchange of information, and ultimately an increase of autonomy from judges and even politicians, a raise of budget and the maximum use of advanced technologies (Bigo 2008a).

In this "useful" frame, security is about life and death, about survival; the conditions of life of the free men depend on the existence of life itself, of the protection of their existence and of the infrastructure of their well-being. Therefore, *liberty and democracy as conditions of life are consequential and derivative, as they depend on security for life to exist.* A "third way" is developed in the academic life, permitting to disqualify the opponents of what has been coined by Etzioni as the "security first" argument. On one side, the traditional discourse of national sovereignty is attacked as a form of egoist and selfish interest of national governments perpetuating the threat they pretend to combat if they do not collaborate together; exit the realists and national sovereignty. On the other side, if the value of protection of life is not considered as the only imperative, then people are naïve to discuss about freedom, because freedom supposes first to be alive; exit the liberals and their concerns on freedom. The "real" question is the management of life globally. A utilitarian model frames the relation to security with the notion of protecting life globally (and not only nationally), even if some sacrifices concerning freedom and individual lives are at stake. The argument of "security first" connected with "global insecurity at the horizon" goes along the route of redefining a moral agenda and legitimacy concerning use of force (Bigo 2011).

Many authors have embarked into it, but a specific research about the consolidation of this discourse shows that it has been popularised first by Amitai Etzioni in two books, which later on will have a strong impact on the way other initiatives, as for example the responsibility to protect, will be reframed after 2001 by the main state actors. The current Obama administration is certainly one of the archetypes of this "life" argument, which goes beyond the traditional idea of state survival and follows the Etzioni's frame. In "How patriotic is the Patriot act" Amitai Etzioni explains that he wants to present the necessity to go beyond a discussion around liberty and security after September 11 opposing the liberals and the realists (2004). For him, this discussion is irrelevant under the new "conditions" of global terrorism. He pleads for what he describes as "the search of *new standards* concerning reasonable and unreasonable judgement and decisions after acts of violence like the one of September 11." He critically discusses the measures of increased surveillance inside the US and marginally the justification of war in Iraq and Afghanistan to see the proportionality and reasonableness of the "answers" both from efficiency and legitimacy points of view. For him, the answer is clear. The Bush administration has been wrong strategically and even morally, because the administration was still conducted by a cold war, selfish state mentality and has dismissed the international. But the Bush administration has addressed a key question that the allies in Europe and Canada did not dare to evoke. The survival of the *human species* facing nuclear terrorism supposes that security comes first, not individual freedoms. Liberalism has to adjust to the new situation of danger. The title of his second book "Security first: for a muscular, moral foreign policy" insists on this new moral for new times (2007). Here, also he is not meagre on criticising the way the Bush administration conducted the first five years of the war on terror and especially the Iraqi part of it, but he wants to save the overall strategy of preventive actions, and accepts the reasoning and technology of risk analysis, which may target suspects of terrorism, without giving them their full rights. As he says, "Security drives democracy, while democracy does not beget security" (2007, IX). The security first argument is based on the primacy of life at the global level (2007, XV). So, security cannot refer, "as followers of narrow realism might have it, only on the security of the United States and its allies. The primacy of life principle places a responsibility on the major powers, not only to ensure basic security to their own people, but also to contribute to the basic security of *other* peoples." It breaks out with the sovereignty of states principle and considers intervention justified when it is possible to answer positively on moral ground to the question: when is it okay to bomb or invade someone else's homeland (2007, 193)?

Arguing that sovereignty as responsibility is the new pattern along the lines of what Deng tried to suggest in 1996 at the UN, Amitai Etzioni proposes that the sovereign state which does not fulfil its obligations can be disciplined by the other states. *The responsibility to protect is then the responsibility to intervene.* Violations of human rights, especially in case of genocide or massive war crimes, are an obvious case. But he insists, the second one is the risk of nuclear terrorism. In both cases, it is necessary, in order to be consistent, to act *before* the crime happens "in a form of war against humanity," even if it may imply a preventive punishment for an act not yet accomplished. *It is the third responsibility, which ensures the first two*, to be different from lip services: *the duty to prevent.*

Security as the duty to prevent?

Those who are responsible, as managers of life, have to act by calculating the risks that the population they have in charge has to be killed, and to intervene under uncertainty, as often exact knowledge is not available, and it will take too much time to be constituted, especially if emergency exists considering the scale of the danger. The consequences of such preventive actions are left in the shadows, as it seems that *the duty to prevent may justify preventive "attacks"* against a country trying to develop a nuclear program and suspected to try to join the club of the nuclear military powers, for example either Iraq or Iran. The targeted killing of individuals suspected of terrorism by a small group of analysts of a powerful coalition of states are also evoked, but only to justify that it is too complicated to arrest and detain them. Killing is unfortunate, but one of the only solutions; drone cohorts are behind the reasoning. As we see, the duty to protect is changed (subverted) into a duty to prevent with all the consequences it implies. Preventive war and duty to protect are mixed together in this narrative of security as protection of humanity. The caveat is that the decisions have to be grounded on claims that are not coming from only one country or a group of countries if the target of the intervention denies it. The international community has to accept the claim, and this claim needs to rely on the best accurate knowledge at the time of the intervention. But, as a consensus of the international community and accurate knowledge are quite impossible to reach, it may be to a muscular leader to decide, in practice, in relying on a risk-based system of information, which is always limited. The duty to prevent goes with a probability of error greater than the previous approach in terms of answer to an act already committed, and it may create the death of some innocents, but it is the price to pay for the primacy of life globally. Some commentators have spoken about the entry into an age of bio-politics for liberal wars, which are fought in the name of peace and protection of life (Dillon and Neal 2008; Dillon and Reid 2007).

Professionals of security are often more direct in their comments and less subtle in their justifications. They consider the academic debate as too "juridical," too "normative." But they agree also with the arguments of prevention. For them, prevention is the key word to have more budget and capabilities, and to escape the previous criticism of inefficiency. If they have had the technology, then the terrorist attacks would have been prevented. In a quite paradoxical way, they have been the victims of the "peace dividend" sequence of argument. If people want to be safe, they have to pay the price, and they have to accept the uncertainty of decision-making and the specific "quality" of the reasoning of anticipation, which change the category of innocence and suspicion. In the same way, some professionals of politics jump to the end of the reasoning concerning responsibility. They do not believe in a responsible international community, but they believe that they are "muscular" and that they have knowledge. Attacks by drones by cyber space are considered as a means to gather intelligence and to "answer" in real time, achieving a real duty to prevent and protect. Intrusive intelligence gathering is also possible. Civil liberties and religious minorities NGOs may be considered as allies of the "suspected" terrorists, and at the very least they may have their assets frozen in order to limit their support. The arrival of the Obama administration has been framed through this more "friendly" international community agenda on the surface, while maintaining the muscular side of US politics. That security creates insecurity by choosing who is to be protected and who is to be targeted, which is forgotten in this narrative by both sides; that a small part of the targeted could mobilise and engage in physical violence because of this targeting, thus creating more insecurity, is also forgotten. And it is as if all the lessons of the cold war about escalation and de-escalation don't apply to the new context. The escalation of counter-terrorism is called struggle against radicalisation, and radicalisation is perceived as a pure ideological move where the other self-radicalised himself. It has nothing to do with a "relation" between counter terrorist policy and the next process of recruitment of clandestine organisations. It has nothing to do with this "preventive" dimension.

As with many "ultra solutions," the lessons learned have been to expand the agenda of prevention, instead of recognising its failures (Watzlawick 1988). The case for a common struggle against global terrorism has been expanded to struggles against organised crime and so-called illegal migration and trafficking. The European Union and the US Obama administration have seen the narrative of security as the protection of humanity through the duty to prevent a superb way to "reconcile;" the ambiguity of the terminologies has been even more exacerbated. But the most important argument on both sides has always been to explain that "cooperation" (even if asymmetrical) is the only possible answer. Global cooperation between security intelligence networks have to work efficiently and have to overcome national interests, because no one state alone can assure its own security. Insecurity is not only a question of nuclear terrorism; this is only the tip of the iceberg. Insecurity has multiple faces; they are all interconnected and they are global. Interconnections between professionals of intelligence, of police, of border guards, of military are a necessity.

The enemy: frame of understanding or form of justification for ready-made solutions?

The doxa of global insecurity: insecurity assemblage and transfer of legitimacy of preventive-coercive actions

We can analyse this previous reasoning as a form of *doxa* in Bourdieuian terms (Bourdieu 1980). September 11, 2001 is seen as the proof of the truth of this narrative about the emergence of a global (in)security by the different groups in competition for assessing the "meaning of the international world," be they professionals of politics, of security or experts from academia. The "classics," as we have called the network of traditional realists, responsible of borders, and the national security strategists, insist on the freedom for the great powers to lead a coalition of the willing; to the contrary, the "neo-moderns," regrouping the humanitarian-military-development nexus, part of the intelligence services, the networks of counter-terrorist professionals, are challenging the "classics" about the necessity of a global coordination for a global security agenda, but they *all* accept that global insecurity is the truth of the contemporary world and that prevention is the solution (Bigo and

Tsoukala 2008). It is important here to insist that all the professionals of security tend to present this agreement, not as a consensus but as evidence, coming from their expertise and inner knowledge, but this assertion has to be challenged. Both classics and neo-moderns have no serious argument concerning the radical transformation of the enemy and the nature of conflicts; it is just a "feeling," a "regression towards the habitus," concerning the end of certainty about the rules of the game and a ready-made justification for using technological solutions conceived under a different frame, as if they were adapted and even conceived for this "new" enemy (Bigo 1994).

This has become the *epitome* (the condensed version of a sacred text) of the dogma of global (in)security and its necessary answer: duty to prevent (Dal lago and Palidda 2010). Deconstructing discourses that trace the origin and spread of the globalization of (in)security from the events of September 11 is important, but it is not enough to dissolve them. What is necessary is to understand that these practices, encapsulated in the duty to prevent, are linked to the rise of transnational guilds of experts of security, who are more and more having the last word over the truth concerning the evaluation of the future dangers and the construction of categories of danger and desirability, and who have common interests in developing this frame of global insecurity as "evidence," as a "fact." Of course, if they have succeeded, it is not because they are all allies in a Machiavellian plot against liberties. It is because they competed for their preferred cause to be given priority, whether this cause be terrorism, organised crime, natural catastrophes or the threat of a pandemic, and because simultaneously they all shared the idea of a global insecurity that must be prevented at all costs. It is in this sense that we can speak of a transnational field of security professionals opposing different professional guilds (police, military, intelligence, customs, security and insurance industry, software and data base provider) attracted by the stake of predicting the future of insecurity. The more conventional inheritors of the cold war legacy are better attached to national sovereignty, border controls, specific human knowledge and ground field practices. The pretenders, the children of the end of bipolarity and the mass development of surveillance technologies privileged the argument of the global traceability of threat and the anticipation of action through prediction software. The trajectory of the last thirty years shows the slow progress of the pretenders and depicts the "neo-moderns" progressively occupying key positions. This is done by dismissing the old-fashioned security thinking and by violently attacking the liberal democratic agenda. They have succeeded by connecting the dots between local heterogeneous insecurities, as if they were the signifiers of a global polymorphic insecurity.

In that sense, the duty to prevent is not a consequence of September 11. It is important to understand the current conjuncture in terms of how narratives have come together from the Iranian revolution in 1979, to the end of the Cold War in 1990, to the fear of illegal migrants in the beginning of the 1980s, and to the fear of local terrorism back in the mid-1960s - how they have merged with the discourses of non-territorial threats (called also a-geographical, transnational, cyber, neither inside nor outside, transversal, global and virtual threats), and finally how they have created the possibility of shifting from one threat to another. It seems as if they are now all aspects of the same generalised insecurity, but for a long time they were independent narratives. Along with the emergence of global networks, these narratives form what I call, following Latour, an *"(in)security assemblage"* (in preference to my previous formulation, "insecurity continuum") (2007; Bigo 1996; Bigo 2011). This assemblage creates the conditions for diverse agencies to extend their operations and to *transfer the legitimacy of their original missions to other domains and scales*: the police go abroad, the military operates inside territorial borders and intelligence services exchange personal data across borders all over the world. Public and private agents work together, creating para-private organisations. The temporary alliances that emerge are the result of the competition that exists between different agencies, each of which considers that what is at stake concerning (in)security is vital. Different agents understand their actions as a response to violence and insecurity whose scale is now "global."

To mobilize the population behind the security agenda (the struggle against global insecurity), it is central to reframe the strategy and to give the enemy different names in order to justify the changes. These two last points are central to understanding the nature of the transformations in contemporary security: reframing the enemy's image is not the point of departure from reality, as shown by the changes in war tactics and by crime evolution, rather, it is the result of transnational guilds of security professionals' various activities and of the de-differentiation of internal and external activities by the military, the police and the intelligence and surveillance industries. The multiple heterogeneous forms of enmities have evolved, but are not the root cause of the transformation of the security field in the Western world. Instead, they are its justification for globalisation.

The paradox of the global enemy from within:
the stealth enemy

However, this "global" security strategy, justified in the name of humanity by its duty to prevent, creates more insecurity than the traditional national strategies. The enemy is no longer a citizen of another state. He is a human, but denied of being such. Instead, he is abnormalised as a deficient human being (irrational, self-radicalised). Unfortunately, he is powerful, as he is everywhere in this globalised world, and he may be hidden among us. Proactive technologies are the only solution for an accurate detection. Surveillance has to computerise and mine data; they must trace patterns and trajectories, must turn the future into the past, as, in the present, no obvious feature exists to spot and differentiate him.

It is not so much the fact that foreigners have been considered as potential enemies after September 11 which is surprising, but more the way this Otherness has been portrayed through private beliefs concerning religion, irrationality, and hatred. The issues of spying, of traitors, of infiltrated enemies are always quite contemporaneous to popular mobilisation campaigns of ultra-patriotism. Nevertheless, in previous moments (First and Second World Wars, Red Scares, McCarthyism, the Cold War, etc.), one was associating this issue of enmity with an undercover war amongst a small number of professionals, concerning ideology, territory, and politics. When the foreigner was targeted as an enemy, it was because he belonged to other governments or to different political regimes. After 2001 and the September 14 Declaration of War on Terror, it is mainly because of his personal profile or his religious beliefs. Otherness is individualised and globalised simultaneously. The enemy is as much private as public. Carl Schmitt is not followed at all, he is forgotten, and with him the distinction between theology and politics.

The world was dangerous mainly because of a human strategy connected with an ideology and with interests, not because of private evil behaviours. However, it seems as if the religious discourse of evil that Christianity had put away with its modernization is coming back, supported by beliefs and by the interests of some political leaders to answer in a very mimetic way to their adversaries. As Michael Rogin, specialist of McCarthyism, reminded us ironically: "it was a long time that the US has not such a powerful enemy if now the US attacks the devil itself and engages into a war against evil" (Rogin 2002). His irony fell short: more and more people answer to polls that they feel that "evil" is surrounding them and that Armageddon is approaching. Some media have made the connection between this feeling of religious unease and the success of Harry Potter, whose sales reach the scale of the Bible, by suggesting that J. K. Rowlings had anticipated a profound desire of a global (but mainly Western) population to be reassured that the fight between good and evil would be difficult, but that good would triumph anyway (Harry Potter and International Relations 2009). The Rumsfeld theology of the Unknown Unknown is now taken seriously in academic books as if he had captured with this phrase the "essence" of the new characteristics of the enemy. But are these characteristics signs of the transformation of conflicts or of a paranoid form of international politics, expanding throughout the world what was previously seen as specifically "American?" How to make sense of this framing of the enemy? Do we have to believe that the nature of conflicts radically changed in 2001? Or is this enemy a "commodified" enemy justifying ready-made solutions?

The idea that the "global" enemy is locally among "us" has changed the way conflict is analysed and constructed. The international war paradigm certainly continues for some distant geographical conflict. Nonetheless, the colonial, counter-insurgency « pacification » paradigm has been reactivated, with the particularity that the counter-insurgency is now geographically relocated into the « heart » of different metropolises (this is the reason the New York World Trade Cente, more than the Washington Pentagon, has been selected to encapsulate the epitome of the narrative, and later on why cosmopolitan London has exceeded Madrid). The enemy among us (different from the enemy within) has created a parallel with previous juridical notions of treason, but this time in a war read as a "global civil war." It has enacted the idea that *suspicion is legitimate* as the enemy is a « covert » enemy, an enemy which does not deserve to be considered as a honourable adversary, a combatant (Begg 2006; Bigo 2005; Bonelli 2005; Cole 2002; Cole 2003; MacLeod and Racicot 2001; Murray and Cowden 1999; Schulhofer 2002; Walker 2008).

Even more importantly, the danger is such that waiting for evidence of the action is not possible anymore. Prevention is enacted as an act before the other acts. It is a temporal move based on the belief that the future can be read as the past, and that it is possible to predict the culpability of a human being before he has acted. I have called this move the dream of the "future perfect" (futur antérieur), where by accumulation of knowledge through data mining, elaboration of algorithms, discovery of patterns and the setting of profiles of risk, the security professionals think that they can allocate a sufficient degree of certainty to a human action in order to consider they can hit or detain first without being illegitimate in being the one attacking. This distortion of time is central to justifying prevention and has to be constructed under the image of the enemy as global and individual, as an "enemy alien" and not a real combatant, already guilty even if he has not yet attacked. The terminologies of preparedness, of signals, of early warnings, of virtual dangers try to fill the gap. The global enemy is nowhere, not detectable, stealthy like the X117 stealth planes, but he is everywhere, already there, already planning the next attack. He has a face but this face is polymorphic and always changing (Dobson, Huysans and Prokhovnik 2006). We may know, but "too late." Speed in the circuit of information is of vital importance. Speed is life, life is speed. The Total Information Awareness of the Vice-Admiral Pointdexter (hereafter referred to as "TIA") is the equivalent of the Jeremy Bentham's Panopticon for the 21st century, but speed and anticipation are replacing the eye on the overall territory (Belasco 2003). The TIA is the dream and the goal of the neo-modern transatlantic guild and the result of the argument of the duty to prevent. With this, they challenge less their official adversaries than their own political professionals concerning who has the authority to pronounce the last word in the assessment of truth about future threats.

George Bush, Tony Blair and at an even larger scale, José María Aznar, put their legitimacy at stake when they pretended to have better knowledge than their security professionals. They were in part victims of the strength of the transversal and transnational networks that intelligence services could mobilise if necessary. The nuclear arms in Iraq, the dodgy dossier of the 30 minutes attacks and the so-called yellow cake of Niger, the death of the nuclear scientist in the UK and the responsibility attributed to ETA in the Madrid attacks have been all challenging for the political professionalsand have shown the tensions between the national professionals of politics and the transnational professionals of (in)security. Certainly, the US neo-cons were the first to realise that they could not control the neo-moderns of the professionals of security, even if they were sharing some risk, especially concerning the quasi-theological argument of the possible unknown of the unknown in terms of threat of nuclear terrorism. They saw how the US professionals of security played against them, and how they resisted by giving different information than the ones of the US government to their transnational counterparts. Jacques Chirac and Dominique de Villepin took advantage of it. But it can be said that, beyond this rift concerning Iraq, in Europe it was mainly after Madrid, on March 11, 2004 and especially after the London bombings on the 7 July, 2005, that the argument which advanced that security was about proactive action, preventive logic and profiling techniques was developed and once again justified a change in the way of policing.

Far from being stabilised, the image of the global enemy has evolved from the infiltrated religious enemy of September 11 and the resonating Islamophobia to the undetectable enemy already inside, home-grown and self-radicalised of post London July 5. Of course, the anthrax scare had already given a sense of enemy among us to the events of September 11, but it is clear that the silencing of this aspect of anthrax has been one of the most important successes of the US government to control the situation internally. The government management of (in)security did not go along that road of generalised suspicion of everyone, including all Americans and including their governmental elites. The lessons of McCarthyism had been learned: they focused on "undetectable," but "visible" (recognizable) enemies. In London, people acting violently were no foreigners having recently infiltrated the territory; they were "home-grown" and surveillance had to take a new step. Sealing the borders was seen as fully irrelevant this time, and the classics were under pressure. The strategy of the neo-moderns was to "seal the future," to determine the worst-case scenarios and to anticipate who had to be put under surveillance by the "science of risk management and profiling." Counter-terrorism truly became an omnipresent issue in the UK, but also in Germany and France. Discourses after 2005 connected terrorism with the radicalisation of "hyphenated citizens," not so much with borders and migration. The intelligence services guilds were taking over the border guards and the homeland security guilds (Bigo and Delmas-Marty 2012). The discourses were about culture, minorities, and integration seen as a path to homogenisation. Internal security came to be seen as a part of every problem facing the Union (terrorism but also crime, illegal immigration, unauthorised border crossings, falsified documents and in fine ways of life and ways of thinking), requiring dangers to be listed and specific techniques to be employed (in particular, searches in data bases which were set up for other purposes, establishment of categories of profiles and of lists of persons to be put under surveillance and sometimes banned from entering a country they had never been to). Under this trend, issues of movement, tourism, migration and asylum have been linked not only to detective police activities, but also to intelligence or even to military issues. *The everyday life has been strategized.* Wearing a veil is seen as a "military" provocation of an invisible enemy or a stealth enemy hiding, having decided to fight "globally" and "in each local place." The de-differentiation between internal and external (in)securities has been put in place with the idea that internal security agencies, which may at times work outside the borders of a country to prevent threats, must cooperate with neighbouring countries to "connect the dots," and that they have to *fusion* their information with military intelligence.

"Fighting," but how? Spotting, identification and selection through profiling more than combat: the rise of "intelligence" between police and army

The task is then less to combat as an Army force and more to police and do intelligence work, in other words, to search for unknown actors, to identify patterns permitting to select categories of individuals possibly belonging to the potential enemies inside the territory and to prevent their actions before they can act. The characteristic of Otherness has to be discovered because the enemy hides it.

It is not Aunt Julie we search for, said Ashcroft, and Obama logic has reinforced the *limited scope of search*. It is not massive stop and search. It is *selective tracing through massive information gathering, intelligence and surveillance with limited controls and arrest*. The question that remains is how to do this, how to select the categories of individuals that need to be put under more severe and intrusive (so labour-intensive work for the agencies) surveillance? Who is "infiltrated into the territory, but nevertheless unknown," who is a "sleeping agent" of a new kind, a "sleeping agent of a non-state actor?" (Ashcroft and Mueller 2001; Brown 2003).

The "classics" inside the professionals of (in)security management often do not like the politics of fear and scapegoating developed by some of the professionals of politics and their pretenders. They don't like the idea of a radically new situation. They don't like ethnic profiling. *What they like is* the possibility, the opportunity given to them to use their tools and *their technologies without traditional limitations*, such as the presumption of innocence, of privacy, data protection and freedom of speech and movement, which are usually protected through judicial control.

In that, they are often more direct in their comments. Some political professionals have often threatened the civil liberties of religious minorities and certain NGOs by treating them like allies of "the terrorists," by using "unselected targets," "by casting the net too far and too large" and by exacerbating tensions within some communities instead of pushing them to collaborate. They often share the view of some NGOs and are strange bedfellows, insisting for a more specific and narrow form of surveillance and control. *They are often the first to give a discourse "balancing" liberty and security. But this discourse is not a "liberal" discourse in the sense of libertarian discourse; it is another form of justification that the European Union has developed more than the US.*

Balancing liberty and security: a metaphor that has political effects

Balancing: a critique of a right of exception?

At times, while addressing the discourse according to which "security goes first," a large group of academics, NGOs and "enlightened" professionals of security have insisted on the exaggeration inherent to "the novelty discourse" and of the threat of WMD terrorism after September 11. They have alluded to the necessity to address the debate from the perspective of democracy and have warned that a "maximum security" argument will actually succeed in destroying the very democratic principles that are to be protected in the first place. These voices have also insisted on the need to consider democracy and individual freedoms as the main objectives and premises of life and have asserted that security measures and practices must not endanger liberal democratic principles in order to avoid falling into a totalitarian or a surveillance state. Instead, one of the predominant arguments that have been more often used is that of the balance between security and liberty, especially in the debates between different national parliaments in Europe. The focus has been put in ascertaining what amount of additional security is necessary to preserve liberty more than a discussion about war powers.

How far or to what extent can this necessary "additional security" infringe individual freedoms (Cannistraro 2003; Darmer, Rosenbaum and Baird 2005; Den Boer and Monar 2002)? Does the state have the right to argue about danger, risk and emergency in order to use exceptional measures for "exceptional times" and to pass emergency legislations? Is it legitimate to adjust the "balance" between fundamental freedoms and security in a context of major global threat? What freedoms can be limited and which ones cannot because of their centrality to democracy? Are the rights to life and protection against torture so absolute that no worst-case scenario can infringe them? (Bigo et al. 2010)

There, the argument mostly regarded as critical of a theory concerning wartime, or concerning the necessity of a permanent exception and a reframing of the constitution and the rules through exceptional measures, has been expressed as the need to find "the right balance between liberty and security" and to develop "proportionality," but is this a coherent argument?

The balance metaphor: a dead-end argument

The way to frame the discussion between security and liberty was to present the situation as if a balance existed with two (and only two) scales of similar values to consider: freedom and security. The balance supposes that liberty and security are "eternal values," that they are easily differentiable, quasi-quantifiable and homogeneous. It is in fact "uncritical": the balance metaphor masks the imbalance that exists between the two dimensions and silences the capacity of political judgement. It has been often used as a bureaucratic argument in different historical periods as well as by many academics. As the CHALLENGE project has showed, it has been one of the most powerful discursive tools at times of limiting the discussions around liberty after September 11, 2001 (Bigo et al. 2010).

First, it is clear that some of the authors who have used the balance metaphor had a rhetorical strategy in mind. By using the term freedom – understood as a series of freedoms in competition – instead of the general principle of liberty, they have actually unified the concept of security and fragmented that of freedom. Simultaneously, they have referred to the term of security in relation to all the practices of war, coercion and protection, both in their collective and individual meanings and in their internal and external facets. Their reasoning leads to the fragmentation of liberty, considered mainly at the individual level, and to the reunification of security, aggregated to safety, protection and to survival, considered both "global" and "personal," intimate. The consequence of this framing is that security needs to trump liberty, because, in fact, security may become freedom itself, the first freedom, which is the freedom from fear to live.

The second implication, more structural, of the framing of a unified security and a fragmented liberty is that danger becomes central. The balance metaphor transforms the dual relationship between liberty and security into a triangle where security needs to be enhanced against liberty because of the eventuality of risk, danger and threat. In this triangular setting between danger, liberty and security, liberty becomes the problem. The main political actors have insisted on the need for security to be completed, to become global, to be developed beyond traditional cooperation and to become the marker of identity of "the civilized values" against "the barbarian ones." However, this claim for a global security agenda is re-engaged with total information awareness, where security is once again without limits, other than some bits of individual privacy. The cursor of the balance has changed. Global trumps local and individual; the protection of humanity justifies sacrifices of some individual rights. To find an adequate balance between security and liberty is transformed into an obligation to choose the "lesser evil."

Michael Ignatieff, using this argument, ended up trying to justify lesser forms of evil by arguing about the acceptable lower limits of coercion, whereas Dershowitz was discussing the special timing and conditions to use torture (Dershowitz 2002; Ignatieff 2004). Here, the notion of balance shows its limitations. The neutralisation of the primacy of freedom and democracy in the name of another value, "security," becomes prevalent, even in the critique.

Is proportionality an error of reasoning? The "techniques" of neutralisation of political judgement

If liberty is a goal advanced by any liberal regime, is security a goal too or just a means to achieve freedom and democracy? This question has not emerged in public debates and discourses. It has been very rare to find any framing of "the balance" into a triangle between liberty, security and democracy. The reason might be that from this perspective, security becomes the problem, not the solution. The balance metaphor has been a way to avoid discussing the relationship between liberty, security and democracy. By choosing freedom (instead of democracy) to frame the discussion, the balance metaphor silences the difficulty to have proper judgement about the most important problem of political violence between adversaries: escalation of violence on both sides.

The balance metaphor transforms a political judgement into a series of techniques that bureaucracies can use. Security and freedom are instrumentalised and transformed into sheets for accountants. Prejudices are drawn into science and technology and "laundered" (money laundering) in order to become results of these techniques and not initial inputs.

The professionals of (in)security love the idea of "balance" and for them this neutrality can be achieved through "technology," especially mass gathering of information and proper filter software that can sort out categories of cases to analyse more in detail. They dream of a rational choice approach which can be proportionate or, in other words, able to assess the good and the bad with a detached and neutral point of view, a depoliticized one. Some professional judges share this idea about neutral techniques: they view Law as a field where these techniques can be used. They put their faith in human reasoning and in the rule of Law more than in a computer, but it is the very same base of reasoning.

Once the debate about the best techniques is started, the judges and lawyers find themselves more or less isolated by insisting on human resources and reasoning, as the other bureaucracies public and private prefer more "productive" techniques. The policemen and especially the intelligence services, including the private companies of profiling software, prefer new high-tech algorithms for their software and new platforms for integrating data. It is a useful segment of a productive market, unlike the technique preferred by the judges.

For the "modern" bureaucracies, in tune with advanced capitalism, the idea is that neutral techniques (interoperable databases and behavioural assessment profiles) will filter in their stead the categories of people likely to be wrongdoers (terrorist, criminals, traffickers, illegal migrants or tax defrauders). These techniques will simultaneously identify the large majority of benevolent people, the bona fide, the trusted ones, that, after having gathered their information, can avoid being searched and put under surveillance. At the transnational scale, a majority of these professionals rely more and more on large data bases, interoperable, which can trace the profile of individuals and associate them with statistical records of previous offenders in order to judge their possible future behaviour. They see this actuarial process as science, statistical knowledge with low levels of errors (false positives and false negatives). They are shocked if people see their actions as ethnic profiling or discriminatory policies against a whole population. They consider that if they look at a specific category, it is because this category presents the highest proportion of offenders and shows a higher risk for their brothers, their kin, to be like them: potential offenders. The profile is not responsible of the result, they say. It has not been created against a category as such and is therefore not dangerous. It protects the individual, it saves time and money by anticipating who can be dangerous, and it permits the other trusted travellers to feel free and travel easily.

Technology, neutrality, and future human behaviour

One key question that remains is concerning this belief in technology and software. Could we monitor the future of human beings by correlating behavioural patterns supposedly shared with other human beings? Would this not be the negation of the singularity of each human being? Would preventing crimes by classifying people in various categories of already suspicious individuals, created through data mining and data retention, not be the opposite of criminal justice logic? I have developed in many texts this idea of monitoring the future as a future perfect, as a "future antérieur," as a future that is already known, under the logic of the worst-case scenario or of the logic of the worst possible vulnerability and its lack of philosophical grounds. Risk-management discourse is now more in favour than ever, after the limits of the worst-case scenario discourse of nuclear terrorism failed to sustain such a politics by itself. It works along the same lines. Risk-management discourse asserts that it is possible to anticipate risk through technology and that human beings are "reproducible machines." They are "information packets" that can be disassociated and re-associated. They are similar to their "data doubles." This anthropology of humanity has effects on the reframing of the notion of freedom.

It seems that the IR literature has mainly been focused on discussions about security, risk and exception and – marginally – on their consequences on freedom, but not so much on freedom itself. Indeed, the question of what we mean by freedom – or by liberty – has been left so far unquestioned. This is evidenced by the fact that while there are several security studies, and even critical security studies, there are no "liberty studies."

What I would want to encourage is the development of "liberty studies" in the so-called global realm, in the study of the international, in the world today, taking into account the frame of a "global security" discourse and one of "freedom of a community of people," of the free men (versus the "unfree"). It is an intellectual project, but that has policy consequences too; a critical reflection about freedom becomes especially crucial when taking into account how the current Obama administration is criticizing "exceptionalism," but is continuing with the same argument about freedom than the Bush administration.

Freedom as a « property » possessed by a group

In his popular book *Whose Freedom?*, Lakoff argues that the main strategy of the radical right in the US was not to develop an "exceptionalist agenda," but rather to reframe the notion of freedom, which was why these measures had such success (2006). However, it is possible that the radical right may not be solely responsible for this realization. It seems that liberty has been reframed by eradicating its linkages with equality, solidarity and social justice, and by emphasizing its links with human rights, civilization, protection of values, community security (humanity) and with the fight for freedom and for child education. Indeed, children lack clarity of judgement and are irrational, weak, sometimes violent and not yet fully human. We need to protect them for their own good, be they put under tutelage or guardianship.

In this frame, freedom ends up being "the marker" of a civilized group fighting to preserve its values and principles against the unfree, the not yet free. Freedom is then a quality possessed by advanced liberal democracies. In this cosmopolitan account, freedom exists naturally, but it needs to be enacted by education. This conception legitimates the engagement into fights and even war "for freedom" or to engage into global policing in the name of freedom. As put by a top military US commander in Afghanistan speaking at KCL:

> [W]e have to win heart and minds. So we have to inoculate them with freedom […] The perpetual peace foreseen by Kant is possible only if we succeed the contamination of the 'virus of democracy and its propagation into authoritarian regimes and failed states..

In a less bio-political metaphor, but having the same idea in mind, many governments and international organizations as well as academics have insisted that it is important to develop "education," "training," "communication" and "universalization" of freedom in order to accelerate the pace, especially when radical clandestine organizations try to reverse the trend and propose cultural enclosures. Freedom(ization) is a competition (against obscurantism). Liberty is a possession, a property of a specific group – us – that the others do not have. This line of thought refuses any constitutive theory of ethics and promotes that we judge ourselves and the others only through the prism of our criteria and standards set up as "universal" in this narrative. We can always ask ourselves the level of obedience and participation necessary for creating the possibility of such a version of freedom to be developed and to become not only an official policy, but also a shared belief amongst participants and many international institutions. Maybe, our first freedom as academics is to discuss this version of (un)freedom we call freedom.

References

Agamben, Giorgio. 2003. *État d'exception, Homo Sacer.* Paris: Éditions du Seuil.
Ashcroft, John and Robert Mueller. 2001. "Address by John Ashcroft, Attorney General of the United States, Robert Mueller, Director of the Federal Bureau of Investigations Delivered at Fbi Headquarters, Quantico, Virginia." *Vital Speeches of the Day* 67(24): 748-750.
Begg, Moazzam. 2006. *Enemy Combatant: A British Muslim's Journey to Guantanamo and Back.* London: Free Press.
Belasco, Amy. 2003. *Total Information Awareness Programs: Funding, Composition, and Oversight Issues.* Congressional Research Service Report RL31786. The Library of Congress.

Bigo, Didier. 1994. *Great Debates in a Small World. Debates in international relations and their link with the world of security.* Cultures et Conflits 19-20: 7-48.

—. 1996. *Polices En Reseaux: L'experience Europeenne.* Paris: Presses de la Fondation nationale des sciences politiques.

—. 2005. "From Foreigners to Abnormal Aliens: How the Faces of the Enemy Have Changed Following September the 11th." In *International Migration and Security. Opportunity and Challenges*, edited by Elspeth Guild and Joanne van Selme, 64-81. London: Routledge.

—. 2007. "Exception Et Ban: À Propos De L'"Etat D'exception." *Erytheis* 2: 115-145. http://idt.uab.es/erytheis/pdf/vf/3.pdf

—. 2008a. "The Emergence of a Consensus: Global Terrorism, Global Insecurity, and Global Security." In I*mmigration, Integration, and Security. America and Europe in Comparative Perspective*, edited by Ariane. C. d'Apollonia and Simon Reich, 67-94. Pittsburgh: University of Pittsburgh Press.

—. 2008b. "Globalized (in)Security: The Field and the Banopticon." In *Terror, Insecurity and Liberty: Illiberal Practices of Liberal Regimes after 9/11*, edited by Didier Bigo and Anastassia Tsoukala, 10-48. London: Routledge.

—. 2011. "*Globalisation and Security.*" In *The New Blackwell Companion to Political Sociology*, edited by E. Amenta, K. Nash and A. Scott, 204-213. Blackwell: London.

Bigo, Didier, Sergio Carrera, Elspeth Guild and Rob Walker, eds. 2010. *Europe's 21st Century Challenge: Delivering Liberty and Security.* London: Ashgate.

Bigo, Didier and Mireille Delmas-Marty. 2013. "Prédiction Et Prévention : Conversation." In *Circulation internationale de l'information et sécurité*, edited by E. Mitjans and K. Benyekhlef, 81-95. Editions Thémis: Montréal.

Bigo, Didier and Anastassia Tsoukala, eds. 2008. *Terror, Insecurity and Liberty. Illiberal Practices of Liberal Regimes after 9/11.* Oxon: Routledge.

Blair, Tony. 2003. "Entretien avec Tony Blair: pourquoi il faut agir aux côtés de l'Amérique." *Le Monde.* July 8.

—. "Speech on the threat of global terrorism." Accessed by October 10, 2011. http://www.guardian.co.uk/politics/2004/mar/05/iraq.iraq

Bonelli, Laurent. 2005. "The Control of the Enemy Within ? Police Intelligence in the French Banlieues." In *Controlling Frontiers: Free Movement into and within Europe*, edited by Didier Bigo and Elspeth Guild, 193-208. London: Ashgate.

Bourdieu, Pierre. 1980. *Le Sens Pratique*. Paris: Éditions de Minuit.
Brown, Cynthia, ed. 2003. *Lost Liberties. Ashcroft and the Assault on Personal Freedom*. New York: New Press.
Bush, George W. 2002. "We Will Make a Stand." *Vital Speeches of the Day* 68(23): 738-741.
Cannistraro, Vincent M. 2003. "The Emerging Security Environment: Preemptive War and International Terrorism after Iraq." *Mediterranean Quarterly* 14(4): 56-67.
Coker, Christopher. 2002. "Globalisation and Insecurity in the Twenty-First Century: Nato and the Management of Risk." *Adelphi Papers* 345(June): p. 7-103.
Cole, David. 2002. "Enemy Aliens." *Stanford Law Review* 54(5): 953-1005.
—. 2003. *Enemy Aliens. Double Standards and Constitutional Freedoms in the War on Terrorism*. New York: New Press.
Dal Lago, Alessandro and Salvatore Palidda, eds. 2010. *Conflict, Security and the Reshaping of Society: The Civilisation of War*. Oxon: Routledge.
Darmer, M.Katherine B., Stuart E. Rosenbaum and Robert M. Baird, eds. 2005. *Civil Liberties Vs. National Security in a Post-9/11 World*. Amherst: Prometheus Books.
Den Boer, Monica and Jörg Monar. 2002. "11 September and the Challenge of Global Terrorism to the Eu as a Security Actor." *Journal of Common Market Studies* 40: 11-28.
Dillon, Michael and Andrew W. Neal, eds. 2008. *Foucault on Politics, Security and War*. New York: Palgrave Macmillan.
Dillon, Michael and Julian Reid. 2009. *The Liberal Way of War: Killing to Make Life Live: The Martial Face of Global Biopolitics*. Oxon: Routledge.
Dobson, Andrew, Jef Huysmans and Raia Prokhovnik, eds. 2006. *The Politics of Protection. Sites of Insecurity and Political Agency*. Oxon: Routledge.
Etzioni, Amitai. 2004. *How Patriotic Is the Patriot Act? Freedom Versus Security in the Age of Terrorism*. London: Routledge.
—. 2007. *Security First. For a Muscular, Moral Foreign Policy*. New Haven : Yale University Press.
Gips, Michael A. 2003. "When Attendees May Be Terrorists." *Security Management* 47(3): 16-18.
Harris, Shane. 2002. "Detecting the Threat." *Government Executive* 34(10): p. 51-58.

Hoffmann, Stanley. 2002. "Clash of Globalizations." *Foreign Affairs* 81(4): 104-115.

Lakoff, George. 2006. *Whose Freedom?: The Battle over America's Most Important Idea.* New York: Farrar, Straus and Giroux.

Lamm, Richard D. 2002. "Terrorism and Immigration: We Need a Border." *Vital Speeches of the Day* 68(10): 298-300.

Latour, Bruno. 2007. *Reassembling the Social: An Introduction to Actor-Network-Theory.* Gosport: Oxford University Press.

MacLeod, A. and J.-P. Racicot, "Where's the Enemy? Security and Identity in Post-Cold War North America". Paper presented at the Colloquium CERI "Does the State Still Manage Security?", Paris, 11-13 September, 2001.

Murray, Shoon K. and Jonathan A. Cowden. 1999. "The Role of 'Enemy Images' and Ideology in Elite Belief Systems." *International studies quarterly* 43(3): 455-481.

Rogin, M.P., (2002), *The War on Evil*, in partly reproduced in *Le Monde* 11 September.

Schulhofer, Stephen J. 2002. *The Enemy Within : Intelligence Gathering, Law Enforcement, and Civil Liberties in the Wake of September 11.* New York: Century Foundation Press.

Schultz, Richard H. and Andreas Vogt. 2003. "It's War! Fighting Post-11 September Global Terrorism through a Doctrine of Preemption." *Terrorism and Political Violence* 15(1): 1-30.

Tenet, George J. 2002. "Worldwide Threat: Converging Dangers in a Post 9/11 World." *Vital Speeches of the Day* 68(10): 290-298.

Walker, Clive. 2008. "Know Thine Enemy as Thyself: Discerning Friend from Foe under Anti-Terrorism Laws." *Melbourne University Law Review* 32(1): 275-301.

Watzlawick, Paul. 1988. *Comment Réussir À Échouer. Trouver L'ultrasolution.* Paris: Seuil.

CHAPTER TWELVE

PROTECTING MIGRANTS' RIGHTS: UNDOCUMENTED MIGRANTS AS LOCAL CITIZENS[*]

FRANÇOIS CRÉPEAU[1]

Politicians adopt contradictory discourses about irregular migrants depending on the audience they are addressing. To conservative voters and security agencies, they toe the "law and order" line and vow to expel these "criminals." To employers' associations, they promise to recruit the labour force needed in our economy. To social workers and NGOs, they insist on the dignity and rights of individuals.

Stephen Legomsky (2009) has shown how these varying discourses give rise to two opposing views of irregular migrants. The first image is of hordes of faceless "illegal" migrants, intent on taking jobs from worthy citizens and engaging in dangerous criminal activities. The insecurity thus created must be firmly repressed through detention and deportation. The second typically takes the form of individual stories, giving migrants an identity and a voice. It insists that irregular migration is a crime neither against persons, nor against property, noting that irregular migrants perform tasks that citizens don't want to do. Hence they should be given a chance to gain access to residence and citizenship.

It is in this second category that this article fits, namely that of a humane approach to irregular migration. Although States retain the power to decide who can enter and reside in their territory, there are democratic bodies within the State that may not want to include immigration status as a relevant criterion to define their constituency.

Why should this be? The answer is based on four points: The first is that, as migration is a constant of civilization, we are all migrants. Secondly, we have witnessed, over the past thirty years, the passage from

---

[*] This paper was previously published in *Inroads* 27 (2010) : 70-79.

irregular migration as a social phenomenon that responded to the economic needs of post-war growth to its construction as a threat to national security. Nevertheless, third, migrants do have rights and the respect, protection and promotion of the rights of migrants and how they compare to the rights of citizens is the next frontier in the development of human rights policies. As a result, finally, at least locally, we may need to reconceptualise citizenship and residence, in order to recognise everyone's human dignity over and above their administrative statuses.

We are all migrants

Migration as a complex phenomenon

Migration is a complex phenomenon that defies caricature. It is a constant of civilization: the history of humanity is that of an endless journey on the various continents of our planet. Over time, it is also a generational phenomenon, triggered by a huge array of political, economic and social factors that cannot meaningfully be altered by short-term politics. It is multifaceted: it may be at once an economic transfer, a vector of social transformation, a challenge to territorial sovereignty, a security concern, a clandestine phenomenon, a key to cultural pluralism, etc. It is also a personal trajectory through different social spaces: despite migration being described in terms of "flows" or "waves," we should never lose sight of the individual voicing her hopes and fears.

Humanity is on an ongoing endless journey. We have always been migrants, since our species appeared around 200,000 years ago in Africa and then colonised all continents. Migration is at the heart of many civilisations, as exemplified by the book of Exodus in the Bible, the Kadesh treaty (1275 BCE) between the Pharaoh Ramses II and the Hittites, Homer's Odyssey, the parable of the Good Samaritan in the New Testament, the Hegira in Islam, just to name a few.

Our settling on the land is recent and unstable. Nomadic populations still exist, such as the Roma. Pilgrimages remain important traditions. Rural exodus, urbanisation and seasonal agricultural work, for example, all include elements of migration. "Expats" and "snowbirds" are all migrants. And we dream of outer space.

Migrants have represented about 3 percent of the world population throughout the last century, although numbers have hugely increased, to over 210 million migrants worldwide today. Migration has always existed, from areas of poverty and violence towards regions of prosperity and stability: the first create push factors, the second pull factors. We can slow migration in the short term, but cannot stop it in the long term, as it responds to a basic human need, i.e. the ability to imagine a future for oneself and one's children. Most of us would try to migrate if faced with the choices of the 210 million.

Global North States design policies intended to control migrations in various ways. In countries like Canada, Australia and the United States, immigration policies are mainly used to realize demographic objectives. In contrast, continental European States' policies have been designed to manage unskilled foreign populations, often considered as cheap labour. But both share common policies, such as the repression of irregular migration and resurgent temporary migrant workers' schemes. These policies create spheres of vulnerability. Temporary migrant workers and irregular migrants are often left at the mercy of employers who can trigger their deportation. This is the case, for example, in Canada, for migrants who come under the seasonal agricultural workers programme or the live-in caregivers programme. This power over the migrant's life generally silences them and creates a huge potential for exploitation including sexual exploitation – a modern form of slavery (*Siliadin v. France* 2005).

Irregular migration results from the interplay of three factors: our hidden low-skilled labour migration needs, the needs of those seeking to emigrate from countries in the south, and our repressive border policies which interfere with the effective interplay of push and pull factors.

Thus, the plight of the migrant illustrates the conflict between the two basic paradigms in international law and policy. Under the traditional territorial sovereignty paradigm, the host State decides who enters and stays in the country, who is a member of the political community. But according to the more recent human rights paradigm, every person has fundamental rights that should be respected by any authority. The conflict sets States asserting their power of exclusion against migrants who try to resist through their rights.

Irregular migrants are extremely diversified

Irregular migrants do not constitute a homogeneous community. Although they used to be generally young, able-bodied, male and unskilled, this picture is changing, becoming more diversified.

The irregularity of their administrative status comes from very different sources. They may have arrived on a temporary tourist, student or migrant worker visa, and decided to stay on. They may have entered the country clandestinely either through "smuggling" rings, or using improper identity and travel documentation. The latter may be forged altogether, or "altered" (the documents are authentic but the identity is that of another person), or entirely valid but the real reason for the travel (i.e., work) has not been disclosed. They may also have been stranded while transiting through the country and trying to access another country.

Indeed, they may have been brought to the country as young infants by their parents who have remained in an irregular situation: although schooled and socialized as any other resident, they then discover as young adults that they have no status in what they consider their country. They may have been apprehended by the authorities on the day they try to enter the country or after twenty years' residence in the country. They may have founded a family, married a resident or citizen, and they may have children who are born citizens of the country. Some have achieved very successful professional lives, integrating themselves easily into the wider community, even publicly recognized for their achievements. Others will remain in the shadows, bonding mainly with fellow irregular migrants or with persons from their country of origin.

All this to say that there is not one pattern of irregular migration. If one takes the time to inquire and research, one will find very different life stories, as compelling and deserving of respect as any other.

The securitized control of migrations

In the period of post-war prosperity, irregular migration was seen as a minor cost to be paid to meet the soaring demand for unskilled labour. It was the oil crisis of 1973 that led to and justified the relative closure of Global North borders to foreign workers. Combined with an increased accessibility to international travel and communications, the number of asylum claims and later of irregular migrants soared. States reacted with a strong anti-asylum discourse and with repressive and deterrence measures against irregular migration.

Deterrence measures attempt to discourage irregular migrants from entering the country by raising the cost and diminishing the benefits of migration. They focus on reducing the entitlements offered to migrants, such as the elimination of appeals in the immigration process and restriction of access to legal aid, labour market and social protection. Migrant smuggling is increasingly criminalised. States resort more to international agreements to facilitate the return of undesirable migrants. In addition, migrants face increased detention (Migreurop 2009). *Preventive measures* are designed to impede the arrival of irregular migrants on "our" territory altogether in order to avoid the possible intervention of NGOs, lawyers, politicians or journalists to fight deportations, since none of these actors will intervene in favour of someone who is maintained abroad. Measures include visa regimes, among which the visa obligation for Mexican and Czech nationals is the most recent Canadian example, an obligation directly triggered by the rise in the number of asylum claims from these two countries. There are also carrier sanctions (fines imposed on transportation companies for bringing foreign individuals without appropriate documentation), the effect of which is a partial privatisation of migration controls. States also resort to interception mechanisms abroad in order to prevent irregular migration: Canada has deployed "migration integrity officers" abroad.

Immigration intelligence is widely shared without effective control on access to the personal information found on such databases. International economic cooperation arrangements – such as the Barcelona Process in the Mediterranean, the Puebla process for Central America or the EU-ACP development agreements – nowadays all contain chapters obliging countries in the Global South to implement migration control mechanisms that "protect" the Global North. Borders and seas are militarized: Guantanamo during the '90s was used to "warehouse" Haitians picked up on the high seas before returning them home; the enduring Pacific Solution in Australia has applied the same mechanism towards migrants coming through Indonesia; the European Frontex agency is patrolling the Mediterranean to the same end. European countries have discussed the idea of an "externalisation" of asylum procedures, which would only take place abroad, in such countries as Libya, Morocco, Albania and Mauritania (Lutterbeck 2006, 69; Huguenet 2004).

All in all, States are increasingly coordinating efforts to set within a coherently articulated strategy their arsenal of measures for preventing irregular movements of persons, including asylum seekers and refugees, and reducing the "burden" of such migration.

These measures proceed from a transformation of the political paradigm, reflected by a new public discourse on migrants. Especially since 9/11, as well as the 2004 Madrid and 2005 London bombings, migrants are considered suspect, dangerous. More than before, they are associated with economic ills (unemployment, welfare state crisis, etc.), insecurity (inner cities, petty violence, organized crime, terrorism, etc.) and identity anxiety (demographic changes, identity markers). The "*us and them*" mentality is at work, creating discrimination and easily manipulated into hatred. Migration is now part of a new international security paradigm structured around the "securitisation of the public space" (water security, food security, energy security, communication security, environmental security, etc) (Faist 2004).

But is it justified? Irregular entry is not a crime against persons or against property: it is essentially the crossing of a virtual line in the sand, which hurts no one in itself. Moreover, the use of smuggling rings is often the last resort, when all other avenues of protection are closed. In history, countless people have been saved by smugglers (remember the movie *Casablanca*). The large majority of irregular migrants pose no security risk (the 9/11 terrorists were not irregular migrants). Although framed as a fight against international criminality, the migration control mechanisms serve more to reassure citizens that governments are taking appropriate action, than to meaningfully increase their security.

Furthermore, measures against irregular migration are inefficient, as they never address a root cause for migration, i.e. the need for exploited labour in the Global North. The exploitation of vulnerable migrants in specific sectors of the economy (construction, agriculture, domestic workers, cleaning or catering services, for example) enhances the competitiveness of Global North economies. These "illegal employers" are an essential pull factor that is systematically forgotten in government discourse regarding irregular migration: the fact that "we" are co-responsible for the phenomenon is never mentioned (International Labour Office 2004; Global Commission on International Migration 2005).

Migrants have rights

Irregular migration is now treated as a form of "international criminality," the implication of which is that irregular migrants shouldn't be recognized any rights. Indeed, not one State of the Global North signed or ratified the 1990 *International Convention on the Protection of the Rights of All Migrant Workers and Members of Their Families*, which details the rights of all migrants.[2] Its "flaw" is to extend many of these rights to irregular migrants.

In international law, as well as in most domestic legal systems, two rights are exclusive to the citizen: the right to political participation, which means the right to vote and be elected to office, and the right to enter and remain on the territory. All other rights in principle apply equally to the foreigner and the citizen, by virtue of their common humanity. Foreigners benefit from the right to equality and to not being discriminated against on the ground of nationality. They are protected against return to face torture and arbitrary detention. Foreign children enjoy specific protections. Foreigners must have access to remedies and due process. They benefit from guarantees even in cases of national security. In Canada, according to article 1 of the *Canadian Charter of Rights and Freedoms*, a differentiation between citizens and non-citizens must be "reasonable and justifiable in a free and democratic society" (1982, art. 1-15).

This is what several tribunals have recently affirmed. The Supreme Court of Canada has curtailed the discretionary elements and the secrecy of the long-term detention without charges of persons subject to a security certificate (*Charkaoui* v. *Canada (Citizenship and Immigration)* 2007). The United States Supreme Court has progressively imposed a due process framework to the detention in Guantanamo Bay of suspects caught in the "war against terror" (*Boudemiene* v. *Bush* 2008; *Sale* v. *Haitian Centers Council 1993)*. The European Court of Human Rights has affirmed that so-called "international" zones in airports are actually national territory where human rights guarantees apply (*Amuur* v. *France* 1996). The British House of Lords has decided that indefinite detention and discriminatory practices in a foreign airport are against basic human rights guarantees (*A and others* v. *Secretary of State of the Home Department* 2004; *Regina* v. *Immigration Officer at Prague Airport* 2004).

In the end, once past the moral panic that followed 9/11, normal legal frameworks slowly reasserted themselves. Our common universal human rights framework has been established by the World War II generation. Its legacy is that law must always prevail over executive power. This was threatened by the modus operandi established for the "war on terror." It is heartening to see courts restricting the application of laws and policies that expanded executive powers against individual freedoms.

Political mobilisation must complement legal guarantees to defend human rights. The history of the 20th century showed that majorities can be wrong and that individuals and minorities must be able to defend their rights against the majority. Marginalized or vulnerable categories of people have always had to fight for their rights: industrial workers, women, aboriginals, national minorities, detainees, gays and lesbians, among others. In modern times, they had to fight through the courts, against the Executive, against Parliament, and often against a majority of public opinion. Migrants are the latest such a vulnerable group.

Who will defend them? One cannot generally expect the Executive or the Legislator to protect the rights of migrants. They are convenient scapegoats for the woes of our societies. They rarely complain and do not vote, so they are legally and politically insignificant. As nationalist populist discourse goes unopposed, public opinion is easily deflected from supporting or even taking an interest in migrants. NGOs, churches, pro bono lawyers and other concerned citizens are thus often left to carry the burden of defending their rights.

Recognising migrants' role in our societies:
Migrants as local citizens

Migrants are an integral part of the city; they should be recognized as such. They would be citizens with a small "c," as they are not nationals; but, locally, they would be considered as citizens, on an equal footing with everyone who also lives and works in the city.

Irregular migrants all work (they can't afford not to); their work contributes to the competitiveness of the economy in several sectors like agriculture, cleaning, construction or catering. They pay taxes on everything they buy or rent, and sparingly use public services. The absence of an administrative status that recognizes the whole range of their rights makes them vulnerable. Restoring a meaningful status to such persons, albeit only locally, would go a long way towards empowering them to fight exploitation and discrimination.

Examples exist of how some local communities already adopt a different attitude on vulnerable migrants. In many American cities (such as San Francisco), the police have decided to ignore immigration status in carrying out their work with fellow citizens to maintain the confidence of all segments of the population: fighting violence becomes impossible when victims or witnesses do not call the police for fear of deportation. In Toronto, all children have the right to go to school whatever the status of their parents, in conformity with a "don't ask, don't tell" policy. In Massachusetts, the State hands out driver's licences without checking immigration status, thus allowing irregular migrants to gain access to many services. In many European countries, resident European citizens can now vote at local elections; but several other jurisdictions also allow resident aliens to vote in local elections: six townships in Maryland; two towns in Massachusetts (Amherst and Cambridge); New York, Chicago and Arlington (VA) for school board elections; and New Zealand for all elections (Earnest 2003; Raskin 1993). In Quebec, the AH1N1 flu vaccination campaign of the fall of 2009 was available to all, irrespective of immigration status. In Paris, "Médecins du Monde" administers 21 medical dispensaries for irregular migrants with the cooperation of the local authorities.

These are all examples that show that a different conception of the place of vulnerable migrants in many host societies is possible. Immigration status is still an important factor at the national level and the power of States to deport migrants in irregular situations is not at issue: it is part of the present international legal regime. However, local governments (regional or municipal) can take a different stand. They don't have to act as enforcers of an immigration policy which is not theirs (for example, by interconnecting their databases to that of the immigration department). In order to appropriately focus on their own priorities (such as fostering social cohesion), they can leave it to be enforced by the immigration authorities.

The key idea is that there should not be any special status (or non-status) for migrants at local level: there would be only one status for all inhabitants of the city or local community. Any person who resides there and participates in the economic and social workings of any society should enjoy a status that allows her to benefit from services commensurate to her contribution and participate in the local political decision-making.

References

A and others v. *Secretary of State of the Home Department*, [2004] UKHL 56.

Amuur v. *France*, 17/1995/523/609, Council of Europe: European Court of Human Rights, 25 June 1996.

Boudemiene v. *Bush*, 553 U.S. (2008).

Canadian Charter of Rights and Freedoms, part I of the *Constitution Act*, 1982 [Schedule B to *Canada Act 1982* (1982, U.K., c. 11)], art. 1-15.

Charkaoui v. *Canada (Citizenship and Immigration)*, [2007] 1 S.C.R. 350.

Crépeau, François and Delphine Nakache. 2006. "Controlling Irregular Migration in Canada: Reconciling Security Concerns with Human Rights Protection." *IRPP Choices* 12(1).

Crépeau, François, Delphine Nakache and Idil Atak. 2009. "Introduction." In *Les migrations internationales contemporaines – Une dynamique complexe au cœur de la globalisation*, edited by François Crépeau, Delphine Nakache et Idil Atak, 7-19. Montréal : Presses de l'Université de Montréal.

—. 1995. *Droit d'asile : de l'hospitalité aux contrôles migratoires*. Bruxelles : Établissements Émile Bruylant/ Éditions de l'Université de Bruxelles.

Earnest, David C. 2003. "Noncitizen Voting Rights: A Survey of an Emerging Democratic Norm." Paper presented at the annual convention of the American Political Science Association, Philadelphia, Pennsylvania, August 28-31. www.odu.edu/~dearnest/pdfs/Earnest_APSA_2003.pdf.

Faist, Thomas. 2004. "The Migration-Security Nexus. International Migration and Security before and after 9/11", Malmö University

School of International Migration and Ethnic Relations, Willy Brandt Working Papers, 2004, online:
www.dspace.mah.se/bitstream/2043/686/1/Willy%20Brandt%202003-4.pdf (last accessed 26 November 2009).

Global Commission on International Migration, *Migration in an interconnected world: New directions for action*, Global Commission on International Migration, 2005, at 32-40, online:
www.gcim.org/attachements/gcim-complete-report-2005.pdf
(last accessed 20 December 2009).

Huguenet, Sophie. 2004. *Droit de l'asile : le projet britannique d'externalisation*. Paris : L'Harmattan.

International Labour Office. 2004. "Towards a Fair Deal for Migrant Workers in the Global Economy." Report VI Paper presented at the International Labour Conference, 92nd Session), Geneva, Switzerland, June 1-17. www.ilo.org/wcmsp5/groups/public/---dgreports/---dcomm/documents/meetingdocument/kd00096.pdf.

Legomsky, Stephen H. 2009. "Portraits of the Undocumented Immigrant: Epiphany through Dialectic." *Georgia Law Review* 44: 2-95.
http://papers.ssrn.com/sol3/papers.cfm?abstract_id=1372171.

Lutterbeck, Derek. 2006. "Policing Migration in the Mediterranean." *Mediterranean Politics* 11(1) : 59-82.

Migreurop. 2009. "'The encampment' in Europe and around the Mediterranean Sea." Accessed November 23.
www.migreurop.org/IMG/pdf/L_Europe_des_camps_2009.pdf.

Nakache, Delphine and François Crépeau. 2010. " Migrants as Local Citizens." *Inroads* : 70-9.

Raskin, Jamin B. 1993. "Legal Aliens, Local Citizens: The Historical, Constitutional and Theoretical Meanings of Alien Suffrage." *University of Pennsylvania Law Review* 141(4): 1391-1470. doi: 10.2307/3312345.

Regina v. *Immigration Officer at Prague Airport*, [2004] UKHL 55.

Sale v. Haitian Centers Council, 113 S. Ct. 2549, 113 S. Ct. 2549, 125 L. (92-344), 509 U.S. 155 (1993).

Siliadin v. France, n° 73316/01, ECHR, 2005-VII.

United Nations Treaty Collection. "CHAPTER IV: HUMAN RIGHTS 13. International Convention on the Protection of the Rights of All Migrant Workers and Members of Their Families." Last modified 18 December, 1990.
www.treaties.un.org/Pages/ViewDetails.aspx?src=TREATY&mtdsg_no=IV-13&chapter=4&lang=en.

Notes

[1] The author thanks Louis-Philippe Jannard, coordinator at the Oppenheimer Chair, for his work on the manuscript. The author thanks the *Pierre-Elliott Trudeau Foundation* and the *Calcutta Research Group* for their part in the preparation of this paper. This paper takes up ideas presented in greater depth in several previous papers (Crépeau, Nakache and Atak 2009, 7-19; Crépeau 1995, 29-38 ; Crépeau and Nakache 2006, 4-5 ; Nakache and Crépeau 2010).

[2] On 5 March 2010, 42 states had ratified the *International Convention on the Protection of the Rights of All Migrant Workers and Members of Their Families* (United Nations 1990).